Reading the Illegible

Reading the Illegible

CRAIG DWORKIN

Northwestern

University Press

Evanston

Illinois

Northwestern University Press
Evanston, Illinois 60208-4210

ISBN 0-8101-1926-9 (cloth)
ISBN 0-8101-1927-7 (paper)

Library of Congress Cataloging-in-Publication Data
Dworkin, Craig Douglas.
 Reading the illegible / Craig Dworkin.
  p. cm. — (Avant-garde and modernism studies)
 Based on the author's thesis (Ph.D.) — University of California,
Berkeley, 1998.
 Includes bibliographical references and index.
  ISBN 0-8101-1926-9 (alk. paper) — ISBN 0-8101-1927-7 (pbk. :
alk. paper)
  I. Poetry. 2. Poetics. I. Title. II. Avant-garde and modernism
studies.
 PN1031 .D97 2003
 809.1 — dc21

                  2002153017

FOR MY FAMILY
AND IN MEMORY OF JIM BRESLIN,
WHO WOULD HAVE MADE THIS
A BETTER WORK

Contents

Illustrations

Acknowledgments

This book, like many others, would not have been conceivable without Marjorie Perloff, to whom it owes everything. As it was being written, Charlie Altieri kept me from forgetting how poetry matters (and he has graciously put up with me when he deserved a much better student). Although they didn't know it, Scott Saul, Christian Bök, and Darren Wershler-Henry have all been models for me, and when I sat down to write, they were the readers I wanted to impress. Ty Miller first introduced me to the demands and rewards of innovative writing, for which I will always be grateful. I couldn't have asked for a better guide. More specifically, and even beyond their irreplaceable help, repeated insights, and the dead-on knowledge that have contributed so much to this work, I am grateful to Anne Wagner and Michael Bernstein for their faith. Al Gelpi, Diane Middlebrook, John Bishop, Steve Goldsmith, and Michael Wood have all indulged and encouraged me in the academy at crucial moments. Outside of academia, and for more than a decade, Mike Golston has proved to be the best of intellectual companions, reminding me of the real work to be done. That work has been a pleasure shared above all with Gregg Biglieri. Bruce Andrews, Johanna Drucker, Kenny Goldsmith, Lyn Hejinian, Anne Jamison, Travis Ortiz, and Joanna Picciotto have all been friends enough to keep me honest and on my toes. And I can't imagine better colleagues, or company, than Ming-Qian Ma, Susan Vanderborg, David Cantrell, Sarah Willburn, Christine Holbo, and Susan Dunn. In addition to being fun company, Susan Howe and Charles Bernstein were patient and kind in answering questions. In ways that are both more amorphous and more crucial, many others, over many years, for many things—but everyone, in the end really, for the poetry: thank you. These are debts that cannot be repaid, least of all with this book. But that does not mean they have ever been forgotten, and perhaps their weight will have been felt, here or there in these pages, in a few moments of true poetry—in Guy Debord's phrase: "the moment of true poetry brings all the unsettled debts of history back into play."

The result of a year's work depends more on what is struck out than on what is left in.

—Henry Adams

. . . in practical terms, the complete shutout of the reader's attention is subverted by most ostensibly antiabsorptive texts, partly by some reader's "paradoxically" keen interest in impermeability. . . .

—Charles Bernstein

I have cultivated my hysteria with delight and terror.

—Charles Baudelaire

Introduction

Our topic is poetry in itself and its kinds, and what potential each has: how plots should be constructed if the composition is to turn out well, from how many parts it is constituted, and of what sort they are, and likewise all other aspects of the same inquiry. An old academic joke provides the best emblem for the historical and thematic concerns that will dominate this book. April is the cruelest month. Choosing one's tongue and point of view, one can call that a *postscriptum* or a *foreword*. For some years, being obliged on occasion to answer the question "What are you working on?" I was embarrassed to have to say, "A book of political economy." Matthew Arnold's war on the Philistines was fought, as everybody knows; but nobody thinks that it was won. *Arma virumque cano.* It is a frequent custom for those who seek the favor of a prince to make him presents of those things they value most highly or which they know are most pleasing to him. May it please Heaven that the reader, emboldened, and become momentarily as fierce as what he reads, find without loss of bearings a wild and sudden way across the desolate swamps of these sombre, poison-filled pages. We are talking now of summer evenings in Tennessee. They order, said I, this matter better in France. This (therefore) will not have been a book. This book was written in good faith, reader. It is paradoxical to make a retrospective survey of a work which never intended to be prospective. Each has his reasons: for one, art is a flight, for another a means of conquering. Robert Cohn was once middleweight boxing champion of Princeton. Critics are rarely faithful to their labels and their special strategies. I say that, as is affirmed in the first chapter, it is meet for this exposition to be both literal and figural. Hermes, lord of the dead, who watch over the powers of my fathers, be my savior and stand by my claim. If it is a merit to have brought psychoanalysis into being, that merit is not mine. In my literary essays I have often spoken of the application of the experimental method to the novel and to the drama. To understand what poetics is, we must start with a general, and, of course, a somewhat simplified image of literary studies. The world is everything that is the case. The evidence of this fact is to be sought, not in the writings of the Critics, but in those of the Poets themselves. Many attempts have been made by writers on art and poetry to define beauty in the abstract, to express it in the most general terms, to find a universal formula for it. In Spring it is the dawn that is most beautiful. Men can do nothing without the make-believe of a beginning. A convenient arrangement for the parts in this book has not been easy to find. There is a longish dull stretch shortly after the beginning of the book. That I was anxious for the success of a work which had employed much of my time and labor, I do not wish to conceal. The Master said: Is it not pleasant to learn with a constant perseverance and application? This is a delicate question, and one for which a good many different solutions might have been given at different periods and seasons. Now is the winter of our discontent. I at last deliver to the world a Work which I have long promised, and to which, I am afraid, too high expectations have been raised. The work now laid before the public originated in indignation at the shallow and false criticisms of the periodicals of the day on the works of the great living artists to whom it principally refers. In English writing we seldom speak of tradition, though we occasionally apply its name in deploring its absence. The history of this work (whose birth in its present shape has been much retarded by the necessity of periodical publication) is briefly as follows. It was years ago, I remember, one Christmas eve, when I was dining with friends: a lady beside me made in the course of talk one of those allusions I have always found myself recognizing on the spot as "germs." I have always been meaning to explain the way in which I came to write certain of my books. For a long time I used to go to bed early. And then went down to the ship. The varieties of aphasia are numerous and diverse, but all of them oscillate between the two polar types just described. Hegel remarks somewhere that all great, world-historical facts and personages occur, as it were, twice. This is the saddest story I have ever heard. To stay cheerful when involved in a gloomy and exceedingly responsible business is no inconsiderable art: yet what could be more necessary than cheerfulness? While I was pondering thus in silence and using my pen to set down my tearful complaint, there appeared to me standing overhead a woman whose countenance was full of majesty, whose gleaming eyes surpassed in power of insight those of ordinary mortals, whose color was full of life, and whose strength was still intact though she was so full of years that by no means would it be believed that she was of our times. In the present state of society it appears necessary to go back to first principles in search of the most simple truths, and to dispute with some prevailing prejudice every inch of ground. The object before us, to begin with: *material production.* This book affirms the reality of spirit and the reality of matter, and tries to determine the relation of the one to the other by the study of a definite example, that of memory. My intention is to tell of bodies changed to different forms. The schoolmaster was leaving the village and everybody seemed sorry. The world is so taken up of late with novels and romances that it will be hard for a private history to be taken for genuine, where the names and other circumstances of the person are concealed, and on this account we must be content to leave the reader to pass his own opinion upon the ensuing sheets, and take it just as he pleases. *License* as permit, as permission from an outside authority; *license* as defiance of authority, as failure to obtain a permit—the introductions of our time have navigated with difficulty between these options. It will be seen that this mere painstaking borrower and grub-worm of a poor devil of a Sub-Sub appears to have gone through the long Vatican and street-stalls of the earth, picking up whatever random allusions to introductions he could anyways find in any book whatsoever, sacred or profane. Criticism, I take it, is the formal discourse of an amateur. Voluptuaries of all ages, of every sex, it is to you only that I offer this work; nourish yourselves upon its principles. This book is not for the overfed. The claim of the author's "intention" upon the critic's judgment has been challenged in a number of recent discussions. It is my purpose in this book to try to trace the origins of certain tendencies in contemporary literature and to show their development in the work of six contemporary writers. The following narrative is intended to answer a purpose more general and important than immediately appears upon the face of it. I have resolved on an enterprise which has no precedent, and which, once complete, will have no imitator. If ye be thus resolv'd, as it were injury to thinke ye were not, I know not what should withhold me from presenting ye with a fit instance wherein to shew both that tone of truth which ye eminently professe, and that uprightnesse of your judgement which is not wont to be partiall to your selves; by judging over again that Order which ye have ordain'd *to regulate printing.* 'Tis hard to say if greater want of skill appear in writing or in judging ill. How you felt, when you heard my accusers, I do not know; but I—well, I nearly forgot who I was, they were so persuasive. It would only be right and proper if this volume were published without any preface, or without any name on the title page, but simply with its own name to speak for itself. It is a trite but true observation, that examples work more forcibly on the mind than precepts. Nothing to be done. *Often cap. often attrib:* . . . a symbol for the first in a series or group. (*Coming in through the open window from the terrace*). I don't know how you found me, but since you're here you might as well come in and sit down.

Although this book was begun while I was a graduate student at Berkeley, it could never have been a dissertation. The requirements for a doctorate granted by the University of California at Berkeley preclude it. In the Graduate Division's "Guidelines for Submitting a Doctoral Dissertation," the section on format sets rigid typographic constraints, regulating font, spacing, margins, binding, paper stock, and even ink. Furthermore, these guidelines pay particular attention to legibility: "any legible typeface, except script, italic, or ornamental fonts, is acceptable for the body of the text," and the rulebook elaborates: "the print should be letter quality with dark black characters that are consistently clear and dense."[1] Additionally, photocopies "must be clearly legible," and the guidelines warn: "pages with illegible or disfiguring erasure or corrections, or with changes likely to be unclear in photographic reproduction, will be rejected."[2] At one point, it declares that any "photocopy must be as legible as the original"—as if such a feat were even *theoretically* possible.[3]

This all sounds, I know, like an overwrought harping on trivialities, or as though I were grandly pointing a finger at the most obvious and expected symptoms of an all-too-familiar bureaucratic pathology. Or perhaps simply as though I have been long nursing some festering and frustrated animosity toward the authority which I was too powerless, or too cowardly, to face while still a student and against which I can now safely rail. But one should at least pause over the fact that the requirements for a dissertation are not adequate to the intellectual rigor one would hope to expect from the dissertation itself. Because in the final analysis, a dissertation—not as the academic project it was, nor as the book it will become, but *as such*—is unable to claim the authority necessary to overrule that authority which grants its status and brings it into being; it can never overcome the theoretical limitations of its own requirements.

And besides, such textual details are never merely trivial. As the following chapters will demonstrate, the very "accidentals" governed by the university's "Guidelines"—type, layout, paper stock, and so on—are far from ever incidental. Indeed, what follows will argue for precisely why details like spacing and margins are important enough for a university to worry about. The embarrassment of such guidelines—and they are certainly not restricted to one instance at one school—is not that the obsessive focus of their scope is petty or unimportant but rather that their importance is unrecognized and untheorized. The problem is not that such requirements are too formal but that they are not sufficiently formalist. At numerous points, and often with an even greater attention to specifics, this book examines the very same elements inspected by the Graduate Division. Unlike the Graduate Division, however, this book proceeds with what I describe in the first chapter as a "radical formalism": one that reads textual details not merely as points of description but rather as inherently significant (that is, both important and signifying) and independent of lexical reference. A radical formalism, that is, reads such details as points of de-scription.

Because those details signify with the same force as lexical denotation, the guidelines that pass themselves off as simply the etiquette of format are in fact a substantial restriction on the semantic possibilities of University of California dissertations. Ostensibly, of course, the "content" of the dissertation is judged by members of the supervising faculty committee and is guaranteed by their signatures, while the Graduate Division merely regulates and regularizes a presentation supposedly incidental to that content. But perhaps it still needs to be said once more (and with feeling): the "formal" elements of a text quite simply cannot be separated from its "content." The matter is ontological: there exists absolutely no "idea," no "result" of my research, that I could communicate without regard to its form even if I wanted to do such a thing (and the same would be true if my work were the presentation of research in molecular biology or algebraic topology). The Graduate Division's proscriptions are thus more than a sign of the conservatism typical of academia; they don't just dull the surface presentation of the text, replacing the flair permitted by multimedia and desktop-publishing technologies with the typewriter style of a government document, nor do they merely discourage innovative and creative intellectual work; they also ultimately regulate within the very jurisdiction they would seek to disclaim: what can in fact be said, as communicable content, by a dissertation at a prominent research institution.[4]

But this present work, written beyond the strictures of a graduate division, is nevertheless—and necessarily—at heart a betrayal of the very values for which it argues. At several points in the following chapters I explicitly address the contradictions that beset a conventionally written advocation of innovative writing, but for now let me briefly suggest why there may be some worth in having this work stand as it is (though like all apologies, the truth of these claims neither sufficiently excuses the fault which they would propitiate nor mitigates the pathetic delusion of the hope with which they are made). If nothing else, perhaps this book will direct readers to a literature that they would not otherwise have encountered, and by dint of its conventionality it may actually create opportunities for those decidedly *un*conventional texts to achieve the results unique to their methods and beyond the ability of a flatly expository work. This book, moreover, may perform as one-half of a dialectical pair, permitting a synthesis of understanding when read in conjunction with the radical writing it discusses. This is hopefully not, in other words, just a reference to certain innovative writings, but also a facilitator, a catalyst that will reduce the risk that the texts it treats will remain inert, or be too quickly passed over.

And so what follows is also a confession of sorts. "Critics are generally poets who have betrayed their art, and instead have tried to turn art into a matter of reasoned discourse, and, occasionally, when their 'truth' breaks down, they resort to a poetic quote."[5]

Moreover, those university "Guidelines" are all to the point, because this book, as the title indicates, is essentially about how we read the illegible. "It is wonderful how a handwriting which is illegible can be read, oh yes it can," Gertrude Stein asserts, and this book begins with a similar faith that the illegible can indeed be read.[6] Rather than orthography, however, it focuses on poetic works that appropriate and then physically manipulate a source text, employing erasures, overprintings, excisions, cancellations, rearrangements, and so on, to render part of the source text literally unreadable. Interestingly enough, as it turns out, the university's guidelines ensure that illegibility would have been a fundamental concern of my dissertation regardless of its topic. Of every University of California dissertation. Bibliography is destiny.

In short, the basic thesis of this book is ███████████████████ .

That synopsis, I should emphasize, is both quite sincere and entirely accurate. At the same time, it is also equally true that there is no single thesis governing this book. If I had only one argument to make we would be well into it by now and looking forward to its conclusion. Instead, I have tried in each instance to allow the specifics of the works under consideration to generate the logic—and necessity—for pursuing particular, contingent, microlevel arguments. Rather than begin with a totalizing thesis for which literary texts serve as convenient examples, I have tried to take the texts on their own terms and permit them to lead me in precisely those directions for which I did not have a guiding thesis, and for which I could not, indeed, imagine one. In fact, I have written this book with a firm belief that even critical writing can be a productive experiment: actively generating unknown results through a process that prevents it from becoming a fixed and predictable report on the already known. Accordingly, a primary goal of the radical formalism at work in this project has been to apply its method of reading to the production of its own writing, and to pursue what could be called a Smithsonian criticism. "In the illusory babels of language," the radical formalist, like Robert Smithson's hypothetical artist,

> might advance specifically to get lost, and to intoxicate himself [or herself] in dizzying syntaxes, seeking odd intersections of meaning, strange corridors of history, unexpected echoes, unknown humors, or voids of knowledge.[7]

Part of what I hope to establish, quietly and unobtrusively, through this book's many close readings is an alternative strategy of reading itself.[8] Attentive to "odd intersections of meaning" and recording "unexpected echoes," the explications that populate the following chapters have led to arguments concerning the philosophy of language, experimental film, neuroptic perception, print technology, noise, sediment, error, censorship, and the temporality of intoxication, to recall only a handful. So what follows is diverse, but it is not simply a cobble of unrelated and isolated essays. In the course of making particular claims, I have also tried to let two broad arguments coalesce over the span of the book. Because these arguments remain more or less implicit throughout (though they are certainly neither collateral nor inconsequential), I want to state them explicitly here.

The range and diversity of topics is, to begin with, all to the point. One of the claims I want to substantiate is that even identical modes of illegibility produce a wide variety of unique local effects. Not only have procedures of illegibility been widely used, but their use has meant a great deal. Put more generally, this is an argument for the way in which the formal elements of a text signify in specific, politically and historically inflected ways. My thesis, in short, is that form must always necessarily signify but any particular signification is historically contingent and never inherently meaningful or a priori. As a concrete example, consider, for the moment, sanserif typefaces. In the early twentieth century, the "functionalism and quiet line" associated with the unadorned and hard-edged sanserif made it de rigueur for those who wanted to signify a futuristic modernity in line with the streamlined look of an industrial machine age.[9] "Futura," the name of Paul Renner's famous sanserif, was not incidental. Indeed, sanserif was so strongly established as the textual look of the Bauhaus that in 1928 Jan Tschichold could write (in a text originally set in the jobbing sanserif Akzidenz Grotesk): "to proclaim sanserif as the typeface of our time is not a question of being fashionable, it really does express the same tendencies to be seen in our architecture."[10] However, with its etymological recollection of the grotto, *Grotesk* (the German word for "sanserif") encodes another story entirely. The sanserif look that Tschichold and his contemporaries took to be a self-evident zeitgeist evocation of radical modernity had originally been revived, at the end of the eighteenth century, as the signifier of the classical, conservative past. For the romantic-era reader, the sanserif—in marked and diametric contrast to a mechanized modernity—possessed unmistakable "associations of rugged antiquity."[11]

The other extended argument, which follows from the shared appropriational strategies of the works I discuss, and which is itself reenacted at times by the radical formalism I have tried to put into practice, is for the supple force of paragrammatic "misreading." In Ihab Hassan's infamous schematic, "misreading"—as opposed to modernism's hermeneutic concern for "interpretation"—is listed as one of the attributes of "postmodernism," and throughout the following chapters I will demonstrate the relation of paragrammatics to a range of poststructural principles, as well as to Georges Bataille's influential concept of general economy.[12] For now, Leon Roudiez's concise definition will do; in his terms, a "paragrammatic" reading is any reading that challenges the normative referential grammar of a text by forming "networks of signification not accessible through conventional reading habits."[13] In the first chapter, I will argue for the political and historical resonance of such misreadings, but in brief, my dual claim is that paragrammatics—as a tactic for both reading and writing—manifests a certain politics within the realm of literature itself, and that examples of literary paragrammatics provide concrete models for the sort of cultural activities readers might then bring to other aspects of the world around them. This book is thus the admission of a certain utopianism; but I would rather maroon myself nowhere than surrender to a status quo with which I am not content, and in which "erasure and palimpsests are reduced to a flat / Surface effect: the afterlife of ethics."[14]

When I began this project I knew of only a few examples of "poetic illegibility," which I took to constitute an interesting collection of rarities. These texts seemed worth the sustained work of a book primarily because even as an habitual reader of "difficult" poetry, and a scholar familiar with avant-garde traditions, I was unable to figure out how to write about them; they stood out as works about which I had nothing to say, and the extremity of their resistance was in itself a strong invitation to make the attempt. One of the rewards of searching and researching through special library collections, however, was to discover how often writers and artists have used such techniques (and there are undoubtedly many more examples than I have found). Moreover, I was surprised to learn that such works were generally unknown even among scholars often accused of narrow specialization, just as even among a poetic avant-garde so often faulted for coterie insularity these works were frequently unknown even when authored by another member of the community—and as you will soon see, these are remarkable, striking, and memorable works at that. One of my hopes for this book, as I suggested above, is that it will direct readers to literature they might not otherwise have encountered, and in large part I intend this book to serve as an initial, critical guide to a tradition which has itself remained largely illegible. To this end, I have included many references in the endnotes to works on which my analyses do not directly focus. Within each chapter, I have kept the focus on one or two works, letting them serve as touchstone exempla for the particular technique of illegibility—erasure, overprinting, writing-through, and so on—around which each chapter is organized. While some readings are obviously limited to the specific text under discussion, readers should keep in mind that many of my larger claims apply not only to other instances of a given technique, but often to phenomena of illegibility in general.

In addition to providing a critical history, this book should also prepare us to be better readers of contemporary writing, because such procedures have only become increasingly ubiquitous and varied in recent years. In particular, many younger poets are rediscovering—or more often than not reinventing—techniques of illegibility. Part of this interest and activity derives from developments in digital technology, which have made the effects

I consider here all the more easy and inexpensive to create and reproduce. As that technology develops, and as the generation of writers just now emerging matures, I hope that this book will lay part of the groundwork needed to effectively engage the literature that will mark the new millennium.

If a specific work discussed in this book is likely to be unknown even to writers who are also part of an avant-garde community, or who have themselves engaged in similar practices, the existence of these *types* of works—the knowledge of a tradition of poetic illegibility—has been part of the poetic imagination of the last thirty years. Even if such works are not a commonplace of the poetic landscape, they have been part of the background against which other, less visually dramatic works have been undertaken, and the force of their pressure on that poetic imagination derives from the same factors that make them important even for the reader who is generally uninterested in innovative writing as such. Because many of the works I address stand on the threshold of legibility, they serve as limit cases that define the field of everything that is readable, and the exceptional extremity of their means, in fact, allows us to better test the claims we would make about all literature. Such works not only put descriptions of "difficult" and "radical" textual practices into better perspective, but they also further our understanding of the constraints and possibilities inherent in the act of reading, the construction of linguistic meaning, and the very nature of language itself. In ways that help us to think through certain ideas more fully, many of these works constitute not merely illustrations, but literal and concrete enactments of theoretical concepts—like Jacques Derrida's *écriture sous rature,* or Martin Heidegger's *kreuzweise Durchstreichung*—that have by now become all but clichéd. Similarly, they allow us to see familiar and canonical examples afresh: Eliot's telling blank space in the last line of *The Waste Land,* where he *om*its the "Om" that in fact begins "the formal ending to an Upanishad"; Pound's groundbreaking replication of Malatesta's epistle in "Canto VIII"; Williams's conclusion of *A Novelette* with the revelatory "OL MPI" (like his reduction of "song" to "son" in *Spring & All*); or Zukofsky's similar transformation in *"A"-7* of a "toilet"—"rent in arrears"—into a literal *vacancy* "to let." What were, for these modernists, isolated instances of literary daring or dramatic special effects, have become for their successors the very procedures by which entire books are written.

where prohibited.

A frustrating and intimidating condition of undertaking this sort of sustained writing project is the knowledge of blind spots which one cannot, by definition, detect on one's own; but I should perhaps make clear, from the outset, a few of the parameters which have knowingly limited this investigation. To begin with, I have not gone beyond quite literal examples of illegibility to consider the many figural uses of the "unreadable." Nonetheless, the works I discuss provide concrete instantiations of such metaphors and thereby put them to the test, giving us a renewed understanding of the powerful imaginative descriptions which have implicated themselves in a rhetoric of illegibility. Indeed, certain conceptual constructions have been so dependent on figures of the unreadable that to reconsider illegibility *as such* has the potential to effect far-reaching revisions in thought. For just one example, recall Freud's discussion of psychic disturbances, which he famously casts in textual terms and which evoke nothing so much as a descriptive catalogue of the works I consider here: "one way [to resolve such disturbances] would be for the offending passages to be thickly crossed through so that they were illegible," another way would be "to proceed to distort the text. Single words would be left out," and "best of all, the whole passage would be erased. . . ."[15]

Because of the claims I make for paragrammatics, I have also limited my discussion to instances of "strategic illegibility" rather than considering issues of textual editing and paleography, such as inadvertent printing errors or the range of illegibilities inherent in manuscripts. However, since those documents and my examples often share the same visual effects, perhaps this book will allow similar instances—as well as an erroneously garbled or damaged message, say, or graffiti on the side of a bus—to be read less as regrettable losses and more as exciting, poetic possibilities. I refrain as well from considering the use of illegibility in graphic design and commercial advertising, where these techniques have an independent tradition and use, although much of what I say will again leave readers more aware of the processes and stakes that confront them when they come across a software manual with illustrations that use the iconic conventions of layout mock-up, or a compact disc like the one marketed by ECM for the Hilliard Ensemble, which sports a cover strikingly similar to Rosmarie Waldrop's presswork. Similarly, while this is certainly not a book about visual poetry in general, certain aspects of its method should prove useful for reading other, more subtle visual effects.

And one final note: while I focus on the visual dimension of written language, my claims about the materiality of language apply equally to the sonic dimensions of spoken language, and much of what follows could serve as a model for listening to the inaudible.

Speaking of which ("unexpected echoes"), if it would be ridiculous to ground the cultural significance of this book in a reading of the Nixon White House tapes as intertexts of the contemporaneous artistic experimentations with erasure and electromagnetic tape, the procedures I discuss here are not without their "real world" civic consequences. The most radical anagrammatic disarticulations are a case in point; in Wisconsin, the governor's power of item veto (itself a genre of "writing-through") extended until recently to "striking individual letters in the words of an enrolled bill" in order to create new words, and the governor is still permitted to delete individual words and eliminate digits in an appropriations bill.[16] While the most recent constitutional interpretation requires that the remaining text constitute a "complete, entire, and workable law," the state supreme court has explicitly declared that the governor can even use such erasures—like Tom Phillips's treatment of a Victorian novel—to change the original legislative intent.[17]

In an essay on Blanchot, Derrida asks: "How can one text, assuming its unity, give or present another to be read, without touching it, without saying anything about it, practically without referring to it?"[18] The question is only complicated by recalling Ludwig Wittgenstein's discussion of metacritical rules: "Any interpretation still hangs in the air with what it interprets, and cannot give it any support."[19] If I have, at times, abjured interpretation in the following pages, it has only been to give onto *reading*.

This is a book about (upon) Marcel Duchamp, in which he is only ever mentioned, as it were, en passant.

Reading the Illegible

Je rêvais croisades, voyages de découvertes dont on n'a pas de relations, républiques sans histoires, guerres de religion étouffées, révolutions de moeures, déplacement de races et de continents: je croyais à tous les enchantements.

    —Arthur Rimbaud

In dreams begin responsibilities.

    —William Butler Yeats

1. Radical Formalism

One Thousand Poppies

Amid poetry's slumbers, avant-garde form has returned, nightly, to the dream of politics. I want to begin by awakening us into—and not out of—that dream. But we should be lucid in our dreaming, because discussions of literary politics frequently stumble on the very sort of grammatical confusions that Ludwig Wittgenstein warns against. This confusion is exacerbated by the common restriction of "politics" to so narrow a reference that it reduces to the question "for whom did you vote?" Such circumscription diminishes the meaningfulness of politics accordingly, and it conveniently avoids the more rigorous, continual, and self-scrutinizing duties of a genuine and fully political life. A "politics" in its broader sense would include all relations of power, however local or miniscule, and the ethics of their distribution. The "political," in this sense, thus extends not just to the personal, as the watchword of a generation of feminist theorists reminds us, but to the most minute particulars of everyday life. From a certain perspective, the scale of those particulars may indeed appear small (after all, it's only a poem), but they are never petty; not only are they coextensive with every other organization of power, however global, but they are also—in and of themselves—just as plenipotent. "In short, everything is political, but every politics is simultaneously a *macropolitics* and a *micropolitics*."[1] To pass over the politics of such details as mere trivia threatens to leave the very imbalances of power one might want to redress both largely unexamined and all the more deeply—and insidiously—entrenched. Worse yet,

3

the disdain for details in the righteous pursuit of "grander" issues risks implicating one, by means, in the very politics that one's ends would seek to oppose. At the very least, such negligence forfeits the unstinting vigilance that political issues most require. "Good or bad, politics and its judgements are always molar, but it is the molecular and its assessment that makes it or breaks it."[2]

The politics of literature, accordingly, is no less fraught. In the narrow sense of "politics," poems are quite simply not efficacious. At best, they may present models from which readers can extrapolate modes of thought or behavior which can then be translated into other contexts and systems. To the degree that poems affect a reader's understanding of language, they have the potential to alter all of those extraliterary relationships that also involve language; but they do not directly influence electoral politics, or feed the hungry, or soften blows. If you want to organize a labor union, say, you don't write a poem: you go out and organize. George Oppen is exemplary. Moreover, political examinations of literature frequently enact an ultimately reactionary two-step: first raising the question in the narrow sense, and then finding literature lacking, all questions of literary politics are dismissed, leaving a status quo in which the meaningful and appropriate aspects of literary politics continue to go unexamined.[3] The danger of taking poetry to be politically efficacious in the narrow sense is not so much a naïveté about what poetry cannot do, but an inattention to what it actually *can* do.

The very importance of political issues, in fact, demands a more sophisticated reading practice. Both Jed Rasula and Bruce Andrews have suggested the requirements for such readings, and given the similarities between their arguments and my own, the outlines of their positions are worth rehearsing briefly here. Following Rasula's terminology (and at the risk of sounding like Henry James) one might differentiate between the politics *through,* the politics *in,* and the politics *of* the poem.[4] The politics *through* the poem would, accordingly, be politics in the narrow sense: essentially false leads, though perhaps occasionally and collaterally achieved by certain rallying songs or the poetic ornaments accompanying speeches. The politics *in* the poem would indicate Pound's discussion of Mussolini, say, or Adrienne Rich's feminist thematics. In chapter 4, I will address the dangers of focusing on the politics *in* the poem and the inadequacy of stopping political analysis at that level without considering the politics *of* the poem: what is signified by its form, enacted by its structures, implicit in its philosophy of language, how it positions its reader, and a range of questions relating to the poem as a material object—how it was produced, distributed, exchanged. Or in Bruce Andrews's terms: "writing *as* politics, not writing *about* politics."[5]

So what follows, I want to emphasize, is at once far more modest than most discussions of the politics of art—making no claims to treat affairs of state, teasing out no thematic subtleties from narratives about social relations—and also far more scrupulous. To extend one's reading to the politics *of* the poem is a prerequisite for a more significantly and fully political or ethical reading, and to that end I want to insist throughout this book on a radical formalism. I adapt the term from Andrews's definition of a "radical praxis," which "involves the rigors of formal celebration, a playful infidelity, a certain illegibility within the legible: an infinitizing, a wide-open exuberance, a perpetual motion machine, a transgression."[6] A sufficiently radical formalism pursues the closest of close readings *in the service of* political questions, rather than to their exclusion. At the same time, it refuses to consider the poem as a realm separate from politics, even as it focuses on "the poem itself." It is a matter, quite simply, of being true to form. As a 'pataphysical investigation of minute particulars, radical formalisms hew to the concrete. Where "concrete" is what the street is made of.

In order to elaborate a more nuanced account of these claims, I want to turn the focus of this chapter to the Internationale Situationniste (IS). The Situationists not only strove to develop a theory and praxis of micropolitical activity that would extend to all aspects of everyday life (including the poetic), but they also explicitly conceived of that activity in linguistic and literary terms. Moreover, they realized that even the most radically utopian experiments would have to be conducted—like the most radically experimental poetry—within certain unavoidable parameters and preexisting structures. Their resulting theory of *détournement* provides a clear explication of the ideological force behind the appropriation and strategic "misuse" of source texts common to the work I discuss throughout this book. In fact, the Situationists provide a historical and conceptual analogue for the revolutionary impulses that have generally been less well articulated in the political discourse around the Anglo-American art and poetry discussed in other chapters. If the Situationists did not, in the end, conclusively answer the questions they raised about the viability of political poetry, their incitements make palpably visible the absence of such aspirations in other arenas, and they also ground the various impulses that did make attempts to reach some answer, beginning from the same questions as the Situationists but taking other, less salient, lines of flight. In fact, the Situationist account may too astringently rationalize the distinctively unconstrainable aspect of poetic illegibility, but it will nonetheless better show that given the dream of politics, a poetry that did not aspire to some degree of illegibility would be a nightmare. One caution, however: what follows will itself be a diversion of Situationist thought. More a bricolage than any attempt to present either an exhaustive or a partisan history, this chapter will extract certain valuable moments from the long, variable, and problematic trajectory of Situationist theory, and it is perhaps most true to their spirit at those very points where the Situationists would themselves have been most ready to denounce and reject it. "Les hallucinations sont innombrables. C'est bien ce que j'ai toujours eu: plus de foi en l'histoire, l'oubli des principes. Je m'en tairai: poètes et visionnaires serient jaloux [The hallucinations are endless. It is precisely what I have always had: no more faith in history, neglect of principles. I'll say no more about it: poets and visionaries would be jealous]."[7]

Gangland and Philosophy

> The art of living presupposes . . . that life as a whole—everyday life—
> should become a work of art.
>   —Henri Lefebvre

> Beauty will be convulsive, or it will not be.
>   —André Breton

"We must multiply poetic subject and objects," proclaimed Guy Debord's 1957 "Report on the Construction of Situations," and thus, amid the left-existentialist milieu of midcentury Europe, with the most improbable inevitability, several artistic and political traditions converged in the Internationale Situationniste. From one direction, it took a place in the history of anarchism and heretical Marxism. In the tradition of the revolutions of Kiel (1918), Turin (1920), Kronstadt (1921), and Catalonia (1936), the IS combined individual self-management with collective violence in the face of authority, rejecting both capitalist and Marxist models in favor of radically antiauthoritarian and autonomous soviets. Moreover, this model of the soviet, with its continually dissolving and reconstituting self-management, was to be applied to everyday life in the form of "constructed situations": ad hoc, specific, creative, and consensus-based reactions to the demands of an environment by small, transient, spontaneously formed collectives of individuals. Or, in Situationist ar-got: "Un moment de la vie, concrètement et délibérément construit par l'organisation collective d'une ambiance unitaire et d'un jeu d'événements. [A moment of life concretely and deliberately constructed by the collective organization of a unitary ambience and a game of events.]" The trajectory of Situationist thought, in short, followed from the political philosophies of Proudhon, Bakunin, and Luxemburg—inflected by the arguments of Georg Lukács, the group around *Socialisme ou barbarie,* and (most significantly) Henri Lefebvre—but with corrections made for the idiosyncratic influence of writers like Fourier, de Sade, Saint-Just, and Bataille.[8] At the same time, it was also heir to the legacy of a number of writers who all predicated their poetry on social critique: Lautréamont (Isidore Ducasse), Alfred Jarry, Arthur Rimbaud, Arthur Craven, and the surrealists who had also followed their lead.[9]

Indeed, from another direction, the IS marks a cycle of the half-life of futurism as it decayed through dada and then surrealism. In 1956, a congress at Giuseppe Pinot-Gallizio's Alba Laboratory gathered fragments of surrealism's centrifugal dissolution; among others, it brought together members from Asger Jorn's Scandinavian CoBrA group (Copenhagen-Brussels-Amsterdam) and its incarnation as the Mouvement International pour une Bauhaus Imaginiste, or MIBI (including Constant Niewenhuys and Jørgen Nash), the German Gruppe Spur, the Movimento Nucleare (Enrico Baj), Ralph Rumney's "London Psychogeographical Committee," and Gil Wolman, who represented the Internationale Lettriste. This latter group, which included the urban theorist Ivan Chtcheglov, had recently splintered from Jean-Isidore Isou's *lettristes.* When a founding conference was held in 1957 at Cosio d'Arroscia, officially merging all of these organizations into the Internationale Situationniste, the lettrists—including Guy-Ernest Debord and Michèle Bernstein—played a key role, and the two would remain central figures in the IS, along with other notable participants, including Attila Kotányi, Jacqueline de Jong, Jeppesen Martin, René Riesel, and their chronicler René-Donatien Viénet.[10] Before its official dissolution in 1972, around seventy members passed through the IS, although the core was kept to a handful at any given time through strict ostracism and regular resignations. Purges were immediate (Baj was excluded upon arriving at Alba and several founding members from the MIBI were dismissed with a few months of the Cosio d'Arroscia conference), and exclusions followed regularly over the years, as Debord mimicked the practice of Isou and Breton at the height of their sectarian zeal. In fact, as with the records of dada, surrealism, and lettrism, the petty and recurrent policing of the official Situationist membership and the endless cataloguing of expulsions is tedious and embarrassing. At best it is an unfortunate side of the juvenile coin with which the energy of such movements is bought, and at worst a symptomatic authoritarianism of even the best-intentioned provocateurs.

Although the founding convention of the IS was held in 1957, the Situationists came to attention only a decade later, when the University of Strasbourg's Union National des Étudiants Français local turned to them for inspiration in its 1966 resistance to administrative authority. After consultation with the Situationists, the Strasbourg student union published Mustapha Khayati's *De la misère en milieu étudiant* (*On the Poverty of Student Life*), and with the beauty of a dada suicide it attempted to dissolve itself as a bureaucratic body. The two major Situationist statements appeared in 1967, with the publication of Guy Debord's *La société du spectacle* (*The Society of the Spectacle*) and Raoul Vaneigem's *Traité de savoir-vivre à l'usage des jeunes générations* (*The Young Person's Etiquette Manual;* often translated as *The Revolution of Everyday Life*). This complementary pair of manifestos stands—both stylistically and conceptually—as the *Tractatus* and *Investigations* of the movement, respectively. However, after the trials and media attention at Strasbourg, Situationist notoriety came less with these publications than with the spread of student unrest to Paris and the revolution of May 1968, when the Situationists joined *les enragés* from Nanterre and put into practice theories that would influence thinkers from Michel de Certeau, Maurice Blanchot, and Jean Baudrillard to the host of Anglo-American "pro-situ" groups that followed in their wake.[11]

Much of what inspired these heirs to the Situationist legacy can be found in Debord's *La société du spectacle*. Over several decades of revolutionary activity, Debord was astonishingly consistent in his arguments, in part because his early judgments would prove so prophetic. Indeed, those judgments are still incisive thirty years after the composition of *La société* because the world he describes has only become increasingly familiar.[12] *La société du spectacle* abstracts and condenses the core of Debord's theories into a lapidary prose honed to 221 numbered theses. With a bitter, sharp etch "comme l'eau-forte sur le fer [like nitric acid on iron]," *La société du spectacle* describes the bleakness of a postwar culture in which capital has so thoroughly colonized the most trivial aspects of everyday life that only an equally thorough revolution of that life can now hope to offer any resistance.[13] Or, in the terms of Jean Baudrillard's related concept of "total revolution," articulated a few years after the publication of *La société:* "Les signes doivent brûler eux aussi [Even signs must burn]."[14] With an argument that parallels Baudrillard's deconstructive link of exchange value and use value—in which the one emerges as a disguised category of the other according to a dangerously supplemental relation—Debord diagnoses the way in which the logic of capital has come to dominate and orchestrate the realm of consumption as it had previously only governed production. Where once, he nostalgically imagines, we lived in an age when time away from work was genuinely outside the demands of capital and beyond its panoptic gaze—when, in short, "no one was looking"—there is now no longer any part of the day, however ostensibly "private" (and including the very understanding of time itself), that escapes the demands of capital. Leisure time and "time off" have themselves been co-opted until there is not a single moment in the day, as William Blake would say, that Satan cannot find.

That satanic permeation is the condition of the "spectacle." Debord frustrates any easy reification of the term by carefully avoiding a single definition; in fact, such a prescription would itself be characteristic of the spectacle's natural inclination to stability and its tendency to freeze, fix, and congeal.[15] Accordingly, in Debord's writing the spectacle is not, I should be quick to point out, merely "show business" (one of the denotations of the word in French), nor is it simply visual media and advertising, or even necessarily visual at all—though none of these are beyond its purview and all are specifically included in the course of Debord's argument.[16] So if the spectacle is defined in one section as "*capital* accumulated to the point where it becomes an image," it is equally "a *false consciousness of time*" and an image-mediated "social relationship between people."[17] Debord's concept of the spectacle, that is, maintains a "family resemblance": lacking a single definition, but constituting a range of descriptive conditions. However diverse the registers of the spectacle's referents, certain of its characteristics clearly emerge over the course of *La société*. The spectacle corresponds to an authoritarian univocality that encourages a passive reception and obedient consumption of its message. Being the "opposite of dialogue," the spectacle is a "monologue" that has no truck with interruptions or alternate presentations.[18] Moreover, against the active production that it discourages, the spectacle maintains a realm of passive reproduction; as "the sun that never sets on the empire of modern passivity," the spectacle strives to render its spectator "*passive,*" "submissive," and "unthinking."[19]

Because such spectacular relationships have extended from the realm of production to that of consumption, Debord casts his resistance to the spectacle with a corresponding focus, turning to the latter with the critical scrutiny traditionally reserved for the former.[20] Picking up on a line from *Das Kapital,* Debord affirms that a "product, though ready for immediate consumption, may nevertheless serve as raw material for a further product."[21] Accordingly, rather than divide consumers from producers, Debord advocates the dehierarchized equalization of the two. In opposition to the spectacle's monologue, Debord calls for a "two-way communication" in which consumers would become (unalienated) producers of meaning in their interactions with commodities, including commodified space and time.[22] These dialogues would be necessarily anti-spectacular, in part, because they would avoid the reflective logic of the mirror (*speculum*). Productive dialogue, for Debord, does not reflect received structures of authority precisely because it generates signification without appeal to previous models or habitual protocols. As "constructed situations" these dialogues, by definition, have arisen on the spur of the moment, contingently, and in unforeseen ways from the material at hand. The Situationist, in this sense, is a *bricoleur,* making do with ad hoc tactics and eschewing predetermined or received strategies.[23] Or, in the terms developed by Gilles Deleuze and Félix Guattari, the Situationists practiced an art of continual deterritorialization. Construing even the spectacular world imposed on us as a "mobile space of play," Debord proposes that since we have no choice but to play along to some degree, we might still make "freely chosen variations in the rules of the game."[24] Bypassing the rote reactions elicited by certain codes and structures, such playful restructuring of the "rules of the game" works to destabilize the implicit authoritarianism of disciplined responses and the hierarchies they establish. The "free construction" of such situations defines "authentic poetry" for Debord, and to this end he advocates an active, playful, creative, and willfully conscious engagement with commodities in ways other than those ordained by the "machinery of permitted consumption."[25] Such creative "misuse" of commodities, codes, and environments establishes the "liberated creative activity" that Debord and the Situationists consider "true communication."[26]

These figures of "communication" and "poetry" are not coincidental, and Debord frequently casts his arguments for political resistance in the terms of communicative and artistic practice. In linguistic terms, the spectacle corresponds to the conventional "conduit" models of communication, in which an addresser (to use Jakobson's terms) constructs and transmits a message to a receptive addressee. Or to translate this hierarchy to a literary model: writers produce texts which readers then consume. "True communication," in Debord's sense, disrupts these hierarchies with an anarchism of mutual production that pushes the dialogue between reader and writer to such a degree of interaction that the very distinction between the two disappears; typically passive readers become "both producer and consumer," as "writing" and "reading" are seen to decline to the same verb.[27] Debord works to "define comprehension as something other than consumption. (*Other then.*) So it's politicizing: a radical *reading* embodied in writing. A writing that is itself a 'wild reading' *solicits* wild reading."[28] Jean-Marie Apostolidès relates this aspect of Debord's critique to the surrealists, invoking Pierre Bourdieu's understanding of "un champ nouveau [a new field]" which is "de l'imaginaire," "expérimental," and where "l'incitation n'y est plus de recevoir les oeuvres passivement, mais de les *produire* pour élargir le champ d'expérience individuel [the provocation there is no longer to passively receive works of art but to *produce* them in order to open the field of individual experience]."[29] Communicating vessels. Where "vessel" is a verb.

Indeed, the defiant activity of words when they refuse to be merely containers for instrumental communication is a touchstone of Situationist poetics, and because "words coexist with power in a relationship analogous to that which proletarians . . . have with power" their resistance is both a model for political activity and one version of a politically aware writing.[30] Throughout this book we will see examples of an active language, and while I will not belabor the point, the political force of their example should not be forgotten. Although, in Debord's analysis, "words *work*—on behalf of the dominant organization of life," they are not mere markers of "unambiguous signals" in an exchange of information because they are not in themselves "informationist."[31] This anti-semantic aspect of language will be examined more closely in chapter 3, but when language exceeds its communicative authority—in those moments when its familiar and overworked utility stutters to reveal its "fundamentally strange and foreign" nature—one catches a glimpse of "*the insubordination of words.*"[32]

Indeed, the question of an insubordinate Situationist linguistics is worth considering. If the Situationist revolution must extend to "every aspect" of life and refuse to any longer "*combat alienation by means of alienated forms of struggle,*" what of the textual realm, in which the "ruler's chief weapon" has always been "the written word"?[33] All reading, of course, involves the reader's production of signification to some degree; the point is that such production is too often routine and disciplined by preestablished and inflexible protocols. Nor, on the other hand, is the "indeterminate" text a guarantor of Debordian dialogue. Even those works which encourage or require creative reader participation can operate in accord with hierarchies and manipulative control; indeed, that manipulation is frequently all the more insidious given its ulteriority. In both cases, the force of the Situationists' response lies in their emphasis on the creative misuse of established codes, existing structures, and inescapable conditions. When that principle of revolutionary activity is translated to language and literature it constitutes a "paragrammatics." In Leon Roudiez's definition, any reading strategy that challenges the normative referential grammar of a text by forming "networks of signification not accessible through conventional reading habits" is paragrammatic.[34] The chapters that follow will consider a series of paragrammatic strategies—from readings that ignore word boundaries, or select and recombine certain letters from words rather than taking them in the conventional order, to readings that proceed vertically down the page rather than horizontally from left to right. Before turning to examples of the Situationists' own paragrammatics, I want to emphasize the political stakes of such activities, which bring revolutionary action to the field of literature, and ultimately to language itself.

Coups de Dé's

> The insubordination of words . . . has shown that the theoretical critique of
> the world of power is inseparable from a practice that destroys it.
> —Mustapha Khayati

The ludic aspect of the Situationists' dialogue with the world around them should not eclipse the imperative with which they playfully misused found objects. Debord and his compatriots understood that any games were wagered against an opponent who would always be one move ahead. Accordingly, their analysis takes into account the fate of opposition in a world so thoroughly colonized by modern capitalist structures that acts of resistance are not only anticipated but have themselves been incorporated as an integral part of the strategy of capital to begin with. In the modern arena, the most outrageous assaults of the political and artistic avant-gardes are no longer merely repressed, or ignored, or even assimilated, so much as they are transformed—according to an increasingly rapid cycle of recovery—into tactics in the service of the very powers they were originally meant to attack. But "l'avant-garde," as Asger Jorn knew, "se rend pas [doesn't give up]." Whether in the street or the pages of a book, we encounter codes and structures that we inherit, inhabit, and cannot simply refuse. These *donées,* however, do not mean that the situation, however dire, is entirely hopeless, and the Situationists offer tactics for playing under precisely such conditions. Indeed, part of the force of the many labyrinths which spiral through the pages of Situationist texts is their representation of structures in which one is trapped and hopelessly lost; if the Situationists no longer make attempts to exit from these mazes, it is because they recognize that the only escape is to transform the geography in which one is (always) already trapped. If the Minotaur, surrealism's totem animal, can no longer simply be killed off, or avoided, he might yet be *détourned* with a deft veronica—with that flash of the red and black flag that flew over Paris in the summer of 1968.[35]

Through his elaboration and examples of such *détournements,* Debord provides a model for productive engagement with given and inescapable forms. *Détourner,* to "deflect" in French, is the verb used to describe illicit diversions: embezzlement, misappropriation, hijack. In the Situationist lexicon the word became a *terme de métier* short for the phrase "détournement des éléments esthétiques préfabriqués [diversion of ready-made aesthetic elements]." The antithesis of quotation, which marks and reinscribes authority, *détournement* pursues a poetics of plagiarism in the tradition of Lautréamont, whose infamous syllogism declares: "Les idées s'améliorent. Le sens des mots y participe. Le plagiat est nécessaire, le progrès l'implique [Ideas improve. The meaning of words plays a part in this development. Plagiarism is necessary. Progress implies it]."[36] Taking what is given and improving upon it, *détournement* unsettles hierarchies by initiating a dialogue in a formerly monologic setting and inscribing multiple authors and multiple sites for the generation of meaning. To maintain that dialogue and prevent it from simply reverting to another monologue, both the ready-made elements and their manipulation must remain evident. Rather than effecting a mere cancellation or negation, *détournement* thus pursues a logic parallel to that of modernist collage, in which elements maintain a simultaneous reference to both their original contexts, which are never entirely effaced, as well as to the new collage composition into which they are introduced.[37] Each collaged element, as Groupe μ writes, thus "necessarily leads to a double reading: a reading of the fragment perceived in relation to its text of origin, and a reading of the same fragment incorporated into a new, different totality."[38] Within that new totality, moreover, the elements of collage—like those of *un objet détourné*—always maintain a certain autonomy, and they resist the subsumption of one by the other; "in collage," as Marjorie Perloff notes, "hierarchy gives way to parataxis."[39]

Where collage might simply acknowledge the conjunction of elements from different registers, however, *détournement* focuses on the deformation of those registers and the frustration of their seemingly natural conclusions; it re-engineers objects and events on their own terms, but counter to their ostensible ends, turning the codes of appropriated elements against themselves. *Détournement,* in short, is a communication containing its own critique. Because that critique disrupts the smooth operation of ideologies, laying bare the seemingly natural structures and logics that would otherwise be taken for granted and then employing them in startling and novel ways, Situationist diversions are frequently приёми остраннения (devices of making strange). In the words of Shklovskii's classic definition of such devices, *détournements,* that is, work to "make the stone *stony*"—so that it can be hurled through a plate-glass shop window or at a police van on the rue Gay-Lussac.[40] As a graffito read in May 1968, when writing spread across the walls of the Sorbonne and Les Halles in a realization of Lautréamont's dream of a poetry one day written by everyone: "Sous les pavés, la plage [Under the cobblestones, the beach]."[41]

With its restructuring of the urban landscape, graffiti may in fact be the most familiar instance of *détournement*. At its simplest, graffiti can turn the sign of impassive corporate power—the solid expanse of an uncommunicating wall, for instance—into a support for the declaration of precisely those voices it would exclude. Depending on the context, moreover, the effect can be more pointed. In my West Berkeley neighborhood, for example, a group of "vegan vandals," as the newspapers referred to them, were active in the early 1990s. One of their interventions strategically painted out letters in a billboard advertisement for yogurt; against a background of smiling, healthy, exercisers, the original copy read "Good Fast Food." *Détourned,* it read: "Goo Fat od." A different group (one assumes) used the same tactic to *détourn* a nearby municipal street sign, which had been posted outside a liquor store as part of a campaign against drunk driving. The sign originally read "DUI: you can't afford it"; with a pun on the name of the car company, the sign now reads "DUI: you can ford it." Like the poetry of May 1968, this pro-situ graffiti follows a strangely proleptic genealogy: it has been inscribed on the city following principles developed from artists who had themselves originally been inspired by anonymous urban graffiti. *Les lettristes* (François Dufrêne, Maurice Lamaître) and *les nouveaux realistes* (Mimmo Rotella, Raymond Hains, Jacques Villéglé), for instance, had been working "au pied du mur [at the foot of the wall]" since the beginning of the 1950s—removing fragments of torn posters and recontextualizing them in ways that were reminiscent of Brassaï's mid-century photographs of reframed and aestheticized Parisian advertisements and graffiti.

One of the artists who worked seriously with those *déchiré* street posters was Asger Jorn, and he indexes graffiti explicitly in his 1962 painting *L'avant-garde se rend pas,* and implicitly in the 1959 *Paris by Night.*[42] I have already noted the central role Jorn played in the founding of the Internationale Situationniste, and I want to consider his *peinture détourné* (diverted painting), which provides a good illustration of the Situationist aesthetic. Exhibited as a group of "modifications" in 1959, with a subsequent series of "nouvelles défigurations [new disfigurations]" shown in 1962, they were constructed by reworking thrift-store paintings of kitsch scenes and high-art imitations. On the realist portraits and landscapes he picked up secondhand, Jorn overlaid his distinctively dripped abstractions and gestural, roughly figured primitivism. In part, Jorn's defacements are the typically hostile and scandalous avant-garde response to emblems of artistic "tradition," displaying the irreverence but not always the ironic good humor with which Duchamp suggested, in the Green Box, that one use a Rembrandt as an ironing board. In many of the *détourned* portraits, however, such as *Fraternité avant tout* and *Les deux pingouins,* the force of those gestures also reveals the aggression of Jorn's response to the static smugness of "high society" and the self-satisfied image the *haute bourgeoisie* has of itself. Not coincidentally, in Debord's terms that mirror image is the very definition of the spectacle; just as the spectacular "commodity contemplates itself in a world of its own making," so through the reflection of the spectacle "the ruling order discourses endlessly upon itself in an uninterrupted monologue of self-praise. The spectacle is the self-portrait of power" which becomes a narcissistic, "uninterrupted discourse about itself, a laudatory monologue."[43]

The irreverence with which Jorn's defacements break the drone of that monologue is certainly gratifying, but his *détournements* go beyond a simple mockery or negation of the original. Unlike Duchamp's *L.H.O.O.Q.,* to which it obviously alludes, *L'avant-garde se rend pas,* for example, is less an act of defacement than the remotivation of an image that would originally have signified with the sort of hackneyed elicitation of habitual response ("nice little girl," say) that leaves such emblems all but unseen. In part, the difference between Duchamp's and Jorn's barbering is an effect of the difference between the singular icon of high art and an anonymous painting. In Jorn's *détournement,* however, even the dirty, brownish pigment added to the figure's bust is applied with a certain soigné delicacy, matched by the care with which he has drawn in the facial hair; these gestures stand in marked contrast to the blunt lettering and childish figures that surround her. Moreover, by suggesting that those figures were scribbled on the wall by the girl herself, Jorn revitalizes the stasis of the original scene with a sense of narrative, and he generates a range of new significations from the tension between the original painting and its *détournement.* The girl's politely neutral and unemotional smile takes on an impish cast, and her direct gaze, perhaps originally even *ingénue,* acquires a certain impertinent defiance, as does the prim pose with hands held demurely and passively in front, pleading a blamelessness blatantly contradicted by the evidence behind her. "Who me?" her pose seems to deny with a faux innocence. Indeed, the jump rope held in those hands is emblematic; on the one hand, a sign of child's play, *la corde à sauter* (jump rope; *ça saute aux yeux* [it's obvious]), cannot, on the other hand — however limply bunched — entirely cancel the whispered confession that her play has *trop tirée sur la corde* (gone too far).

That same combination of impudence and abnegation also colors Jorn's own puerile scribblings, which themselves carry a certain disavowal. Although the difference between marking the photographic reproduction of a painting and irrevocably marking the surface of the painting itself is not inconsequential, Jorn quotes Duchamp's audacity rather than effectively reenacting it.[44] Originally, *L.H.O.O.Q.* was also an act of остраннения, although it has itself become familiar in turn; Debord was not alone in noting that "les moustaches de la Joconde ne présentent aucun caractère plus intéressant que la première version de cette peinture [the Mona Lisa's whiskers are no more interesting a feature than the original version of that painting]."[45] Jorn's *détournement* gains interest because it extends not just to the found painting, but also to Duchamp's mustache: redirecting its original purpose and putting it to new uses so that it can again be meaningfully seen. Because of the rapidity with which the most defiant gestures are recuperated — the high-art status of dada's anti-art statements being a case in point — effective revolution must be continuous, which is precisely why *l'avant-garde se rend pas.* To this end, one should of course not regard Jorn's *détournements* as finished objects to be read like traditional paintings; they record his own engagement with a painting and should be a spur to the subsequent *détournement* of his own diversions. Accordingly, the implicated but unintegrated status of original and *détourned* elements in Jorn's paintings—their "dialogue," in Debord's terms—helps to forestall his work's lapse into a readily assimilable stasis; Jorn keeps the two far enough apart that the new work switches constantly between its original elements and their deflection, sparking like a cylinder between the two poles of a dynamo. In *L'avant-garde se rend pas,* that tension is maintained in large part through the recursively homologous structure of the painting: Jorn's illicit scribbling is *mise en abîme* in the implied scene of the girl's own illicit scribblings.

Jorn negotiates a similarly undecidable ambivalence in his 1962 disfiguration *Les deux pingouins* (*The Two Penguins*), which again underscores the difference between his work and the original painting even as it connects the two, bringing them close enough to engage in a meaningful dialogue. Although many of Jorn's titles amount to no more than uninspired calembours—*Le barbare et la berbère* (*The Barbarian and the Berber*), or *La vie d'une nature morte* (*The Life of a Still Life;* literally, a "dead nature"]), for instance—they often repay attention.[46] A title like *Arbre arbitraire* (*Arbitrary Tree*), for example, nicely evokes de Saussure's famous illustration in the *Cours de linguistique général* and underscores precisely the way in which the arbitrary, unmotivated nature of the sign can be remotivated so that *arbitraire* can in fact generate ~~arbitraire~~. "I always go for a title that has the maximum number of meanings, yet applies to only one single object," Jorn has remarked, and "les deux pingouins" is worth considering beyond its obvious reference.[47] At one level, Jorn merely insists upon the humor inherent in the original portrait: a man starched in a formal "penguin-suit" and looking—as does a penguin—"à fois guindé et comique [simultaneously stilted and comical]." But why only "deux" penguins, when each panel ghosts a doubled image so that there are really four penguins visible in the painting? The answer, it turns out, is close at hand. Unlike English, French actually does have two "penguins"; outside of ornithological texts, *pingouin* and *manchot* are used almost interchangeably. Moreover, Jorn hints at this other penguin by leaving one of the man's hands manifestly visible even as his arms have been obscured and shortened into rough approximations of wings. "Un manchot" also denotes a one-armed man, and it would have described not only the figure in the painting but also the condition of Jorn himself working in the one-armed medium of oils rather than the two-handed mode of ceramics with which he divided his artistic time. A hand in the bird, in other words, is worth pushing the two. If Jorn's own "hand" is visible in the drips and rapidly worked figurations on this painting, it never entirely effaces the realist hand of what was there "avant [before]" (as the first panel of the diptych is inscribed). Idiomatically, *il n'est pas manchot* denotes "he's good with his hands," and this is precisely the distinction that separates Jorn's gestural painting, with its studied primitivism, from the more or less awkward (or is that aukward?) techniques of his thrift-store sources.

Thus, in accord with the Situationists' valuation of productive insubordination, Jorn unsettles the hierarchies of signification within his modified paintings; he (mis)uses certain elements by both frustrating their presumed signification within a particular semiotic system and emphasizing their potential to generate meanings within other, separate regimes. Jorn's interventions, that is, remotivate certain images (rope, bird, hand, etc.) so that they become elements in a linguistic code that works independently of, or even against, their ostensible visual use as represented images. Similarly, part of the force of the sources Jorn appropriates is that their representationality provides a background against which his abstractions are able to signify as oppositionally opaque and insubordinate marks that cannot be assimilated to a referential discourse. (Were Jorn's source one of Pollock's drip paintings or one of Malevich's suprematist compositions, that is, the force of his own marking would be quite different.) The point is worth emphasizing: to merely disrupt the illusionistic surface of his sources would simply reinstate one authority with another, and the distinctly *détourné* quality of Jorn's interventions derives from the way in which he prevents any given framework from wresting a secure authority. This sense of Situationist "dialogue" emerges not just from the implication of particular elements in multiple signifying systems, but also from Jorn's method of complicitously inscribing himself and his own insurrectional gestures into the space of even the most complacent original painting. As we have seen with both the *mise en abîme* graffiti of *L'avant-garde se rend pas* and the announcement of one-handed skill in *Les deux pingouins*, Jorn draws analogies between his own activities and those of his subjects, thus unresolvably complicating the relation of process and product in such a way that neither painting nor (over)painted can secure an unambiguous priority or uncontested authority over the other. So even when the original portrait threatens to disappear beneath the splatter and drip of Jorn's modifications in the second panel of *Les deux pingouins*, the play of Jorn's title helps to sustain the dialogue that Situationist *détournement* requires. By showing his hand, as it were, Jorn invites the viewer to recognize the puns, but the full force of those puns' meaning requires the viewer to simultaneously recognize both levels of the *détourned* painting, without allowing one to either take precedence or collapse entirely into the other.

In a number of other *détournements,* Jorn also insists on making visible what is effaced, even as he displays the obscurant overpainting. In several works, Jorn images and emphasizes ducks; among the 1959 modifications, for instance, one finds *Le lac des canards* and the hilariously ridiculous *Le canard inquiétant.* As with the penguins, this avian subject matter is not incidental. The French *canard,* like the English "duck," denotes not just the waterfowl but the cotton canvas of the painting itself—what realism attempts to render invisible and what Jorn returns to view. At the same time, the wet and fluid oil with which he further obscured the duck of the original canvases, as evidenced by its drips and runs, might well have evoked the adjectival sense of *canard—très mouillé* (all wet)—and idiomatic phrases like *mouillé* and *trempé comme un canard.* The pictographic graffiti in *L'avant-garde se rend pas,* it turns out, are far from gratuitous: a bird and a one-handed man—*canard et manchot*—in dialogue with Jorn's other *détournements* and once again leaving their conversational trace on the surface of the painting.

Message in a Bottle

Life is an anarchy of clair-obscur.

　—Georg Lukács

The perfection of suicide is in ambiguity.

　—Guy Debord

In 1957, just as the Situationniste Internationale was coalescing, Jorn and Debord collaborated with the lithographer and printer V. O. Permild to make two extraordinary books, *Fin de Copenhague* and *Mémoires.*[48] To some extent, these works recall Gil Wolman's *récit détourné* (diverted narrative) "J'écris propre," which had been published the previous year in the proto-Situationist journal *Les lèvres nues.* Like Wolman's story, these books announce themselves collage works "entièrement composé d'éléments préfabriqués [composed entirely of prefabricated material]"; but to that scavenged, fragmented, and sutured language they add line illustrations, photographs, and Jorn's distinctive overpainting of drips, spatters, and runs. In the case of *Mémoires,* which is divided into precisely dated sections, the collage elements are salvaged from a variety of books, popular magazines, and souvenirs from Debord's lettrist days, which it recalls with the unrelenting "melancholy of a world passing away."[49] In the case of *Fin de Copenhague,* which is at once more styptic and humorous in its critique of spectacular culture, all of the material was purportedly raided from a single news kiosk and assembled in a single, inspired day.[50] For all of its improvisatory haste, however, the text's wit and economy of means is superb; if a movie advertisement appears to reference *la société du spectacle,* for instance, its placement is motivated both because the title— *Vera Cruz*—rhymes with the *cruise* liner that appears on the same page, and also because "super<u>scope</u>" graphically echoes the "<u>Cope</u>nhagen" written *super,* or above it.

Constructed as *détournements* of found material reorganized to tell new stories, the language of these books also undergoes its own analogous *détournement.* Specific calembours, as we have seen, work effectively to maintain the dialogue of Jorn's modifications, but paronomasia, as such, is integral to Situationist practice as well. At the level of the word, the pun itself is a *détournement.* Puns differ from polysemy or mere homophony by holding two registers simultaneously in play and dialogue with one another, rather than simply switching between them. The graphemic or phonemic ensembles of the word are hijacked in a pun so that the apparent direction of reference—the semantic telos of the word—is diverted from its ostensible destination. That signified is not simply bypassed, however; a trace of its semantic vector always remains as the word gestures towards both its original and modified meaning at the same time. The pun, in short, is a word beset by eidetic memory. In their collage books, Jorn and Debord work to create contextual registers with such precise semantic fields that the pull of reference causes words to hover in suspended resonance between the balanced play of competing forces. Or perhaps the effect of these words is less like a *champ magnétique* and more like the undecidable movements of subatomic particles simultaneously swerving towards discrete and irreconcilable states of affairs, tracing their clinanimatic paths between subatomic matter under the sway of a gravitational semantics.

Examples of these puns, and the degree to which Jorn and Debord carefully balance their simultaneous references without privileging one over the other, will emerge in the course of this chapter. To begin with, I want to concentrate on the way in which *Fin de Copenhague* emphasizes its status as a book by punning on elements of its formal structure. Originally bound in flong, made from what is apparently a Danish newspaper, the covers sport a large advertisement for shaving products. The front cover is dominated by a headline that reads "¡barberspejlet! [shaving mirror!]," and the back cover is taken up by the image of a man looking in the mirror as he shaves. The starkly blanched face of that shaver thus both literally and figuratively *a une mine de papier mâché*.[51] Moreover, being bored and being shaved are the same in French (*être rasé*), a coincidence that Jorn and Debord exploit to connect the book's covers with its opening lines: "Copenhague[:] je passais mon temps . . . [avec] la sensation d'être écrasé de fatigue [I have passed the time . . . (with) the feeling of being crushed with tedium]." To further underscore the connection, that somewhat melodramatic "écrasé [crushed]" literally inscribes "rasé [shaved]." Razor blades, in any case, are central to the construction of the collaged pages of the book; the banalities and boredoms of Copenhagen are referenced in *Copenhague* through the collagists' shavings (*copeaux*). With the addition of the advertising copy, these sliding references accumulate at a dizzying pace; the display line at the bottom of the front cover opens "år [year]," suggesting the scar (Danish *ar*) of a shaving cut that might come from the product advertised as the "skarpeste klinge [sharpest razor]" or "blad [blade]" — a Danish homonym which itself neatly collapses the straight-edge and the "newspaper" (*blad*) that was cut to assemble the very book that contains it. This self-reflexiveness is underscored by the cover's image of self-reflection — a man looking at himself in the *barberspejlet* — and, in a line erased so that one must in fact look through it, the caption below that shaver invites one to "gennem [look through]." Taking the cue and figuratively looking straight through the book from that line to its parallel position on the front cover, the reader finds the interlingually punning "videre": an adjective in Danish, meaning "broader" or "wider," and in Latin the infinitive of the verb "to look." Beyond the obvious mockery of spectacular culture in *Fin de Copenhague*, these more subtle anaphoric and cataphoric references ask the reader to strop, look, and listen carefully.

This type of bibliographic self-reflexiveness also inscribes the book's authors into the very weave of their work's material, repeating the way in which we saw Jorn implicate himself within the signifying networks of his paintings. *Fin de Copenhague* was published as an *edition de luxe* limited to 200 copies: "Ein Wertvolles Buch [A Valuable Book]," as one of its own pages announces in bold gothic type. In accord with art world practice, Jorn signed each copy by hand, but the book is wittily countersigned by its very construction and design. Binding is the art of gathering signatures, of course, and the "signature" of the third collaborator, for instance, appears not only in the colophon, but also *mise en abîme* under the movie advertisement with a collaged bit of business stationary from his printing firm: "Permild & Rosengreen." Similarly, with a shift (сдвиг) across word boundaries, Debord's name explicitly emerges from an advertisement copy for a "store kolde bord [big deli spread]." The other inscriptions, however, are less obvious. To begin with (d'abord), in this work of cuttings (des bordes), the printing is bled: most of the collaged images project beyond the margins, and the overlapping painted designs all overflow the edges and run off the page; the layout, that is, continually déborde (overruns) the margins. Additionally, those flows of ink color-in the outskirts and surrounding areas (abords) of the collaged or schematized city maps that fill several pages, as well as the approach (abord) to "Mt Kilimanjaro" on another. Jorn's name implicitly appears throughout the book as well; as a work comprised of newspapers (journaux) documenting a single day's work (journée), Fin becomes a page in Jorn and Debord's collective logbook (journal de bord)—a nautical reference corroborated by the weather charts, sea maps, and cruise advertisements that it contains.

Given that nautical context, in fact, the semantic drifts of appropriated language in Fin de Copenhague suggest—or derive from—a central Situationist concept: la dérive (leeway, drift, adrift).[52] As a Situationist terme de métier, "dérive" denotes "une technique du passage hâtif à travers des ambiances variées [a technique of transient passage through varied ambiences]."[53] Or, in other words, disoriented wanderings, usually through abandoned buildings or city streets. Developed by Chtcheglov, Rumney, and other "new urbanists," that playful, unmotivated wandering—a "déambulation [aimless ambulation]" in explicit contradistinction to a "promenade [stroll]"—proceeds regardless of habit or the coercions of civic planning, and without any goals other than attunement to the lure or repulsion of the landscape and a surrender to its possibilities.[54] A dérive thus charts microclimates of "psychogeographical space" according to an ecology of emotion rather than established architectures or physical distance:

> Une ou plusieurs personnes se livrant à la dérive renoncent, pour une durée plus our moins longue, aux raisons de se déplacer et d'agir qu'elles se connaissent généralement, aux relations, aux travaux et aux loisirs qui leur sont propres, pour se laisser aller aux sollicitations du terrain et des rencontres qui y correspondent.

> *In a dérive one or more persons during a certain period drop their usual motives for movement and action, their relations, their work and leisure activities, and let themselves be drawn by the attractions or the terrain and the encounters they find there.*[55]

In short, Rimbaud's *dérèglement* applied to urban travel. The Situationists thus join the crowd of all those other *promèneurs,* flaneurs, and drifters of unreal cities: De Quincey, de Nerval (Labrunie), Baudelaire, Whitman, and most importantly, Aragon and his surrealist comrades. Against that tradition of the *faire aller,* however, *les dériveurs* are not passively awaiting the prurient thrill of a *choc* from around the corner, or voyeuristically hoping to glimpse *une scène chatouillement,* or even necessarily exploring new and uncharted territory; they are out to actively create the situations of their drift. Indeed, if not sufficiently lost or drunk to effect the proper disorientation of a nonlaminar flow, they could always resort to technologies of *dérivant,* such as following the map of one city while in another.[56]

The spread and drift of the paint that flows through (and off) the pages of Jorn and Debord's Situationist books obviously mimics the *dérive.* Accordingly, Greil Marcus reads Jorn's painting in *Mémoires* representationally: the "seemingly blind strips of color turn into avenues, then Debord's words and pictures change Jorn's avenues into labyrinths."[57] To some extent, and for certain pages, this is certainly correct, but as *Fin de Copenhague* manifests, Jorn's apparently abstract painting is also figurative in another sense; the distinctive liquid overlays in these books index other referents as well. Indeed, the look of those designs is familiar not so much from Jorn's canvases—though you can see them there as well—as from the autobiographical scenes of Debord's films. Glimpsed in frames of *Sur le passage de quelques personnes . . .* (1959) or *Critique du separation* (1961), they are in fact the very mise-en-scène of the artistic and revolutionary bohemian world inhabited by Debord and Jorn. With drips, splashes, smears, and fingerprints, Jorn stains the pages of their books as though they were café tables set amid the scuff and debris of Situationist haunts like Chez Charot, Café de Mabillon, Chez Moineau, or one of the other seedy café bars around the Saint-Germain-des-Prés where Gil Wolman recounts vomiting "copiously."[58] Where, moreover, crowded, careless, inebriated patrons—attempting to negotiate the closely spaced and unsturdy tables—sent liquid sloshing over saucers onto unlevel tabletops, leaving it to ring and pool haphazardly, where hands unsteady from too little sleep and too many drinks misjudged, or gestured overemphatically, and where, later, they idly drew in the spill and splatter with burnt-out matches, tracing through the cigarette ash that speckled the whole in its turn.

I do not mean to be gratuitously discursive here; far from incidental, these very details of everyday life "at the cafe terrace" are central among the narratives written into Situationist books and woven between their fragments.[59] With their wine-tinged memories, the pages of Jorn and Debord's books record a lost world of habit, gesture, and etiquette: in short, the sense of the *6yt* or *vie quotidienne* that was so central to Situationist theory. Fulfilling the dream with which Chtcheglov had helped launch the IS, Jorn and Debord, in other words, were building the hacienda "where the wine is finished off with fables from an old almanac." Or, as Situationist style might have repeated, where old almanacs are finished with wine. Indeed, the contemporaneous issue of the journal *Internationale situationniste* (no. 3) proposes a three-dimensional novel, cut into fragments and pasted on bottles of rum, allowing the reader to follow its narrative at whim; *Mémoires* and *Fin de Copenhague* essentially reverse this scheme, printing rivulets of rum on the pages of a fragmented novel.

The construction of Situationist texts, if not the construction of situations themselves, was done under precisely such conditions—and under the influence. By recalling the very space and story of their own construction, these books fulfill a key principle of Situationist aesthetics: "la principale force d'un détournement étant fonction directe de sa reconnaissance, consciente ou trouble, par la mémoire [the main force of a detournement is directly related to the conscious or vague recollection of the original contexts of the elements]."[60] As Debord notes in the foreword to the 1993 reproduction of *Mémoires,* the book "était en grande harmonie avec la vie réelle que nous menions alors [was in full accord with the life that we then lived]." And that life was consumed by drink. The IS was founded "in a state of semi-drunkenness," and a survey of the photographs documenting the meetings and conferences of CoBrA, the lettrists, and the IS reveals one constant among shifting sites and personnel: the ubiquitous bottles of alcohol, glasses of wine, and beer steins.[61] Debord's own drinking, in particular, is well known; "c'est un fait," he writes, "que j'ai été continuellement ivre tout au long du périodes de plusieurs mois; et encore, le reste du temps, avais-je beaucoup bu [it is a fact that I have been continuously drunk for periods of several months; and the rest of the time, I still drank a lot]."[62] Debord devotes the entire third chapter of his autobiography, *Panegyrique*—a work of overwhelming melancholia cut only by megalomania—to alcohol, which he claims "a été la plus constante et le plus présente [has been the most constant and the most present]" thing in his life.[63] In particular, writing and drinking come hard upon the other in Debord's account: "J'ai écrit beaucoup moins que la plupart des gens qui écrivent; mais j'ai bu beaucoup plus que la plupart des gens qui boivent [I have written much less than most people who write; but I have drunk much more than most people who drink]."[64] When Michèle Bernstein quips, with all the bitterness of the dregs, that Debord's purges extended to those who set "their wine glasses on the table in a bourgeois manner," her sarcastic figure is not incidental. *Fin de Copenhague* and *Mémoires* record the marks those glasses left in a different manner.[65]

Indeed, lest the point be missed, *Fin de Copenhague* renders graphically explicit the equation of spilled alcohol with Jorn's poured paint. In addition to a scotch label which floats at the top of one page (anticipating Gil Wolman's "scotch art" by six years!), the book features several illustrations of tilted bottles, either pasted in at horizontal angles and threatening to spill or actually emptying out onto the page. Even if, in contrast, "les bouteilles se couchent [the bottles are hidden]" in *Mémoires,* they resurface a decade later, when they could be seen in reserve behind the barricades in the summer of 1968: emptied, drunk dry, *détournés,* refilled with petrol and stopped with rags to make Molotov cocktails. Jorn and Debord's books make a plea for that revolution, and Situationist intoxication is intimately bound to their revolution of everyday life, although they did not, perhaps, foresee the way in which the consumption of alcohol would be a necessary prerequisite for revolutionary action: the tools of the alcoholic and the street-fighting *bricoleur* linked in direct proportion to one another. However, when they had *Mémoires* bound in a heavy-gauge sandpaper they would have foreseen the implicit pun. This binding was ostensibly meant to destroy the books next to *Mémoires* on the shelf with each use, thus aggressively undercutting utility with a codexical potlatch; but bound in *papiers de verre* (literally "papers of glass"), the book not only evokes *spectacles,* and makes a witty allusion to the shaving-glass cover of *Fin de Copenhague* (even incorporating a tactile replication of the shaving man's unshaven stubble), but it also becomes a fitting receptacle for the liquids—whether alcoholic or incendiary—it contains.[66]

As an emblem of both the revolt against the state and the revolution of everyday life, the spirituous, in Situationist books, is thus always imbued with politics. Since none of the commentators on Situationist books mentions even the thematic prevalence of this subject, I want to conclude this section by making clear how thoroughly the flavor of that politicized alcohol extends through *Mémoires* and *Fin de Copenhague,* which—even beyond Jorn's painting and the visual figures of bottles—are soaked in alcohol. With what may indeed be "all the pleasures of the summer," or at least "all the necessary conditions," the very first page of *Fin de Copenhague* features a Danish drink menu printed in boldface:

5 slags øl
17 slags vin . . .
solbaerrom
perbermyntelikør
1,31 pr. genstand

5 fine beers
17 fine wines . . .
flavored rum
mint liqueur
1.31 each

After this aperitif, the underlined "Drink—£300" similarly stands out in the center of a later page, and in one opening the bilingual copy from a Dubonnet advertisement, glamorizing an ethos of "dissipation," mirrors a statement at the top of the other page: "Dix minuets après, l'émotion étant / dissipée, on buvait le champagne [Ten minutes later, the emotion having / dissipated, the champagne was drunk]." Such references are even more common in *Mémoires*, where the first page metatextually announces: "il s'agit d'un sujet profondément imprégné d'alcool [it's all about a subject deeply drenched in alcohol]." The collaged fragments which follow corroborate this opening claim. On one page Debord declares, rather pompously, "the wine of life is decanted, and the dregs alone remain of that pompous cellar." He then turns from the metaphoric to the literal a few pages later, admitting that in fact "il reste du vin [there's still some wine left]." "Nous bûmes," Debord recalls, "outre mesure de toutes sortes de vins [we drank beyond measure all sorts of wines]," and among "tous les sirops somnifères du monde [all the world's somniferous cordials]," he queries "Moi, ivre? [Me, drunk?]." Debord records being "sous l'influence de l'alcool [under the influence of alcohol]" or "pas ivre en ce moment [not drunk at the moment]," and he differentiates like a connoisseur of intoxication among "boire [drinking]," "en train de boire [in the midst of drinking]," and "Après boire [After drinking]."[67]

The suffusion of these books with alcohol unsteadies other quotes as well. Part of the collaged material in *Mémoires*, for instance, draws from a soft-porn story, but in its intoxicated new context, the alcoholic and orgasmic blur in a beautifully tight fit—"Beau comme le tremblement des mains dans l'alcoolisme [Beautiful like the trembling of hands in alcoholism]," as Lautréamont would write in a line appropriated by Debord.⁶⁸

Puis les secousses s'espacent, s'atténuent, s'apaisent . . . . Elle se mit à trembler, sans répondre . . . . Ainsi les grandes convulsions pas encore entièrement apaisées . . . . A un moment, si je ne l'avais retenue, elle se serait affalée sur le sol en proie à des convulsions

Then the tremors diminish, attenuate, calm . . . . She set to trembling, without answering . . . . Thus the great convulsions were no longer entirely soothed . . . . At one point, if I hadn't restrained her, she would have collapsed on the ground in the predatory grip of convulsions.

Alcohol similarly flavors other apparently random elements of these collages. The recurrent pirate references from Robert Louis Stevenson are motivated not only because they represent an ethos of criminal and anarchic counter-market lifestyles, but also because they're done in with drink ("La boisson . . . [les a] expédié"), singing "Yo-ho-ho! et une bouteille de rhum [Yo-ho-ho and a bottle of rum!]" to the end—a line that echoes through *Mémoires* to serve as a refrain for Debord's book as well as Cochon-Rôti's song. The description of being "se dessèche [parched]" becomes equally charged in *Fin de Copenhague,* where the recurrent weather maps reveal an alcoholic logic: they predict how wet and dry the coming days and weeks will be, bringing together cool drafts and the draughts of *alcool.* If Jorn and Debord's collaboration was spontaneous, and hence without "drafts" in the artistic sense, it would nonetheless have gone through a series of proofs (*épreuve* if not *teneur*), and indeed, even the degree symbols on the repeated meteorological charts begin to look like indications of proof rather than temperature. All of which, significantly, merges in the homophonic play on the English "fan" and the French "fin" in the Dubonnet page—a linguistic drift beautifully complicated when the tide turns away from phonetics: a tail "fin," in French, is, significantly, *une dérive* (and one should not forget the image in *Fin* of an airplane, with its tail fin silhouetted). In the end, the phonetic difference between *la* fin *de Copenhague* and *le* vin *de Copenhague* (wine from Copenhagen), or the graphic difference between the actual title and *Fine de Copenhague* (brandy liqueur from Copenhagen), is provocatively slight.⁶⁹ An issue for connoisseurs.

Wasted Time

Le meilleur, c'est un sommeil bien ivre, sur la grève.
— Arthur Rimbaud

Life can never be too disorienting.
— Guy Debord

We have seen that alcohol is not simply a biographical accouterment, nor merely incidental to the mise-en-scène of Situationist haunts. Associated as it is with the politicized transformation of everyday life, and working to effect the heightened *détournement* of punning language in Situationist books, alcohol is also intimately bound with another central theme of Jorn and Debord's books, and one of Debord's central objects of critique: time. Alcohol can fundamentally alter one's relationship to time. In a banal sense, it can obviously organize time, as in the "cocktail hour," or through the association of particular drinks with particular times of the day, but the effects can be more profound as well.[70] I want to be clear that I do not mean by this the flush and rush of the first drink (which can of course revive and excite one about the future), nor do I mean to suggest the petty inebriation of the first few (the draughts of the weepy drunk, bringing the past into the present like cases carted from the cellar to be relived); I mean a true, thorough, richly dark intoxication. Intoxication to such a degree that it effects a type of continuous present: not like Stein's, starting again and again, but one that stretches and suspends the present. And thereby obliterates it. The effect, in short, of looking up from the glass at the clock with a shock. We speak of "forgetting all about the time," but the shock is that we have forgotten all about time itself. Or rather, that we have recognized a new experience of time unmoored from its regulation by that clock: time stupored to the point where it forgets itself in an ethyl blind.[71] That point "est au delà de la violente ivresse, quand on a franchi ce stade: une paix magnifique et terrible, le vrai goût du passage du temps [lies beyond violent drunkenness, when one has passed that stage: a magnificent and terrible peace, the true taste of the passage of time]."[72]

This effect of a time reorganized by alcohol, one should note, is quite different from Gilles Deleuze's elaboration of time's reorganization by alco*holism*.[73] In his terms, "Alcoholism does not seem to be a search for pleasure, but a search for an effect which consists mainly in an extraordinary hardening of the present."[74] Debord in fact exemplifies precisely this alcoholic time in *Panegyrique,* with its frequent use of "j'ai bu." "The alcoholic," Deleuze argues, "does not live at all in the imperfect or the future; the alcoholic has only a past perfect (*passé composé*) . . . . as if the softness of the past participle came to be combined with the hardness of the present auxiliary."[75] To harden rather than obliterate the present, however, would run counter to Situationist dreams; a present frozen and brought forward into the future like an artifact—a spectacle displayed in the museum of time—would fail to constitute a "situation" in Debord's terms. "Situations are conceived as the opposite of works of art, which are attempts at absolute valorization and preservation of the present moment."[76] While Deleuze recognizes that there is also the time of alcoholic need, in which "every future is experienced as a future perfect (*futur-antérieur*)," his discussion of Lowry, surprisingly, passes over the intoxicated time of alcohol itself: the "circumfluent" and "paralysed" time described in the final pages of *Under the Volcano*.[77] With a nostalgic gloss appropriate to Debord's tone in *Panegyrique,* Deleuze proclaims: "alcohol is at once love and the loss of love. . . . *object, loss of object and the law governing this loss.*"[78] One cannot help but hear the example he refrains from giving: time and the loss of time. In that loss of time situations are found.

For all their experimentation and radicality, Jorn and Debord's collaborations fail to extend their understanding of revolutionary time to the level of the book itself. Debord, predictably enough, critiques linear and sequential narratives; such "a chronology of events" evokes "an inexorable movement that crushed individuals before it."[79] *Mémoires,* however, enacts precisely such chronologies with its finalized and sequential dating of material corresponding neatly to its standard, linear, codexical sequence (spine to the left and pages turned one after the other from right to left). In contrast, the discontinuous and fragmented pages of *Fin de Copenhague* work against linearity to the extent that their parataxis blocks the smooth transition from one page to the next. Indeed, one might read the structure of *Fin* as a model for anarchist soviets: a federation that resists the subservience of the individual page to either an overall design or to an irrelevant autonomy. The pages in *Fin,* that is, deny precedence but share recurrent motifs, thus creating a spatial analogue to "individual and collective irreversible time which is playful in character and which encompasses, simultaneously present within it, a variety of autonomous yet effectively federated times."[80] In the end, however, the conventional understanding of the page as "a sort of enclosed space" which follows on another in an orderly "succession of artificially distinct moments" like the "accumulation of equivalent intervals" or spatialized examples of "time cut up into equal abstract fragments," is too ingrained to be offset by an exacerbation of their discrete enclosure of space.[81] The layout of pages even in *Fin de Copenhague* ultimately enacts the very structures Debord critiques.

This may seem a rather petty and harsh assessment of Jorn and Debord's work, arrived at only after interrogating the most trivial and incidental aspect of a book which otherwise, as I have just been arguing at some length, displays an exemplary Situationist practice. But the significance of such details, and the unflinching attention they require, is precisely the lesson a radical formalism might learn from that Situationist practice. The dream of politics requires both a sleepless watch, an insomniac vigilance Argus-eyed and lidless, and also—as the title of Michèle Bernstein's manifesto announced in the premier issue of the IS—"Pas d'indulgence inutile [No useless leniency]." We awake into the dawn of the dream of politics with precision, and "oui, l'heure nouvelle est au moins très-sévère [yes, the new hour is, at the very least, quite severe]."[82]

Rien ne se passe d'essentiel où le bruit ne soit présent.

    —Jacques Attali

There is no such thing as silence.

    —John Cage

2. The Politics of Noise

Unmasking the "Face of the Voice of Speech"

"How often do critics consider poetry as a physical act? Do critics look at the print on the page, at the shapes of the words, at the surface—the space of the paper itself?" Having posed these questions, Susan Howe accusingly answers: "Very rarely."[1] In the last chapter, we saw the consequences of overlooking precisely such details; having tested the relation of certain physical poetic acts against the specific political claims of the Situationists, this chapter will turn to a more general examination of the political dynamics of the text at those moments when it threatens (or promises) to become illegible. As in the previous chapter, I will continue to explore the degree to which textual and bibliographic details can motivate the work within which they not only signify and provide material support, but also continually offer points of resistance, contradiction, and the necessity— for both readers and writers—of making irrevocable ethical decisions. By way of example, I will focus on the writings of Howe herself, who began her artistic career as a visual artist and has in fact been one of the rare exceptions to the critical blindness towards the most visual acts of poetry. In her important scholarly work on American literature, and especially on the manuscripts of Emily Dickinson, she evinces a close attention to visual prosody: the look of texts on the page and their necessary imbeddedness in the materiality of that page through details like size, cut, color, and watermark.[2] "Messages," as Howe wittily asserts, "must be seen to be heard to say."[3] One might, of course, question the extent to which Howe reads her own poetic concerns into earlier writings, but whatever the answer, her treatment of others' works stands as a good model of how her own poems, and their visual prosodics, might be considered.

The unconventional look of Howe's pages is the most immediately noticeable aspect of her poetry; the inconsistent leading and spacing of the earlier poems has given way to cut and scored-through type, over-printing, lines set at conflicting and intersecting angles, and even type set backwards and upside down. Surprisingly, this is one aspect of her work which critics have consistently noted but failed to seriously address.[4] In part, this may well be due to the difficulty of talking about visual prosody; we lack a sophisticated critical tradition and ready vocabulary. In fact, when such matters are considered at all, any radical deviation from a print-ing norm is generally taken to be a more important classificatory element for poetry than the underlying theoretical conceptions of representation, performance, or the relationships between text, space, sound, and so on. Critical accounts all too often class together essentially different writings under a single rubric like "visual poetry," which is somehow meant to en-compass everything from ancient Greek *technopaginae* to the work of the Brazilian Noigandres group in the middle of the twentieth century to Flash animated digital poetry. So, by way of approaching what Howe's visual techniques accomplish, I want to start by very briefly situating her work in terms of what it specifically does *not* do in comparison with other experi-ments in typography and spatial composition.

Just as Howe's scholarly project in American literary history has in-volved "unsettling" the "European grid on the Forest," her poetic project has involved unsettling the grid of the page.[5] While Howe's earlier field compositions and word grids challenge their audience's reliance on con-ventions of reading (left-to-right, top-to-bottom), her subsequent turn to rotations and inverse mirrorings, in works such as *The Articulation of Sound Forms in Time* and *Eikon Basilike,* confound a reader's expectations by eliminating the very directional axes on which those conventions are based. Moreover, when such radical disruption gives way to palimpsests which render some words entirely illegible, it becomes clear that Howe's graphic maneuvers are not, like the texts of poets as diverse as Louis Zukofsky and Denise Levertov, at the service of finely modulating a vocal realization of the poem—and this is true despite Howe's virtuoso readings of her own poems. Those pages which are left "to be read by guesswork through oblit-eration" do not constitute a guide to greater syntactic clarity or a score for performance, and this in itself is an important distinction between Howe's work and the majority of even visually experimental writers.[6] Additionally, the viewer of such pages is immediately aware that in contrast with the Italian or Russian futurists—or even contemporary commercial advertising and design—Howe does not exploit the "expressive" potential of varied inks and types, or even, like Mallarmé, different fonts.[7]

One section from Howe's long poem "Melville's Marginalia," however, does make a more direct allusion to what is perhaps the most famous example from the history of typographic innovations: Apollinaire's "Il pleut" ("It's Raining"). This visual rhyme should serve to emphasize the distance which separates Howe's work from that of other twentieth-century experimentalists. "Melville's Marginalia," in part, is a consideration of the life of the Irish writer James "Clarence" Mangan. Explicitly noting the "feminine softness of his voice," Howe translates the rain of ghostly feminine voices from Apollinaire's page into the "verbal phantoms" raining down on her own.[8] Mangan, a figure who "has been all but forgotten" in the current academic memory, is one of the "Writers in these publications" which Howe plunders for her material and "Whose name appears and disappears forever"—quite literally—into the near illegibility beneath the "Churchyard and grave": "voix . . . mortes même dans le souvenir" indeed.[9] As Howe argues, however, this "relative unacquaintance" was not always the case, and "Melville's Marginalia" is saturated with over half a dozen bemused and reverential anecdotes describing various encounters with Mangan. These snippets, like the "gouttelettes" of Apollinaire's second line, could each be entitled "merveilleuses rencontres de ma vie."[10] Two such droplets, in fact, frame the "verbal phantoms" section and foreground the significance of its allusive layout; the previous page contains a citation which describes the "spectral-looking" Mangan as a phantom figure "who never appeared abroad in sunshine or storm without a large malformed umbrella," and the text which follows the section concludes: "Sometimes, even in the most settled weather, he might be seen parading the streets with a very voluminous umbrella under each arm."[11] With the repetition of this odd detail, readers—like Mangan—are indeed prepared for the rain.

Rather than pursue the thematic correlations between these two poems, I want to emphasize the fact that Howe's poem, by calling attention to the rain in this way, both evokes "Il pleut" and also emphasizes the dissimilarity between the texts. The raining words in Howe's poem, to quote from its second vertical distich, move in their "liquid clearness" from the "sky" to the "horizon" in "pure lines"; the *line,* that is, forms Howe's basic unit of both prosodic and spatial composition, and deviations from the conventional horizontal axis in her texts arise primarily from the manipulation of lines rather than of individual words or letters. Moreover, her lines are also "pure"; Howe's visual constructions are dominated by a geometrically strict linearity. In contrast, the words and lines in *Les Calligrammes* curve and circle in uneven waverings; diagonals are generally formed by angling individual letters rather than the rotation of a conventionally typeset line, and the printing of some of the calligrammes ultimately gives way to the "whirlwind handwritten" text of an even more aggressively alinear hand-lettering.[12] Apollinaire's appeal to the calligraphic (beyond, even, the calligrammatic) has been similarly exploited by writers from Aleksei Kruchonykh to Robert Grenier, and it is conspicuously absent from Howe's oeuvre.[13] One should also note that the illustrative aspect of this section of "Melville's Marginalia" is entirely atypical; Howe's writing is generally not—like that of Apollinaire or George Herbert—shaped, pictorial, or even schematic. Accordingly, the relationship of image and text in Howe's disrupted pages is, as I hope to show, more rich and sophisticated than in the vast majority of so-called "concrete" poetry descending from Apollinaire.[14]

While some of the more visually innovative pages from William Carlos Williams's *Paterson* or Charles Olson's *Maximus* poems may be an inspiration closer to home, one precedent for the look of Howe's essentially linear constructions can be found not in some modernist or postmodernist avant-garde, but rather in Samuel Richardson's mid-eighteenth-century novel *Clarissa Harlowe*. (See figure 1.) *Clarissa* is not one of the source texts for "Melville's Marginalia," but a comparison of a page from each reveals similarities which are both striking and significant (as well as uncanny; note the central exclamation in the fourth stanza of Clarissa's poem: "O my Miss Howe!").[15] (See figure 2.) Both pages share an identical overall layout: five horizontal sections above a smaller indented grouping, flanked on the right by a vertical fragment and on either side at the bottom by fragments angled to form a "V." With descriptions that evoke the visual surface of some of Susan Howe's work, Clarissa's writing in this section of the novel appears in a series of papers and "scarce broken letters" found "torn among fragments"; after she "tears, and throws . . . these rambling papers . . . in fragments," they are transcribed, reconstructed, and described as "Scratch'd thro' " and "Torn in two pieces," and they then culminate in the graphically represented dislocations of "Paper X."[16] Clarissa's letter is written immediately after she has been raped, and the text's shift from prose to disrupted verse is obviously meant to be emblematic. The spatial

PAPER X.

LEAD me, where my own thoughts themselves may lose me;
Where I may doze out what I've left of Life,
Forget myself, and that day's guilt!—
Cruel Remembrance!—how shall I appease thee?

   —Oh! you have done an act
That blots the face and blush of modesty;
   Takes off the rose
From the fair forehead of an innocent Love,
And makes a blister there!—

   Then down I laid my head,
Down on cold earth, and for a while was dead;
And my freed Soul to a strange Somewhere fled!
   Ah! sottish Soul! said I,
When back to its cage again I saw it fly;
   Fool! to resume her broken chain,
   And row the galley here again!
   Fool! to that Body to return,
Where it condemn'd and destin'd is to *mourn!*

Death only can be dreadful to the Bad
To Innocence 'tis like a bugbear dress'd
To frighten children. Pull but off the mask
And he'll appear a friend.

O my Miss Howe! if thou hast friendship, help me,
And speak the words of peace to my divided Soul,
   That wars within me,
And raises ev'ry sense to my confusion.
   I'm tott'ring on the brink
Of peace; and thou art all the hold I've left!
Assist me—in the pangs of my affliction!

When Honour's lost, 'tis a relief to die:
Death's but a sure retreat from infamy.

I could a Tale unfold—
Would harrow up thy soul!

   Then farewel, Youth,
      And all the joys that dwell
   With Youth and Life!
      And Life itself, farewel!

By swift misfortunes
How am I pursu'd
Which on each other
Are, like waves, renew'd

   For Life can never be sincerely blest.
   Heav'n punishes the *Bad,* and proves the *Best.*

Figure 1. Samuel Richardson, *Clarissa* (1747)

A FRENCH ETON or, Middle-class Education
and the State

Less can be immediately good taste Prose

critque radical radical visible subsurface

To cry with *Oberman*

we are all <u>terrae filii</u>

All my

estate

or property

authors

quotations

Between real authors

and the makers of dictionaries

blunders

books"

Government says Burke

(to go back to Burke again)

"is a contrivance of human wisdom

to provide for human wants"

Subject of the idea (to quote from *The Excursion*)

Figure 2. Susan Howe, "Melville's Marginalia" (1993)

portrayal of this distracting, visually confused and over-articulated layout mirrors the accompanying verbal descriptions of Clarissa's distracted, confused, and inarticulate thoughts; with conflicting axes breaking in on one another, the physically violent disruption of "Clarissa" conflates both the body of the text and the body of the character into a "word flesh crumbled page."[17] As the novel's subtitle promised, this is a work "Particularly *shewing* the Distresses that attend . . . Misconduct" [emphasis added]. The visual aspect of Richardson's page, that is, enacts a thematic aspect of the narrative but without any claims to a pictorial representation.

Howe structures her own writing within a thematics of mythical and historical violence: Pearl Harbor, the colonizations of America and Ireland, pursuits and exterminations, captivities and expulsions, regicide, revenge. In her works, these specters fuse with the violent silencings that haunt the history of literature itself, to become "Battles . . . fought ferociously / on paper."[18] Howe's poems, moreover, refer explicitly to their own place in the textual records of such violent histories. Constructed—like most academic essays, and including this chapter itself—only at the expense of other writers' "Texts / torn from their contexts," and filled with "words / torn to pieces by memory," her poems physically appropriate and dissect the language of others, often with a deft *détournement:* "I can compose my thought," a line from "Melville's Marginalia" reads, and then continues: "I will dismember marginalia."[19] Figuring poetry and sentences as, respectively, "a play of force and play / of forces," these poems ultimately begin to absorb all textual practices into the terms of violent action, so that even the seemingly innocuous transliterative or transcriptive act of recording the numeral 1 as the letter "i" encodes, in Howe's formulation, an "eye for an eye."[20] Her poems thus link together, to quote two lines themselves linked in the poem "Scattering as Behavior toward Risk," the "violent order of a world" with an "Iconoclastic folio subgenre."[21] The poems, that is, mate their themes to the visual violence of the image-*breaking*— the icono*clasm*—of Howe's disrupted folio pages. On the fragmented and indeterminate surfaces of those pages

War

approaches its abstract form   Play
of possibilities

probabilities

[. . .]

Confusion

of lines bisecting   shred
after shred.[22]

"I had unleashed a picture of violence," Howe explains in reference to the most graphically extreme pages of her poem *Eikon Basilike,* and as her fragmented pages participate in the very processes of violence which they critique, they graphically enact the destructive and deconstructive elements of her project with a visual foregrounding that forces the reader to confront these themes as well.[23] Moreover, Howe's radically disrupted page situates its readers in a position from which they might more empathetically respond to the issues of power addressed by their thematic treatment of personal and cultural violence. Faced with the aggressively restive, almost alien language of her pages, readers are likely to find themselves grappling with a discourse from which they are excluded and about which they must struggle to say anything at all; they may come one step closer, that is, to the position of Howe's personæ: Anne Hutchinson, Hester Johnson, Ophelia. In the process, those readers must directly and personally come to some kind of terms not just with their response to power, but also with what Howe has called our culture's strong "contempt for powerlessness."[24] In both cases, the two denotations of "apprehension" — "visual perception" and "anxious unease" — come together on the page of Howe's poetry.

To view Howe's poems, like Clarissa's letter, as the visual record of their narrated violence is an analogic reading, and this is one way to interpret the typographic space of her poetry in general. The visual surface of her pages illustrates at a literal, physical, and spatial level the much more complicated lessons of the texts' thematic, semantic, and conceptual planes. Howe's mirror pages and repetitions of inverted and reversed text blocks, for example, echo both her own ironic citational techniques as well as what her *détournements* teach her readers about the historical abuses and dangers of language: that the same words can always be turned around, or made to say the opposite, that the voices of others — like the type on the page — can be all too easily manipulated and twisted. Similarly, Howe illustrates the link between "Lenses and language."[25] As her own "reading through" source texts reminds us, language is always reflected and refracted through other points of view. Howe's poetry questions received perspectives and centers of power as it attempts to occupy, or at least to approximate, traditionally neglected positions, a point driven home when readers must physically rotate the page or crane their necks to make out exactly what is being said in a visually decentered field. According to her statement for the New Poetics Colloquium, part of Howe's project has been to recover "voices that are anonymous, slighted — inarticulate," and the occasionally illegible surfaces of her texts physically embody her thematic point that voices can — even if incompletely — be lifted from the brink of erasure, obscuration, and obliteration.[26] By showing "the face of the voice of [their] speech" through her disruptive visual prosody, Howe attempts to reveal "the machinery of injustice" to readers who must visually consume the edgy lyrics of a radical, visionary sensibility whose "whole being is [itself consumed] by Vision."[27]

"Incoherent inaccessible muddled inaudible": one poem catalogues those voices that Howe attempts to recover while simultaneously hinting at the unconventional linguistic form their recovery takes: "Irascible unknowable disorderly."[28] This association between politically marginalized figures and the "noise" of her difficult poetic parallels Howe's thematic connection of noise and political violence. The first poem in Howe's collection *The Europe of Trusts,* for example, opens with the autobiographical statement: "For me there was no silence before armies," and later in the volume she specifically registers guerrilla resistance and political struggle as "noise and noise pursuing power."[29] Such intersections of marginalization, violence, and noise are precisely the nexus explored by Jacques Attali in *Bruits (Noise),* his "essai sur l'économie politique de la musique [essay on the political economy of music]." Attali's book is typical of a certain genre of French essay writing, but despite its cursory treatment of widely scattered and selective evidence, and a tendency toward glib oversimplifications, its historical investigation of sonic culture succeeds in positing an innovative cultural model that allows one to read music as an anticipation of social change. Sound arranged into music, Attali argues, "simule l'ordre social, et ses dissonances expriment les marginalités [simulates the social order, and its dissonances express marginalities]."[30] He then traces the threatening noises at the edge of the dominant social order to mythical scenes which strongly evoke the milieu of Howe's earlier poetry: the edges of the forest beyond the hamlet in some dark fairy tale, the itinerant piper of some medieval legend, the banshee, *la mandragola, die Lorelei, rusalka.*

Listening to the noises at the margins, in many ways, sets the parameters of Howe's project, and the violence which she hears there continues the logic of Attali's own investigation. In contrast to music, which he glosses as a channeling of noise, "*le bruit est violence:* il dérange. Faire du bruit, c'est rompre une transmission, débrancher, tuer. Il est simulacre de meurtre [*noise is violence:* it disturbs. To make noise is to interrupt a transmission, to disconnect, to kill. It is a simulacrum of murder]."[31] This association, in Attali's analysis, extends beyond the tropes and metaphors of information theory: "le bruit a toujours été ressenti comme destruction, désordre, salissure, pollution, agression contre le code qui structure les messages [noise had always been experienced as destruction, disorder, dirt, pollution, an aggression against the code-structuring messages]."[32] This potential to disrupt the message, to unsettle the code of the status quo, is what makes noise more than simply the record of violence. Noise is also, as Attali argues, the potential for new social and political orders. Accordingly, Howe's poems can be read as "waging political babble" with their programmatic recovery of the noises of historically stifled voices through a "critique radical radical visible subsurface."[33] In Howe's case, the political "battle" becomes inextricably intertwined with the "babble" of noise. That connection, and the importance of the battle, is precisely why the experimentalism of poetics like Howe's—and her "bluntly uncompromising and problematic" visual prosody in particular—cannot simply be dismissed on account of its difficulty in favor of the less arduous and less discomforting strategies of more conventional verse.[34] So, before returning to the politics of the critique mounted by her poetry, this essay will continue to look closely at the "babbles" which rise to its radical, visible surfaces.

Listening to the "Visible Surface of Discourse"

> Vigilance! Les récupérateurs sont parmi nous!
> —graffito, Paris 1968

One day, in the mid-1950s, in a Harvard University laboratory, John Cage walked into the supposed silence of an anechoic chamber, only to hear the persistence of sounds from his own nervous and circulatory systems; he would write: "Silence . . . is nonexistent. There always are sounds . . . . Something is always happening that makes a noise."[35] Illustrating this assertion with the famous composition *4'33"*, Cage translated the white canvases of Robert Rauschenberg from a visual to an auditory medium. In both cases, the works foreground the material circumstances of their art: what must always already be present before any "message" can be relayed. When asked what a canvas would look like if she had to paint her writing, Susan Howe responded: "Blank. It would be blank. It would be a white canvas. White."[36] As her answer might hint, Howe's visual prosody does in fact retranslate Cage's version of Rauschenberg's "audible silence"—although without the radical minimalism of either—into the terms of textual language.[37] That final translation answers an emphatic "yes" to Cage's query: "If sounds are noises but not words are they meaningful?"[38]

The even, straight, oddly clinical lines of even the disrupted page from *Clarissa* grate with the epistolary pretense of that novel and throw into contrast the differences between the "tangled scrawl" of a handwritten letter and the typeset book page.[39] The linear uniformity of the type in Richardson's book marks both the medium and the mediation of print; "print settles it," Howe notes in "Melville's Marginalia," and she further signals this gap between the manuscript and even the most scholarly transcriptions both implicitly, with quotations from the editorial apparatuses of fac-simile editions, and explicitly, with phrases such as "printing ruins it."[40] In contrast, say, to Emily Dickinson's orthographically expressive fascicles, the calligraphy of which Howe reads so attentively, Susan Howe's own ma-nipulations draw attention to the *printer's* art: struck and cut type, the lead-ing and the set of lines. Indeed, the predominantly linear and blocked type in Howe's work can, like Richardson's, be read in its composition as a refer-ence to the compositor, and such references are reinforced by the refusal of some pages to operate on the conventional assumption that the visual text is a score for the voice. To appropriate Peter Quartermain's assessment of one of Howe's poems, the disrupted page "emphatically and unabashedly draws attention to itself as text, as written rather than spoken language."[41]

Such visual references to the typographic are again consonant with an explicit thematic subject which Howe has engaged throughout her liter-ary career: the material production of texts. One of the first pages in *Eikon Basilike* opens with the lines "No further trace / of the printer"; the en-tire poem, however, like so much of Howe's recent writing, is constructed primarily of precisely such traces.[42] These poems foreground not only "the printers faults," itself a faulty line due to lack of an apostrophe, but also the so-called "accidentals" of written language: conventions of capitalization, abbreviation, spelling, and alphabet.[43] With all of these elements, Howe calls attention to the very conventions which, when slightly torqued or an-tiquated, themselves call attention to the illusion of the transparency of the printed page, and she thus emphasizes her own works' status as printed artifacts. Even without such visual markers, many of the fragments in her poems constitute the remnants or evocations of inscriptions, dedications, colophons, and printers' advertisements—what might appear, in short, to be the "driest facts / of bibliography": signatures and the stamps of bor-rowers, pagination, watermarks, the frontispiece and flyleaf, the cropping and binding, all manner of codicological measurements and descriptions: condition, copy, edition, provenance.[44] "I have taken the library," one text announces; "I am at home in the library," another counters, perhaps refer-ring to Howe, perhaps to James Mangan, and certainly to itself.[45] Indeed, even on those pages of "Melville's Marginalia" that do not have the con-fused look of palimpsest, the visual layout of centered columns of equally lengthed lines moving paratactically in fragmented units creates the ap-pearance of larger, originally coherent texts read through a narrow window. These pages give the reader the impression of browsing through library catalogues, skimming over title pages, flipping and scanning as the eye and the mind catch isolated words and phrases. In short, this visual layout situates the reader in a position which simulates that of the poem's subject: the roving librarian Mangan who, instead of classifying, browses and dreams irregularly.[46]

In addition to foregrounding the material pages of other books, Howe's poems frequently draw attention to their own pages as well, in part by conflating the space of the page with an evocation of the distinctly Northeastern rural setting which recurs throughout her work. This sylvan mise-en-scène is linked in part, of course, to her concern with "wilderness" and a certain historical and colonial "American" landscape, with what is culturally marginalized and at the margins of culture. Moreover, this setting also consistently and insistently identifies the material origins of her own pages in the wood pulp which has been the common ingredient in the manufacture of paper since the end of the nineteenth century. Within this "land of pages" where "Leaves are white," Howe collapses "passage" with *paysage* as she constructs a general logic that associates "the tracks of the rabbit" with "scribbling," "forest trails" with "lines," and forest "streams" with "ink."[47] Even more insistently, the second section of *The Nonconformist's Memorial* opens by suddenly drawing the reader's attention to the visual image of the wavering drift of print at the right-hand margin of the text; the first three lines read: "Arreption to imagery // of drift meadow edge / of the woods here."[48] The final locative self-reflexively references the line break itself and the conflation of "words" and "woods," "meadow" and "margin" at an "edge" where the "white" "December / Snow" of the following stanza blurs with the "pale bright margins" found later in "Melville's Marginalia"—a poem which itself then records Howe's attempt to follow the (printed) foot*prints* of Melville through the traces of his own marginal pursuits as "Tracking a favorite writer / in the snow . . . / of others."[49] Moreover, the poem suggests that such trackings mark their place by "The leaf s turned down": the leaves, that is, of both the pages and the trees from which those pages come.[50] Howe's poems constantly remind their readers that like "leaf," the words "folio," "biblio-," "book," "codex," and "paper" all reference—etymologically—writing's material origins in fibrous plants.[51] The specifically ecological import of such references is nicely sized up by the anxious repetition in the title of the opening poem of Howe's collection *The Europe of Trusts:* "There Are Not Leaves Enough To Crown To Cover To Crown To Cover."[52] With an echolalia that itself evokes the concatenous verse form of a "crowne" (in which the last line of a stanza is repeated in the opening of the next), the threat of exhausted resources hovers behind a string of terms that all refer to both foliage and bibliography; a "crown" denotes the upper canopy of tree leaves as well as an oversized (15 × 20-inch) sheet of paper.

Indeed, in addition to stationery references such as "White foolscap" and "ass skin," Howe's oeuvre also includes many more explicit references to the specific paper on which the poems themselves are printed.[53] Like the phrase "bark of parchment," for instance, the "sylvan / imagery" of the poem "Pythagorean Silence" makes what Jerome McGann has insightfully read as a reference to "the material origins" of the page in forests which no longer exist.[54] The poem opens:

> We that were wood
> when that a wide wood was
>
> In a physical Universe playing with
>
> words[55]

This trope of the "word forest" recurs throughout Howe's more recent work as well, with lines that emphasize "the wood siege / nesting in this poem"—a poem where in fact "Language" becomes not a "food" but "a wood for thought."[56] An entire section of the book-length "Articulation of Sound Forms in Time" is entitled, significantly, "Taking the Forest," and its implicit transformation of the "wood" into the "word"—a graphemic and phonemic proximity which reminds readers that in the "physical Universe" printed words are never far from the transformed wood of their page— is concretely illustrated by one of the pages from "Melville's Marginalia." (See figure 3.) With the "rewrite" literally inscribed into the jumbled letters which open the fourth line of this page, the poem invites the viewer to "see" the "coffin" and "sew"—the cover and binding—as well as the "wood" on which the "word" physically, typographically, comes to rest after its lyrical permutations through anaphora which itself may also remind the reader that the emphasized "coffin," resonating between "tomb" and "tome," was a technical term in both paper manufacturing and press printing.[57]

Writing out of a diverse experimental tradition in American poetry which is unified in part by its attention to the "materiality of the signifier" (a phrase which already sounds rather tired), Howe reinvigorates a consideration of the material conditions of poetry. Howe's visual prosody cooperates with her poems' thematics to reference the status of her works as artifacts in printed books, and she joins other cross-genre artists such as

Coffin th ſa

Coffin th se a

Coffin th s wooĐ

ŕ e wr t ebly quell

in pencil s c atte

but poetry

Coffin th se Ⱳ

Coffin th se w

Coffin th se wooĐ

Figure 3. Susan Howe, "Melville's Marginalia" (1993)

Johanna Drucker and Tom Phillips who have focused on what was still, surprisingly, the primary material medium of poetic texts in the late twentieth century: "The figment of a book."[58] In the terms of information theory, that is, Howe foregrounds both the data and the channel of their transmission. Moreover, by referencing the page and the book through particularly restive and disruptive means, Howe also signals the noise in that channel. One can see this nexus clearly come together in a double pun suggested in "Melville's Marginalia"; the section of the book which contains this poem opens with an epigraph from Melville's Bartleby: "I like to be stationary." The homophonic play on the scrivener's materials and his immobility is then troped in "Melville's Marginalia" itself with a quote from James Mangan, whom Howe takes to be the "progenitor of the fictional Bartleby":

> there is a prospect of ultimate repose for most things; even the March of Intellect must one day halt; already we see that pens, ink, and papers are—stationary.[59]

As Howe understands, stationery—the pen, the ink, the paper—is not, as Mangan suggests, always "immobile," but it is always "static": that is, the "noise" in the channel of poetry.

Howe also hints at the ubiquity of that static with one of the pages from *Eikon Basilike*.[60] As if mapping trajectory lines of motion, the chrono-photographic convention developed in painting by the futurists (recall Balla's *Leash in Motion* or Duchamp's *Nude Descending a Staircase*), the sequential but irregularly patterned lines of text which fan from the lower left-hand corner of the page can be read as representing or reenacting the fall of a tree, replete with the reverberation of its impact: the jarring "aftershock / Aftershock." The image on this page, indeed, contains its own caption: "So falls," one of the lines reads, "that stately l Cedar." Beyond the rare mimetic iconicity of this page (repeated at the level of the line with the "stately," upright, unfelled caesural mark which separates "stately" and "Cedar"), the visual layout of the page encodes a sort of rebus into the background of the text: "if a tree falls in the forest . . . ?" The proverb recasts as an interrogative the statement by Attali which I took as this chapter's epigraph: can we ever escape noise, and if so, does anything significant occur in its absence? This page's off-kilter set of lines, overprinted type, and mentions of "rabble" and "peculiar spelling" suggest the answers: when trees fall to produce books, one medium of lexical signification, they do indeed, necessarily, make noise.

When Howe makes manifest the "visible surface of Discourse" by explicitly linking the *faktura* (фактура), or materiality, of her texts with their medial noise, she highlights what the Russian futurists called *zvukopis* (звуколись), the "noise emitted by the surface of the work of art."[61]

One emblematically noisy surface can be found on a page from "Scattering as Behavior toward Risk," an examination of which will also illustrate once again the way that Howe's poems present a concept through both a denotative and an analogously visual arrangement of their words. (See figure 4.) This page is filled with terms that refer to the sphere of communication ("discourse," "Meaning," "Narrative," "the sayd," "Watch-words," and so on), and the repetition and emphasis of "common" ("in common," "communism," and twice with "common-wealth") gesture toward "communication" through the Latin *comunis* from which they all directly descend.[62] Additionally, in the context of "Saxon harmony sparrow that lamentation," which suggests Bede's famous account of the conversion of King Edward, "aboord" might well evoke the Anglo-Saxon *abeodan,* "to deliver a message." As in any system, however, noise proliferates hand in hand with an increase in the terms of communication. With the accretion of words like "muttering," "lamentation" (with its own etymological roots in barking and nonsense), "brawling" (which in its proximity to "lamenta-

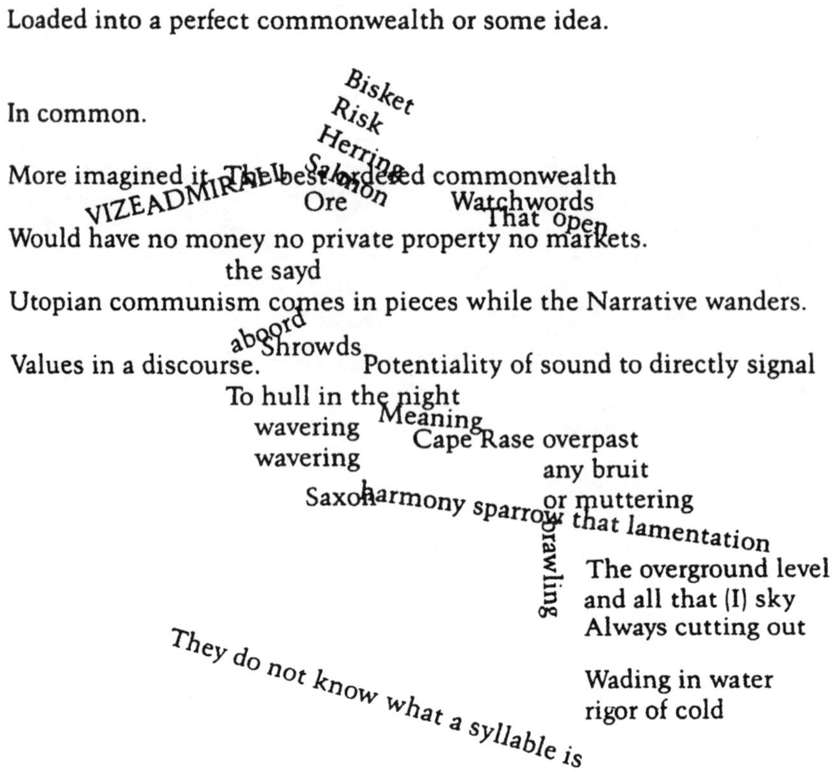

Loaded into a perfect commonwealth or some idea.

In common.

Bisket
Risk
Herring

More imagined it. The best ordered commonwealth
VIZEADMIRAL Selonation Ore on Watchwords
That Open
Would have no money no private property no markets.
the sayd
Utopian communism comes in pieces while the Narrative wanders.
aboord
Values in a discourse. Shrowds Potentiality of sound to directly signal
To hull in the night
wavering Meaning
wavering Cape Rase overpast
any bruit
Saxoharmony sparrow or muttering
that lamentation
brawling
The overground level
and all that (I) sky
Always cutting out

Wading in water
rigor of cold

They do not know what a syllable is

Figure 4. Susan Howe, "Scattering as Behavior Toward Risk" (1990)

tion" evokes "bawling"), and "bruit" (which in French, of course, is simply
"noise"), the poem builds up a vocabulary of incoherent utterances which
suggest that this page is far from a realm of "perfect" or "Utopian" communication. Moreover, the phrase "the potentiality of sound to directly
signal" not only brings into question the possibility of perfect communication, but also evokes the phrase "signal-to-noise ratio," the very measure
of the impedance in a channel carrying data.

That impedance, which Howe might call the "impediment of words," is
precisely what Michel Serres—playing on the French term for "static interference"—has identified as the "parasite, the Demon, the prosopopoeia of
noise."[63] Serres's parasite is that term which is always (already) present in
any medial technology and which, paradoxically, is actually necessary for
any communication or exchange of data to take place at all. In this sense,
one might again translate Attali's polemical assertion, this time into the
terms of information theory: nothing significant (or *signifying*) occurs in

the absence of noise. Attali provides the following definition of such medial "noise":

> Un bruit est une sonorité qui gêne l'écoute d'un message en cours d'émission. Une sonorité étant un ensemble de sons purs simultanés, de fréquences déterminées et d'intensités différentes. Le bruit n'existe donc pas en lui-même, mais par rapport au système où il s'inscrit: émetteur, transmetteur, récepteur. Plus généralement, la théorie de l'information a repris ce concept de bruit (ou plutôt la métonymie): on y appelle bruit pour un récepteur un signal qui gêne la réception d'un message, même s'il peut avoir lui-même un sens pour ce même récepteur.

> *Noise is a resonance that interferes with the audition of a message in the process of emission. A resonance is a set of simultaneous, pure sounds of determined frequency and differing intensity. Noise, then, does not exist in itself, but only in relation to the system within which it is inscribed: emitter, transmitter, receiver. Information theory uses the concept of noise (or rather, metonymy) in a more general way: noise is the term for a signal that interferes with the reception of a message by a receiver, even if the interfering signal itself has a meaning for that receiver.*[64]

In relation to the conventionally set page (like the one you are reading now, for instance), the page from "Scattering," like many of Howe's poems, is inscribed with examples of Attali's "bruit" and Serres's "parasite": misaligned and skewed type, archaic word forms and apparent misspellings, stutterings and omissions, reduced leadings, palimpsests, and a whole host of irregularities which move the text beyond opacity to a near illegibility in which readers—as the last line complains—sometimes even "do not know what a [particular] syllable is." Such medial noise is one of those "Values in a discourse" which "shrowd" "Meaning" in a message that is always "wavering // wavering" between coherence and nonsense.

Howe realizes that "Letters sent out in crystalline purity" are always received "Muddled and ravelled" to some degree, because, inevitably, "messengers falter."[65] With the recognition that there can never be static-free channels, Howe's aggressively "noisy" work resists the temptation to elegiacally view the dynamics of medial systems as mechanisms for loss. Rather, it celebrates their falterings and disruptions as an "ecstasy of communication." With an ear attuned to the pleasures of noise, Howe writes from out of the static: ex-static, indeed. The visually prosodic extremes of Howe's poems amplify the noise accumulated in her source texts, and they serve to remind readers that not only her own poems, but all the works contained in the libraries she mines for her material, all those books to which her readers will return, are infested with parasites, however much they indulge in the illusion of the transparency of the page. If conventional texts can be seen as attempting, always futilely, to suppress the parasite, to exorcise the Demon, then—accordingly—one can read a wide range of contemporary texts, like "Scattering" or "Melville's Marginalia," as instead *emphasizing* their medial noise.

By explicitly making the noise in the channel and the noise of the channel itself into data—that is, making them a part of the message ("Sound," as Cage might have characterized it, "come into its own")—Howe briefly short-circuits the parasitic economy and reminds readers that the facile distinction between "message" and "noise" must ultimately deconstruct itself.[66] Serres's Demon haunts a space at the margin of all technologies of the word, a space which he names the "torus": that point at which data deteriorate to noise, and from which noise itself always suggests some signification. As Howe pushes syntax and sound to the margins of intelligibility and coherence she explores the jagged edge of that torus with a language that is highly evocative, if at times no longer conventionally "meaningful," and her visual prosody does the same. Indeed, even when eliminating lexical meanings altogether—as in an unintelligible palimpsest—the visual surface of the black ink on the white page still operates in a space of difference. The material text cannot ever completely escape from the republic of signification; it simply crosses the border from the canton of "literary" to that of "visual" art.

Just as Howe's poetry works in this way to unsettle any facile relationship between "message" and "noise," so Attali's work cautions that noise is not in and of itself necessarily radical or subversive. Noise can indeed undermine power structures, but it can also "absorber la violence et à réorienter les énergies violentes [absorb violence, and . . . redirect violent energies]," or be played into the hands of the very orders which it threatens: "monopoliser le droit à la violence, provoquer l'angoisse pour sécuriser ensuite, le désordre pour proposer l'ordre, créer le problème que l'on peut résoudre [monopolize the right to violence; provoke anxiety and then provide a feeling of security; provoke disorder and then propose order; create a problem in order to solve it]."[67] This is precisely the danger, as I have already suggested in the first half of this chapter, when experimental writing like Howe's stands as a foil to conservative new formalisms. But there is another, perhaps more serious, risk as well. "Un réseau peut être détruit par des bruits qui l'agressent et le transforment," Attali argues, only "si les codes en place ne peuvent normaliser et réprimer ces bruits [A network can be destroyed by noises that attack and transform it, if the codes in place are unable to normalize and repress them]."[68] Even critical and scholarly work that pays close attention to the disruptive possibilities of visual prosody runs the risk of neutralizing the very disruptive potential it identifies. Such work must try to avoid co-opting those disruptions for its own rhetorical ends, and might instead attempt to communicate noise in the way one might communicate a disease. There is a strong temptation to recuperate the resisting and unsettling potential of "noise" as a "message" which can be absorbed into the very code it challenges, so that it can then be safely consumed by traditional hermeneutic strategies as simply another part of the message's "meaning." This chapter—indeed this entire book—is itself a prime example of the way in which noises get accepted into the system, get inside us, become, in short, *les parasites:* infecting, spreading, and disabling, but also structuring, adapting, mutating, mimicking, colonizing. The very look of texts like Susan Howe's "transmit," in Jerome McGann's terms,

> the simple signal of an emergency or a possible emergency. Stop. Look. Listen. They are Thoreauvian calls to awakening. This may be a special and relatively localized awakening—to the resources of language, to new possibilities for poetry—or it may involve more serious ethical and social questions.[69]

This chapter has been the signal of an emergency as well. Beyond a simple crisis of faith, it has sacrificed its principles—enacting the conservative rather than the liberating potential of *les parasites,* exhibiting "power" rather than "force" in Deleuze and Guattari's terms—and its redemption lies in the degree to which that enactment has in fact led to a local awakening: to your recognition of its failure. But not, perhaps, its failure alone. Because you are implicated and complicitous as well; this has been a litmus test, registering the point at which you identified its self-contradictory claims and the disjunction between *what* was being said and *how* it was being said in a text for which the subject of each was in fact the other. Stop. Look. Aggression, progression, recombination, return. Listen carefully.

The book is only a sort of optical instrument which the writer offers to the reader to enable the latter to discover in himself what he would not have found but for the aid of the book.

    —Marcel Proust

Les phosphènes prenaient soudain une intensité tel que, même les yeux ouvert, ils formaient devant moi un voile . . . .

    —Rene Daumal

3. Destroying Redness

The Carnal Eye: Self-Portrait in a Complex Mirror

In "The Critic," one of C. K. Williams's trademark miniature narratives, he writes of a homeless man "who had a battered loose-leaf book he used to scribble in for hours on end / . . . writing over words that were already there—/ blocks of cursive etched into the softened paper, interspersed with poems in print he'd pasted in."[1] In Williams's poem, some of those specific local effects of Susan Howe's poetry that I examined in the previous chapter—the collage of appropriated texts and their occasional overprinting—have become both a symptom and a comprehensive strategy of textual production. Indeed, a sometimes unrelenting production: after filling the notebook, Williams's scribbler would "start again: page one, chapter one, his blood-rimmed eyes as rapt as David's doing psalms." Taking not just descriptions of such texts, as in Williams's poem, but actual books that were in fact produced by "writing over words that were already there," this chapter will look more closely into the red and "blood-rimmed eyes" of both the writers and readers of the illegible. When the technique that Howe and others have used on occasion becomes the predicate for an entire compositional strategy, the extremity of the overprinted page—as it approaches a true and total illegibility—makes clear the implications inherent in every instance of the overprinted word. As we shall see, those implications extend beyond the obsession of Williams's scribbler and his psalmic rapture to the darkest theological linguistics.

Published in the same year (1987) as Williams's poem, Charles Bernstein's chapbook *Veil* contains blocks of text constructed by overtyping lines until the layers of words form a shimmering screen of partially obliterated writing.[2] (See figure 5.) *Veil* opens with an epigraph from "The Minister's Black Veil," and as in Hawthorne's story, the "veil" in question is the weave of the printed text(ile) itself, so that "writing veils the appearance of language; it is not a guise for language but a disguise."[3] In a mechanized version of Williams's anonymous writer, the journal-like transcriptions of Bernstein's "freely composed" stream-of-consciousness language appear as if the same sheet were reinserted in a typewriter and run through two to four cycles of typing, with the cylinder perhaps having been given a quarter turn before he would "start again." In addition to casual diaristic musings, the writing frequently meditates on the material specificity of its process:

> *italics just to give verve no i think the single face type does all i need at this point is the gradula occluding of the process but if I kept a carbon i wdda been happier maybe a xerox will help reveal the layers* [sic].

Electrostatics do not, unfortunately, help at all, and as readers *face the veil* in *this much tighter mixture of ENJAMBMENT* they have *a hard time following* the text through the *haywireness of superimposition* and *images really run amuk.* With concentration, however, the book *gives a sense of . . . trace . . . felt behind LARGE SCREENS* which the reader ultimately can *see dimly through* as the writing *peeks a boo* to *let a hidden essay emerge* in a constantly switching dialectic of revelation and concealment. Those glimpses work to *excite the curious EYE level scrutiny wch makes the lines CRISS CROSS* until the reader once again *cant make out* the *typing* laid *over and over the same material in a variety of* ways to form *overprint with a density* so great that language *itself is tangible and one feels* the physicality of type.

The opacity which follows from that physical type stands in marked contrast to the dominant Anglo-American tradition of twentieth-century typographic design, which maintains an unobtrusive clarity as its aim.[4] This aesthetic was most forcefully advanced by Stanley Morison, who over a long and influential career repeated his insistence that "any disposition of printing material which, whatever the intention, has the effect of coming between author and reader is wrong."[5] Championing Morison's aesthetic, Beatrice Warde provides what is perhaps its best summation in her famous and frequently repeated metaphor of the crystal goblet; she argues that typographic design should aspire to the state of "crystal-clear glass, thin as a bubble, and as transparent."[6] Declaring that "printing should be invisible," she concludes that "type well used is invisible *as* type."[7] In contrast

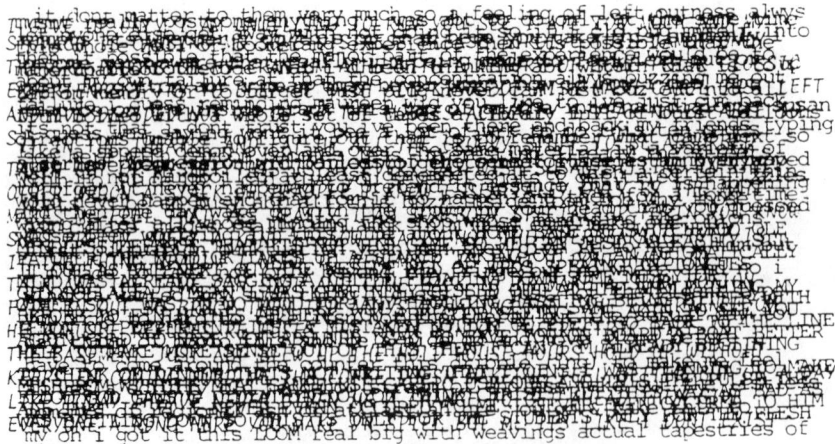

Figure 5. Charles Bernstein, *Veil* (1987)

to this ideal design, in which "the mental eye focuses *through* type and not *upon* it," a work like *Veil* "is something to be looked at, not *through*."[8] The point is obvious but significant: the illegibility in *Veil* arises because its writing—like all writing—is not, contra Warde, transparent. Through their manifest materiality, Bernstein's "veils" are thus *not the theory but the actual* practice of a poststructural linguistics *writ large,* so that, as Wittgenstein might say to Warde, "this crystal does not appear as an abstraction, but as something concrete, indeed as the most concrete, as it were the hardest thing there is."[9] Or as Bruce Andrews more bluntly writes: "Crystalline purity—or transparency—will not be found in words."[10]

The lessons of *Veil,* however, are not just a reminder of the "materiality of the signifier" (that familiar if frequently forgotten story whose moral has never been well learned and rarely really taken to heart); to leave the work at that would underestimate its interest, and ignore its distance from works as diverse as Bob Brown's "readies" or Guillaume Apollinaire's *calligrammes.* Were the mere assertion of the signifier the only point, one page, if not one line, would surely suffice. Surprisingly, the different pages in *Veil* each display a wide and distinctly different range of effects. The ornately italicized second poem, for instance, appears spun as a filigreed latticework of pure surface, while the fourth poem is far less uniform; it manipulates spacing, adds a layer of italic type in one section, and briefly suspends an otherwise regular overlay of capitalized lines to create an astonishing sense of textured depth and three-dimensionality.[11] (See figure 6.) The poem proceeds with a fluid ebb and swell of alternating coagulation and expanse,

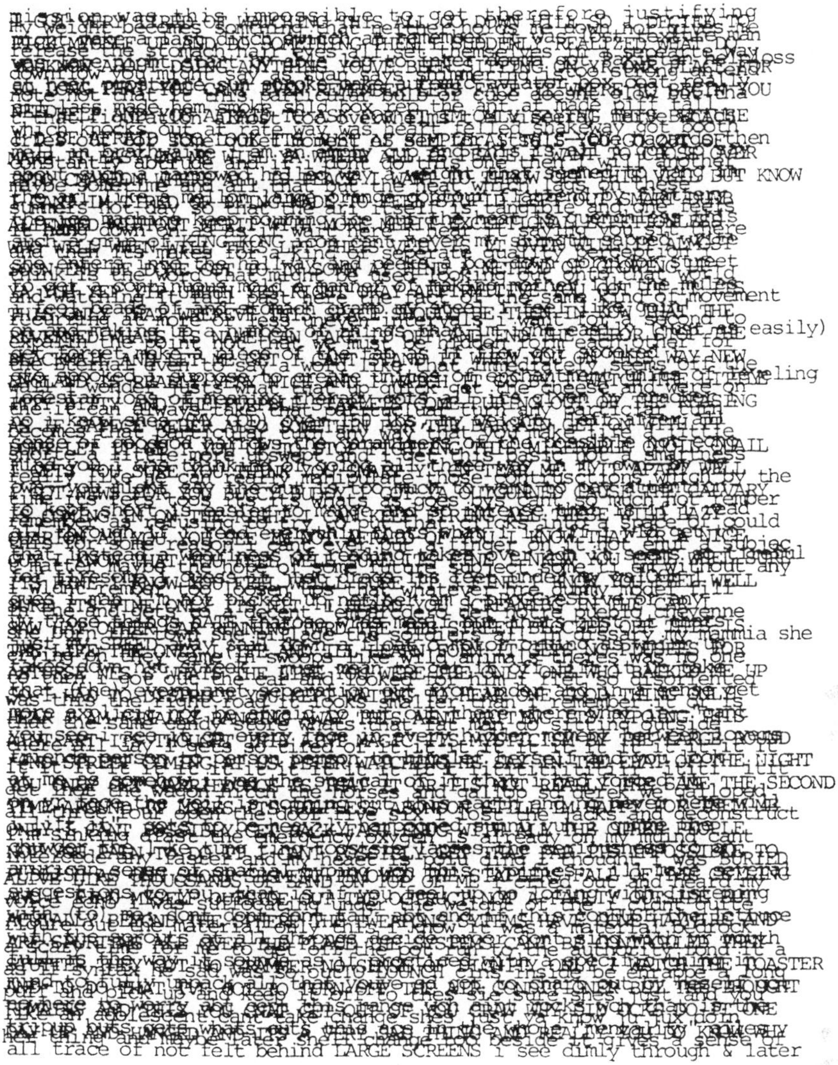

Figure 6. Charles Bernstein, *Veil* (1987)

so that the experience of reading is to move through lines of type which pass like wave fronts cresting and troughing as the text intermittently clouds over completely—and then breaks briefly clear. Indeed, the experience of *reading* is worth insisting on; whatever their initial impressions, the poems in *Veil* are surprising less for their illegibility than for their ultimate intelligibility. With patience and concentration, almost all of the text can be deciphered, if only bit by bit, so that Bernstein's palimpsests do not so much prevent reading as redirect and discipline usual reading habits.[12]

Veil, that is, films and smudges Warde's elegantly transparent glass, leaving it nicked and scratched perhaps, but not shattered. Transparency, as Bernstein argues in his essay "Artifice of Absorption, "is "one technique for producing absorptive works," and the reader's

> Absorption is blocked by misting
> this glass, or by breaking it, or
> by painting on its surface. Any
> typographic irregularity

can thus disrupt that transparency.[13] In contrast with "tranquil looking pages that render up their content with the least possible interference," works like *Veil* transform Warde's crystal goblet into something more like Gertrude Stein's "not ordinary" "blind glass," or Marcel Duchamp's "delay in glass."[14] The delay in reading comprehension necessitated by overtyping renders the ordinary language of Bernstein's texts decidedly unfamiliar, and it mitigates against the possibility of scanning the page in ways to which we have become accustomed. In Ron Silliman's account, we are conditioned to ideologies of textual transparency that create the illusion of the "disappearance of the word" in the service of strategies for consuming texts solely for their summarizable "content": "In its ultimate form, the consumer of a mass market novel such as *Jaws* stares at a "blank" page (the page also of the speed-reader)."[15] By retarding the automatic process of reading, much less any speed-reading, and frustrating that illusion of the blank page, Bernstein's overprinting is a perfect example of Viktor Shklovskii's classic приём остраннения: the "device of making strange" or "not ordinary," which operates primarily by prolonging the processes of perception. To combat the "habituation" of "automatic" perception, and instead "impart the sensation of things as they are perceived, and not as they are [familiarly] known," Shklovskii argues that the defamiliarized art object works "to make forms difficult, to increase the difficulty and length of perception."[16] Or, in Jean Cocteau's version, the poem *"dévoile, dans toute la force du terme. Elle montre nues . . . les choses surprenantes qui nous environnent et que nos sens enregistraient machinalement [takes off the veil,* in the full sense of the word. It lays bare . . . the astonishing things which surround us and which our senses usually register mechanically]."[17]

For one example of this defamiliarizing effect, consider how the blocks of text in *Veil* reconfigure the ostensibly neutral and familiar page which surrounds them and which "our senses usually register mechanically." Like several of Bob Grenier's contemporaneous works, such as the box of cards which make up *Sentences* or the poster-sized broadside *Cambridge M'ass*, Bernstein's "veils" were originally produced on an IBM Selectric typewriter.[18] For both writers, the specificity of the typewriter serves to reinforce the colloquial and process-oriented tone of their works. In Grenier's poems, however, the sparse type energizes the white *espace* of the page around it, while Bernstein's overprinting sculpts that negative space into rivers and amorphous shapes, and seems to open up space *between* the page and the layers of print. As the reader makes the focal shifts necessary to decipher the poems, the black type and white page undergo figure-ground reversals so that the white spaces coalesce into Rorschach-like forms. This effect is all the more apparent in the book's endpapers, which mechanically submit a section of the third poem to four levels of increasing enlargement, so that the bibliographic detail of binding becomes a witty literalization of Xexoxial Edition's title-page device: an old-fashioned compound microscope. The magnified and reproduced text on these pages undergoes a double loss of "definition": fewer words are left to denote as their letters lose crispness and begin to show the imperfections of the type's cut and the liquid bleed of ink into the fibers of the paper. As the letterforms appear to spread and merge into irregular and viscid pools of ink, the white space around them takes on an increasingly positive figuration of its own. In all of the poems, moreover, readers who simply want to untangle the jumble of those letters must attend so closely to the details of the quotidian standard typeface that they become aware of the strangeness of the type itself, and the surprising affinities and distinctions between different characters: the spiny flick of normally unnoticed serifs, or the arch of the kerns, the precise calculus of parabolic bows, the angle and extension of a hairline crossbar, the slightest change in weight.

If the restive opacity of these poems prevents their reader from being absorbed by the seemingly effortless flow of semantic content, it also redirects the reader from that illusionistic immediacy to the even more highly absorptive process of physical decipherment, which requires a concentration and attention far more total and intense than does the conventional page.

In "Artifice of Absorption," Bernstein's sustained and self-illustrated argument for the way in which the artifice of language itself leads to both a semantics and politics of literary form, he discusses this sort of redirection to a "hyperattentiveness" at some length:

The antiabsorptive does not so much prevent
absorption as shift its plane
of engagement—forcing
a shift in attentional focus.[19]

Appropriate to the compositional techniques he deploys in *Veil,* Bernstein describes this shift as a process that "enmeshes / into a dysraphic whole" of " 'overlay and blending.' "[20] When readers give that enmeshed overlay the "attentional focus" it demands, the poems in *Veil* yield up their language in revelatory and reveiling bursts. As the absorbed eye finds the proper focus, whole lines and partial phrases, discrete words and morphemes, individual letters and fragments of type appear in sudden, momentary clarity, before again submerging into the thick of print—only to be replaced by other sections surfacing and dissolving in turn. "It is as if one had altered the adjustment of a microscope. One did not see before what is now in focus."[21]

In charting the limits of visual perception in this way, the experience of reading a page from *Veil* is very much like viewing a film which has been edited into a rapidly changing and radically discontinuous sequence, such as an extended clatter montage or the op art experiments of "flicker films."[22] The illusion of continuous motion in cinematic images, of course, depends on the persistence of vision and the mental conflation of slightly different images into a unified whole. Normally, the mechanics of cinematic filming and projection maintain a pace which keeps the discontinuity of frames below the limit of perceptibility and allows the viewer to smoothly fuse discrete images. These rates, however, can be manipulated to reveal the flicker of discrete bursts of light from the projector, create superimposition effects, or even suggest animation (as with the famous awakening of the lion statue in Eisenstein's *Potemkin,* for instance). Furthermore, when a series of single frames is entirely unrelated, the projected film appears as a blur because the eye and mind are only able to process some of the images, and the optically overpowering techniques of extremely rapid montage take advantage of that limit. Formally, the poles of this editing spectrum correspond, in linguistic terms, to hypotaxis and parataxis. Even in the most radically paratactic series of grammatically unrelated single frames, however, the eye still does register some of the static images, which nictitate before the eyes like those words which suddenly appear legible in the scrim of *Veil's* mesh. Just as in the next reading those words might remain invisible while others appear in their place, each screening of a radically montaged film reveals a different sequence of perceived images, depending largely on optical mechanics such as when viewers blink, how long it takes them to focus, and so on.

The analogy is not exact, since Bernstein's text is not composed of grammatically unrelated words which would correspond to the pictorially discrete frames of a filmstrip. Indeed, as *Veil* wavers on the threshold of perceptibility, that limn is manifested by the difficulty of following a related sequence of words; their hard-won clarity is almost impossible to maintain because the slightest shift in optical performance or reading environment constantly threatens to make the briefly legible text disappear. The graphic forms of writing in *Veil* are so difficult, the increased "difficulty and length of perception" so extreme, that the reader is repeatedly made aware of the most minute aspects of visual perception, which the habitual reader can usually afford to ignore: the general situation of the reading space, the sculptural dimensions of the book, and the physicality of the reader's entire body, which can no longer be ignored in an illusion of direct mental engagement with the writing.[23] Specifically, *Veil* amplifies the sense of bodily presence in a specific environment: the precise distance and angle of the book, the gentle curve of the page—suddenly so three-dimensional—as it arcs from its binding towards the hand holding it at the edge, and every tremor of that hand, and the shadow it casts, and the shading of the pages' center fold, the quality of the light source and its angle of incidence, its reflection or refraction from a chemically sized sheet, halation, the weave of its paper and the sheen of its ink, the waverings of heated air, the breeze from a window, a passing shadow, motes.

Moreover, "it is the spectator who is the real sculptor in the void, who reads the book between its lines," as Jean-Paul Sartre writes, and Bernstein's book becomes a literalization of Proust's "optical instrument," which enables the reader to experience the bodilyness of the physical eye itself: the optical illusion of figure-ground reversals, hypnagogic effects, the detection of movement beyond the periphery of registered images, pupillary vacillation, the persistence of vision in afterimages and the visual renewal of a blink, the error made during a return sweep, drift and tremor, the subtle but incessant pixilated shimmer of the visual field, fatigue of the ciliary muscle, saturation, the flattenings of non-foeveal vision and the aporia of the *punctum caecum,* saccades and scans, flashers, floaters, and all of those luminous patterns which attend even the clearest vision.[24] Of course all printed poems depend on vision, and any of these effects could make a difference in the experience of reading; but such effects are rarely critical to basic visual comprehension; with a work like *Veil* these normally trivial mechanics of vision can entirely undo the reader's tenuous grasp on legibility. *Veil* does not create these optical phenomena (although the strain from reading should not be discounted), but it does open the reader's awareness to a fuller range of visual experience than we usually admit. Accordingly, in this "poetics of optics," the poems in *Veil* become the most intimate physical portraits of their readers: mirrors of the eye looking at itself.[25] But a *speculum obscurum:* "veil" and "oeil" are only ever separated by a grapheme.[26]

This glaucous portrait of the psychophysics of the optic nerve is not how we are accustomed to imagining the eye. Evoking the old adage that the eyes are "windows on the soul," William Blake's visionary optics echoes the more conventional view in his declaration at the conclusion to *A Vision of the Last Judgement:* "I question not my Corporeal and Vegetative Eye any more than I would Question a Window concerning a Sight. I look thro' it and not with it."[27] Blake's concern, of course, is mystical, but the same trope recurs in Warde's quite practical discussions of typography. In contrast to the view changed by "grimy panes," she argues that readers should take "no more notice of the type and layout than they would take of a polished window-pane between them and a view," because the "book typographer has the job of erecting a window between the reader inside the room and that landscape which is the author's words."[28] The simile of the window, of course, was readily available for both Blake and Warde from its famous appearance in Leon Battista Alberti's foundational *De pictura,* where the *espace* of the panel painting is metaphorized as a "window on the world." As Joseph Masheck has established, the textual history of Alberti's treatise is complex, and as his simile ascended to the status of dogma its frequent reiteration was (and continues to be) fast and loose, but it is worth noting here that Alberti's reference is to an open (*aperta*), rather than a paned, window. Additionally, Fernand Braudel provides an important historical reminder: "fifteenth-century window glass was not very translucent and was anyway uncommon . . . . What glazed windows there were would hardly have revealed an undistorted, transparent view."[29] Whatever the view through the window, however, Alberti would have its orthogonals corrected by the "how-to-do-it apparatus of a thin 'veil' (*velum*) of semi-transparent cloth . . . for translating, as with Dürer's famous gridded frame in the next century, three dimensions into two."[30] In a passage that should recall Silliman's argument for the "disappearance of the word," which it parallels, Louis Marin describes the dialectic between the veil and the window in optical terms that are particularly apposite to my argument:

1/ Le tableau come surface-support n'existe pas: le regard humain n'est filtré par nulle grille ou tamis interprétatif pour se saisir du monde naturel.

2/ Pour pouvoir représenter le monde naturel, le tableau comme surface-support existe: sur et par lui s'opère l'exact dédoublement de la réalité. L'oeil humain ne reçoit que le double du monde.

D'où la nécessaire position et la nécessaire neutralisation de la «toile» matérielle et de la surface «réelle» dans l'assomption technique, théorique, idéologique de sa transparence: c'est l'invisibilité de la surface-support qui est la condition de possibilité de la visibilité du monde représenté. La diaphanéité est la définition technique-théorique de l'écran plastique de la représentation.

(1). The painting as material medium does not exist: human vision is not filtered by any grid or interpretive screen in order to comprehend the natural world.

(2). In order to be able to represent the natural world, the painting as material medium exists: the accurate partitioning of reality comes about on and by that material medium. The human eye takes in only the double of the world.

From these propositions it follows that the material canvas and the real surface must be posited and neutralized in the technical, theoretical, and ideological assumption of its transparency: the invisibility of the material medium is the very condition of possibility for the visibility of the represented world. Transparence is the technical/theoretical definition of the opaque screen of representation.[31]

Rather than colluding with an ideal transparent view—either in the mimetic sense of realist conventions or the spiritual sense of Blake's visions—Bernstein's own "veils" are closer to those in Duchamp's *Fresh Widow* than to any "grille ou tamis interprétif." Literalizing Alberti's metaphors of how we represent what is known (no *n*), Duchamp teases out the play between *velum* (veil) and *vellum* (leather) in his version of the "gridded window": a miniature french window in which the glass window panes—like the widow's pain—have been veiled with black leather.[32] Continuing the metaphor in these new terms, the eye in its carnality—like the small windows of Duchamp's sculpture—comes to be understood less as a clear pane and more as "a little curtain of flesh."[33] The minute particulars of a work like *Veil* perform an ocular defenestration, forcing the question for the reader by making one "see with not through the eye."[34] If we first look *at* the text rather than *through* it, in Warde's terms, we must still first look *at* the pellicle of the eyes, rather than through *them*. Just as *Veil* opacates any transparency of writing by defamiliarizing reading material *qua materia,* it also occludes the illusion of the transparency of vision and insists on the materiality of sight itself. Against the Emersonian dream of a "transparent Eye-ball," *Veil* proves that in contrast to the habitual and mechanical registration of external images, even the gross and vegetative "Eye sees more than the Heart knows."[35] I am not suggesting that we mistake the reconfigured or expanded conceptualization of vision for something closer to "true" sight. The point is more modest: an opening of the (visual) field to multiple, even competing and contradictory, "scopic regimes" rather than simply replacing one with another.[36] By enacting Bernstein's understanding that the "eye is not a passive mechanism for intercepting the image of objects," the overprinted poems in *Veil* lead their readers to differentiate, like Wittgenstein, between the alternate demands made by the inescapable idealism of the pellucid "mental" or "geometric eye" and the inescapable carnality of the corporeal "physical eye."[37]

Stan Brakhage has spent his career, as both a filmmaker and a writer, insisting on that corporeal eye. The central figure in American experimental cinema, Brakhage has made hundreds of films in the last four decades, but he is also something of a poet manqué; he frequently refers to film in linguistic terms and writing in visual terms, and his writings, whether essays or epistles, repay the attention usually reserved for "poetry."[38] Moreover, his frequent references to poets include not just figures like Pound and H. D., Olson and Creeley, Robert Kelly and Michael McClure, but "poets' poets" as well: Cage, Zukofsky, Davenport, and Stein — precisely, that is, the tradition from which Bernstein himself emerges.[39] In part through the puns and visual portmanteaux of his own writing, but more systematically in the construction of his films, Brakhage attempts to "untutor" the geometric eye and imagine instead a vision unruled by the social disciplining which conditions us to ignore certain material and retinal information and to regard the eye as a transparent window.[40] In doing so, he employs a number of techniques to produce filmic equivalents for many of those optical phenomena I have just catalogued, which he refers to as "closed-eye vision."[41] To cite just a few examples: rapidly intercut clear and colored leader creates flashes and flares; baking and bleaching 8mm stock to bring out the emulsion grain, as well as emphasizing the lower definition created by optical printing, suggest the pixilation of the visual field; the dust, hair, and scratches visible after that printing, like the interventions of paint flicked from a brush onto the surface of the film or scratches etched into the emulsion, all simulate the dance of entoptic imperfections and phosphenes, those scintillating patterns and specks of light which are "subjective images generated within the eye and brain rather than by light from outside."[42] These effects actually have their place in the poetic tradition; one might recall Arthur Rimbaud's poem "Les poètes de sept ans," in which the young poet, truly *un voyant,* shuts and rubs his eyes with such force that he sees spots ("ses yeux fermés voyait des points") and quite literally has visions ("pour des visions écrasant sone oeil darne"). Similarly, in an extraordinary passage from one of the versions of "La crevette," Francis Ponge figures phosphenes, not coincidentally, as particles of type:

> Admettons-le d'abord, parfois il arrive qu'un homme à la vue troublée par la fièvre, la faim ou simplement la fatigue, subisse une passagère et sans doubte bénigne hallucination: par bonds vifs, saccadés, successifs, rétrogrades suivis de lent retours, il aperçoit d'un endrout à l'autre de l'étendue de sa vision remuer d'une façon particulière une sorte de petits signes, assez peu marqués, translucides, à formes de bâtonnets, de virgules, peut-être d'autres signes de ponctuation, qui, sans lui cacher du tout le monde l'oblitèrent en quelque façon, s'y déplacent en surimpression, enfin donnent envie de se frotter les yeux afin de re-jouir par leur éviction d'une vision plus nette.

> *To begin with, let's acknowledge that people, with their vision disrupted by fever, hunger, or simply fatigue, sometimes undergo a fleeting and no doubt benign hallucination: they notice—from one spot to another across the field of vision, shifting in a particular way, by animated, jerky, successive backward leaps followed by slow returns—a type of tiny marks [symptoms], barely delineated, translucent, in the shape of rods, commas, perhaps other punctuation marks, which, without concealing the whole world from them, do obliterate it in a cetain way, moving around there superimposed, and finally making people want to rub their eyes in order to rejoice in these marks' eviction from a clearer vision.*[43]

The futile paradox presented in the last phrase should be clear; while phosphenes occur spontaneously whenever there is an absence of strong external optical stimulation, they are perhaps most familiar from what one sees when applying pressure to closed eyes.[44] However, any number of conditions can elicit phosphenic display, from the extremes of electroshock, traumatic impacts to the head, and a wide variety of drugs, to the physical states named by Ponge, simple eye movements, a powerful sneeze, or even loud noises.[45]

Brakhage specifically refers to the latter stimuli in his short 1987 film *Loud Visual Noises*. The looped and erratically hand-painted film, which creates foudroyant displays of visual pyrotechnics, is coupled in its video version with a soundtrack of untuned radio signals, the crackle, hiss, and screech of electromagnetic tape, and a wide sampling of audio static. Indeed, "noise," in its information-theory sense, is all to the point for "closed-eye vision." Phosphenes "presumably reflect the neural organization of the visual pathway"; that is, they are part of the noise in the optical channel.[46] In terms that could apply equally well to the experience of reading *Veil*, Brakhage describes the effect he strives for in his films:

> You are seeing yourself seeing. You're seeing your own mechanism of seeing expressing itself. You're seeing what the feedback of the mind puts into the optic nerve ends that cause them to spark and shape up like that.[47]

Brakhage thus provides the optical equivalent to John Cage's aural revelation in the anechoic chamber: an experience of the operation of the nervous system as it records itself rather than any external stimuli.[48] Instead of attempting to filter out the noise in the neuroptic channel, Brakhage amplifies all of that "grainy visual 'noise' perceptible when we are in a dark room or have our eyes tightly closed," and which arises because there "is always some residual neural activity reaching the brain, even when there is no stimulation of the eye by light."[49] Brakhage explicitly relates "the grainy shapes of closed-eye vision" to the emulsion grain of film, which is in general more apparent in the 8mm medium that Brakhage prefers.[50] Ernie Gehr's 1970 film *History* provides what is perhaps the most extreme example of this recognition that, in Lenny Lipton's words, the "background [visual] noise of motion picture systems is very much like that of the eye-brain."[51] As with many of Brakhage's films, which envision technology in terms of the corporeal eye rather than rationalize the eye in terms of the machine, *History* collapses the materiality of the medium and the materiality of vision. Investigating "the articulation of the chemical, mental/optical, and mechanical factors that make the film image," Gehr produced the work by replacing the camera lens with a piece of black cheesecloth and exposing the film to dim illumination.[52] A print was then made from the developed film, and light was allowed to seep in around the sprocket holes of the optical printer, disrupting the uniform intensity of the film stock's illumination and adding another source of nonreferential images (or at least images that refer only to the presence of light itself). The result is a forty-minute-long film that records no external objects, but rather displays the resolution of the emulsion's grains in a tremulous field of excited, scintillating, silver haloid crystals.

Those crystals are an image of the shards to which Warde's crystal is always reduced: the inescapable background noise of the ocular system at work — regardless of any object of perception, however "transparent." Those material opacities of vision, however, are potentially more significant than simply waking us up to the world around us (as Cage might put it) — no matter how spectacular the new impressions we come to notice may be. To begin with, recall the terms in which designers refer to transparency. Morison defines typography "as the art of *rightly* disposing printing material," and we have seen how he accordingly describes the "misuse" of that typography in equally ethical terms ("wrong").[53] Warde, who understands typography to be "not so much an aesthetic as a moral problem," makes this position explicit, and both she and Morison employ a peculiarly religious vocabulary of typographic orthodoxy, heresy, and redemption.[54] In an exactly contemporaneous essay on typographic theory, Eric Gill recognized that his peers found it "exceedingly difficult to keep morals out of art talk," and in this moralistic context the arguments for limpidity repeatedly situate their ideal typography in the anthropomorphized terms of "obedience" and "self-effacing humility" before the "meaning" of the text.[55] Moreover, this language of servile utility perfectly echoes the simultaneous call made by theorists like Warde and Morison for the social deprecation of the typographer, who was to serve artists and clients, and their "meaning," without interference.

The practical role of those professional typographers was changing rapidly in the early decades of the twentieth century in accord with Taylorized industrial management and new developments in automated and electronic print technology. Beyond mere aesthetics, writers like Warde and Morison were reacting to such changes, as well as to institutional and pedagogic reforms in the training of typographers in both vocational "arts and crafts" schools and, to an even greater extent, in academies like the Dessau Bauhaus, where Moholy-Nagy, van Doesburg, Bayer, and Schmidt propagated new theories of both print design and professionalization. The wedding of "craftsperson" or "tradesworker" to "artist" in the ideologies of both the socialism of the aestheticist "guild" and the revolutionary industrial "laboratory" of international constructivism was a union that the proponents of transparency wanted annulled. Their idea of the dutiful society of the print shop served as their model for the larger social order, which in turn would deploy the "rightly" printed word by way of disciplining citizens into a complacent service to church, state, and commerce.[56] Printed norms know to keep their place in generic terms — never confusing the look of a catalogue with that of belles lettres — just as typographers know not to confuse themselves with "artists," and just as all good citizens know to keep their place in political terms. In short, without "interference," either in optical or political terms, "conservative," both in the historical recovery of unobtrusive typefaces as well as the maintenance of a social status quo, and certainly no "revolution of the word" — or the world.

Additionally, the class and social connotations of the "crystal goblet" are not insignificant. Consider the famous first paragraph of Warde's essay, which sets the tenor for her metaphor of transparent type:

> Imagine that you have before you a flagon of wine. You may choose your own favourite vintage for this imaginary demonstration, so that it be a deep shimmering crimson in colour. You have two goblets before you. One is of solid gold, wrought in the most exquisite patterns. The other is of crystal-clear glass, thin as a bubble, and as transparent. Pour and drink; and according to your choice of goblet, I shall know whether or not you are a connoisseur of wine. For if you have no feelings about wine one way or the other, you will want the sensation of drinking the stuff out of a vessel that may have cost thousands of pounds; but if you are a member of that vanishing tribe, the amateurs of fine vintages, you will choose the crystal, because everything about it is calculated to *reveal* rather than to hide the beautiful thing which it was meant to *contain*.

The obvious excesses of a "solid gold" goblet costing "thousands of pounds" (in 1932 at that) is less interesting in itself than the fact that its ostentation is so closely linked with the rhetoric of display that runs through the paragraph (*ostendere:* "to display"). The crystal goblet — her model for typographic characters — not only reveals the character of the wine, it reveals the "character" of the drinker as well, and *conspicuous* consumption, in both cases, is precisely the point (*com* + *specere:* "to see thoroughly"). Although she gives no indication of the allusion, Warde's figuration of writing as wine, which she repeats elsewhere, might seem less a mark of leisured dissipation and more a witty and oblique metaphoric play if one recalls the supposed origin of the fifteenth-century printing press in the mechanism of the winepress.[57] Wine itself, however, is not merely the point in Warde's little story; it is the costly wine favored by daydreaming "connoisseurs." Perhaps like Guy Debord. Though unlike the bars and living rooms in which Debord was purported to turn against those who put "their wine glasses on the table in a bourgeois manner," Warde's "crystal"— even leaving aside the sheer wealth implied by someone who can afford to spend thousands of pounds on stemware—connotes the mise-en-scène of a social function requiring the best manners. The proper crystal, then, is not beside the point when the subjectivity of "unselfconscious transparency" expressing "unintermediated thought" has been elevated, as Richard Lanham has argued, to "a cultural ideal for Western civilization. The best style is the style not noticed; the best manners the most unobtrusive": the "consummate reticence and rare discipline," that is, which designers like Morison demand of an "obedient" typeface.[58]

I do not want to be reductive about discursive affinities; my argument is not, of course, that these connections are necessary, or unavoidable, or somehow immediately causal: reading a book set in Garamond does not automatically render one docile in the face of state authority, and struggling to read a visually resistant book like *Veil* does not send its reader into the streets to take up the struggle of political resistance. At the same time, I would not want to ignore or separate off the convictions which have historically attended aesthetic ideologies, nor do I want to discount or underestimate the very real effects of metaphor, for which Lakoff and Johnson have argued, on our understanding and our actions—particularly when, as Lanham's argument suggests, further metaphoric slippages between graphic design, linguistics, and philosophy are easily and commonly enough made. As a caveat against such slippage, Bernstein's writing against typographic and ocular transparency works as a reminder, frustrating any uncritical move to related theories of transparent communication and the various social dreams which have accompanied such theories. Indeed, part of the force of the conversationally *un*literary and casually personal language which makes up the "veils" is to emphasize the fact that even the most seemingly unmediated language—those colloquial styles which are construed as "direct" and "unselfconsciously transparent," from Coleridge and Wordsworth's claims in the *Lyrical Ballads* to the confessional mode of television talk shows—must always be instantiated in an "obstinate physicality" which can prevent the reader's absorption into the illusion of simulated immediacy.[59]

Moreover, Western philosophical enterprises have been so torqued on visual metaphors, and what Martin Jay records as "the ocular permeation of language," that redefining the nature of perceptual experience surely has the potential for far-reaching revisions of thought.[60] Understanding that "the Eye altering alters all," Blake suggests the power such redefinition might have: "How different their eye and ear! How different the world to them!"[61] Given the possibility of that "different . . . world," I want to recall some of the further stakes which inhere in how works like *Veil* affect the ways in which we conceptualize vision. The partial significance of that conceptualization can be gleaned from the many recent publications on the political and philosophical implications of various "scopic regimes.[62] Most of these studies emphasize the ideology of "Cartesian perspectivalism": the fixed-point perspective which has formed the "dominant" and in some accounts "even totally hegemonic, visual model of the modern era."[63] These works vary widely in methodology and theoretical position, reaching conclusions that are often more contradictory than in league with one another, and it would be a mistake to level them to an equivalence or make them into the platitudes they are themselves sometimes too quick to claim; my point is only that from a certain remove the status of vision and visuality in all of their arguments is felt to be fraught and to bear significantly on diverse non-optical realms. Nor do I intend to rehearse or substantially modify those arguments here, other than to note that transparency haunts perspective both etymologically (*per specere,* "to look *through*") and also conceptually; as Joel Snyder has argued, following from Erwin Panofsky's claims in *Renaissance and Renascences in Western Art,* "the sense of transparency of the picture surface . . . is an essential precondition for the development of linear perspective."[64] Transparency takes its place along with perspective as part of an idealized and ordered ideology of vision that also includes the "lucid, linear, solid, fixed, planimetric, closed form" of a rationalized sight.[65] One might think of Man Ray's 1923 sculpture *Object to Be Destroyed* (later reconstructions optimistically entitled *Indestructible Object*) as the emblem of such a rationalization: the human eye affixed to the automated and precisely regulating mechanism of a metronome. Against such a visual regime, accordingly, the disordering of Brakhage's "closed-eye" vision and the opaque carnality of the eye offers an alternative, or at least a point of resistance.

Because they establish the terms of our relation to the world (whether that relation is conceived of as conjunction or separation), our senses of perception are obviously quite intimately bound with our understanding of subjectivity. Accordingly, in an atmosphere informed by the scopic theories of Foucault and Lacan, many of the recent attempts to historicize visuality have considered the role of vision "in the production of subjectivity."[66] With those general and often sweeping accounts as a background, I want to turn to the writings of Ludwig Wittgenstein, which Bernstein knows well and which, surprisingly, have been left out of the debates over "scopic regimes." Throughout a career that started with a "picture theory" of language and continued with recurrent ruminations on "seeing as" and the optics of Köhler's gestalt psychology, Wittgenstein echoes the classic pleas for a defamiliarized perception as he repeatedly enjoins: "don't think, but look!"[67] All of his writings evince a belief in the power of visuality, whether liberating or captivating, and crucial passages—such as those in the *Tractatus* (5.5423), the *Brown Book* (169), and the *Investigations* (2:193), for instance—turn on the physiology of ocular response. Indeed, the mechanics of perception which lend figures like the Necker cube their interest for Wittgenstein are some of those made apparent by reading a work like *Veil*, in which words "hidden in a tangle of lines" first appear with certain aspects hidden and others visible, and then reverse these fields on subsequent viewings.[68] In the end, figures of visuality come to be so pervasive in Wittgenstein's work that readers can scarcely help but feel the weight of the pun which emerges in his discussion of "the pupil's capacity to learn" a change in "his *way of looking at things*," where the "pupil" might be understood as part of the ocular system which Wittgenstein, like Brakhage, is trying to "untutor."[69] "We find certain things about seeing puzzling," Wittgenstein concludes, "because we do not find the whole business of seeing puzzling enough."[70]

A comprehensive account of the status of vision in Wittgenstein's oeuvre would certainly be rewarding, but for now I want merely to demonstrate the stakes involved in scopic regimes by focusing on two of the alternative visual models that he offers. The first occurs in a famous passage from the *Tractatus Logico-Philosophicus*:

5.631 . . . .

Wenn ich ein Buch schriebe "Die Welt, wie ich sie vorfand", so wäre darin auch über meinen Leib zu berichten und zu sagen, welche Glieder meinem Willen unterstehen und welche nicht etc., dies ist nämlich eine Methode, das Subjekt zu isolieren, oder vielmehr zu zeigen, dass es in einem wichtigen Sinne keine Subjekt gibt: Von ihm allein nämlich könnte in diesem Buche . n i c h t die Rede sein.

5.632   Das Subjeckt gehört nicht zur Welt, sondern es ist eine Grenze der Welt.

5.633   Wo in der Welt ist ein metaphysisches Subjekt zu merken?
Du sagst, es verhält sich hier ganz, wie mit Auge und Gesichtsfeld. Aber das Auge siehst du wirklich n i c h t.
Und nichts am G e s i c h t s f e l d lässt darauf schliessen, dass es von einem Auge gesehen wird.

5.631   . . . .
If I wrote a book "The world as I found it," I should also have therein to report on my body and say which members obey my will and which do not, etc. This then would be a method of isolating the subject or rather of showing that in an important sense there is no subject: that is to say, of it alone in this book mention could not *be made.*

5.632   *The subject does not belong to the world but it is a limit of the world.*

5.633   Where in *the world is a metaphysical subject to be noted?*
You say that this case is altogether like that of the eye and the field of sight. But you do not *really see the eye.*
And from nothing in the field of sight *can it be concluded that it is seen from an eye.*

At issue in these propositions is Wittgenstein's concern with the solipsistic subject, emblematized by the monocular eye, to which he would return later in his career and continue to investigate in terms of the visual field. Furthermore, in the particular context of the *Tractatus,* this section rhymes with similar discussions of the meta position of all those things—from the rules which govern logical operations to the laws of ethics—that cannot themselves be explained by the explanatory structures they make possible.[71] Wittgenstein's notoriously difficult and gnomic writing lends itself to radically different and conflicting interpretations (commentary tends, even more than usual, towards becoming "my own private Wittgenstein"); what interests me at the moment, however, is not the ultimate philosophical import of the passage, whatever it may be, but rather how hinged that meaning is on the transparency of vision and the suppression of the carnal eye. Unlike the geometric eye of rationalized sight, which one can direct and focus at will, the physical eye, as we have seen, is one member of the body which does not always obey the will as it continually generates images and opacities on its own. That optical noise, moreover, does indeed manifest itself *in the field of sight* so that one really does see the eye and actually can conclude its presence.

The point is not that Wittgenstein has been lax by choosing an unfortunate metaphor, which might be corrected by substituting a more accurate one; throughout his writing, visual models are far too frequent and integral to permit so easy a dismissal. For just one other example of how inextricably intertwined such models are with the "hard rock" of the riverbed of Wittgenstein's thought, consider a passage from the *Blue Book,* in which he returns to the rigidity of the *Tractatus* and begins to test its propositions with the "play" (in both relevant senses) of language games. In this particular passage, Wittgenstein is attempting to understand what it would mean "to think what is not the case" (or more poetically, to ask: "How can something be the shadow of a fact which doesn't exist?"):

> But what do you mean by "redness exists"? My watch exists, if it hasn't been pulled to pieces, if it hasn't been *destroyed*. What would we call "destroying redness"? We might of course mean destroying all red objects; but would that make it impossible to imagine a red object? Supposing to this one answered: "But surely, red objects must have existed and you must have seen them if you are able to imagine them"?—But how do you know that this is so? Suppose I said, "Exerting a pressure on your eye-ball produces a red image." Couldn't the way by which you first became acquainted with red have been this?[72]

Wittgenstein here counters his earlier assumption of ocular transparency with the phosphenes of Brakhage's "closed-eye vision": those images produced by exerting pressure on the eyeball. Additionally, in the context of subjective visual experience, the punning example of "my watch" is not merely incidental. Again, my concern is not to advance any argument for a particular understanding of the philosophical issues—negative ontology, intentionality, the "grammar of wishing"—for which Wittgenstein enlists this *Gedankenexperiment,* but rather to note that he once more makes recourse to the subjective details of a particular scopic regime, which is necessarily implicated in those "larger" philosophical concerns. Finally, exerting a pressure on the visuality of his language, one cannot quite exorcise the ghost of "re[a]dness" from this passage, particularly in the context of a later discussion which employs the prop of a sheet of *paper* that can still be "re[a]d" despite the "imagery" which "shows us something less definite" and "hazier."[73] Keeping the indefinite imagery of Bernstein's *Veil* in mind, I want to turn, in the following chapter, to some similar experiments in overprinting and consider what it would really mean to destroy readness.

> . . . more and more my own language appears to me like a veil that must be torn apart in order to get at things (or the Nothingness) behind it . . . . Is there any reason why that terrible materiality of the word surface should not be capable of being dissolved?
>
> — Samuel Beckett, letter to Axel Kaun

4. The Inhumanness of Language

Destroying Readness

In his philosophical investigation of the "bewitching" and "seductive" nature of language, Wittgenstein states: "A *picture* held us captive. And we could not get outside it, for it lay in our language and language seemed to repeat itself to us inexorably."[1] Taken literally, this proposition might serve as an apt description of Rosmarie Waldrop's *Camp Printing*, which submits the texts of some of James Camp's fairly conventional lyrics to a series of repetitive overprintings. Unlike the palimpsests of different texts in *Veil*, each page of Waldrop's book reiterates a single poem. Nevertheless, the range of visual effects and the degree of illegibility is even more dramatic. The book opens with the slightly out-of-focus blur of a single duplication and progresses — adding a layer with each page and increasingly bringing the texts into vertical alignment — until eight levels of text have accumulated. The almost filmic sense of animated print accreting before the reader's eyes imparts an illusion of textual activity to the process of turning pages; the opening sequence emphasizes the codicological structure of the book and at the same time undercuts its usually static impression.

This sequence is followed by a page which effects the almost total cancellation of its text beneath a smear of twenty-two printings made along a carefully maintained horizontal axis, after which the layering in the poems becomes less extreme but more compositionally varied. Texts appear to vibrate, stipple into the texture of magnified brushstrokes, and sweep across the page in arcs that recall the lines of force in chronophotography and its futurist imitations.[2] (See figure 7.) Repeating itself to us in-

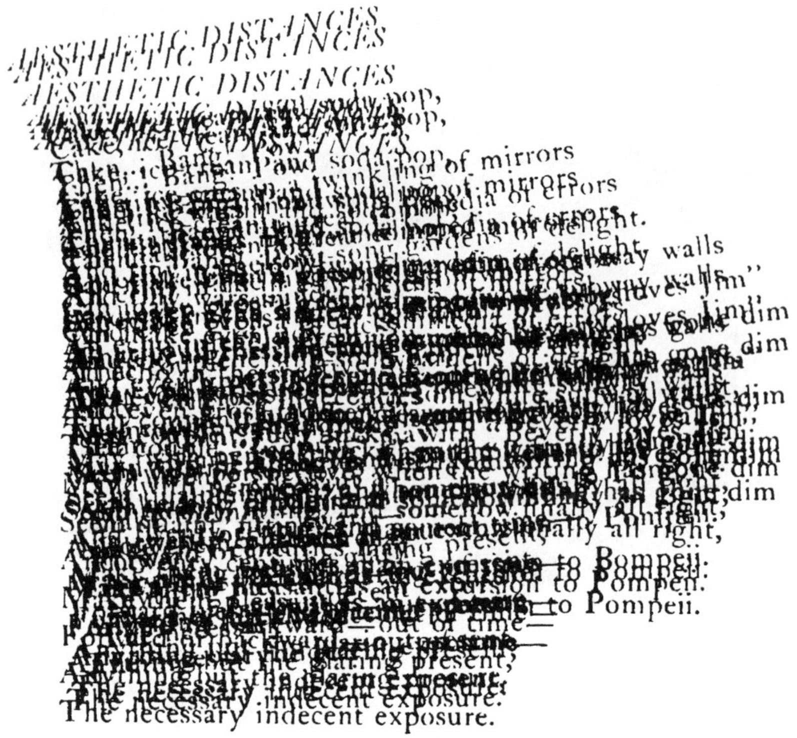

Figure 7. Rosmarie Waldrop, *Camp Printing* (1970)

exorably, the language in these poems approaches the pictorial. In part, such works produce abstract forms by exploiting the visuality of writing for compositional ends, a potential realized in more legible ways by the *calligrammes* of Apollinaire and the collages of cubism and futurism. "Writing" in these poems, to appropriate Plato's famous line from the *Phaedrus,* "is very much like painting."[3] To speak of the "purely visual" nature of such texts, however, or to close off their *reading* by classifying them as "visual" art, would be a mistake—and not just because writing is itself (always) already a visual art.

The ideal of a "perfect" language, one operating exophorically to communicate a "content" of purely referential signifieds, would depend—as the quotations from Silliman and Marin in the previous chapter have implied—on the absolute transparence of the medium: not just the "disappearance of the word" into a "blank page," but ultimately the disappearance of even that page itself.[4] As the material of the medium asserts itself with an increasingly intrusive opacity, the exophoric possibilities diminish in proportion. This ratio, however, need not be construed elegiacally.

As I will try to make clear in this chapter, the materiality of the medium makes available alternative strategies for pursuing signs along routes of signification, and it thus allows language to function anaphorically and cataphorically—gesturing forward and backwards within the economy of the text. This shifting dynamic between opacity and transparence, between the material and the meaning it subtends, explains in part why so many difficult and visually unconventional works seem self-referential or metatextual. *Veil,* as I noted earlier, contains undeniably self-reflexive passages, but as *Camp Printing* manifests by its use of poems from a different context, even phrases with no explicit reference to their production take on an added charge when they are the only readable words in an otherwise illegible page. The examples are numerous, but consider a poem I have already mentioned, in which "errors" immediately suggests the overprinting which *mirrors* duplicated lines into a *twinkling* sweep of words objectified into AESTHETIC DISTANCES from which most are *dim* but a few can be made out in the *indecent exposure* made *necessary* by the mechanics of the printing process used to make the overlay.

As a text moves even further towards complete illegibility, the diminishing denotational capacity of its words helps to foreground the potential of the medium itself to signify, regardless of any specific "content" at all. Consider, for instance, the information carried by typeface and conveyed by even the smallest fragments of letterforms. Bernstein's "veils," for example, appear as typewritten works—with all the connotations of that machine—even before their words can be made out. Similarly, were the poems in *Camp Printing* composed in a black-letter gothic they would be distinctly different poems because they would convey distinctly different cultural information, just as would the connotations of a particular word substituted for its synonym. Such examples could be multiplied, or expanded to include more subjective responses, but I instead want to indicate one of the physical aspects of these poems which signifies even when the typeface itself has been rendered illegible. Compare the indecipherable lines of Waldrop's most heavily overprinted poems with Man Ray's "Lautgedicht" ("Sound-Poem").[5] (See figure 8.) The aesthetics of cancellation will be addressed elsewhere in this book, but for now simply note how *laut* this seemingly muffled poem actually is. Without access to a single word, the viewer immediately knows something of the poem's genre and subject (and one is quite sure that it is a *poem*); it is neither a haiku nor an epic, for instance, and it is likely to be more conventional than experimental, more lyric than narrative. Regardless of such reasoned speculations, the poems

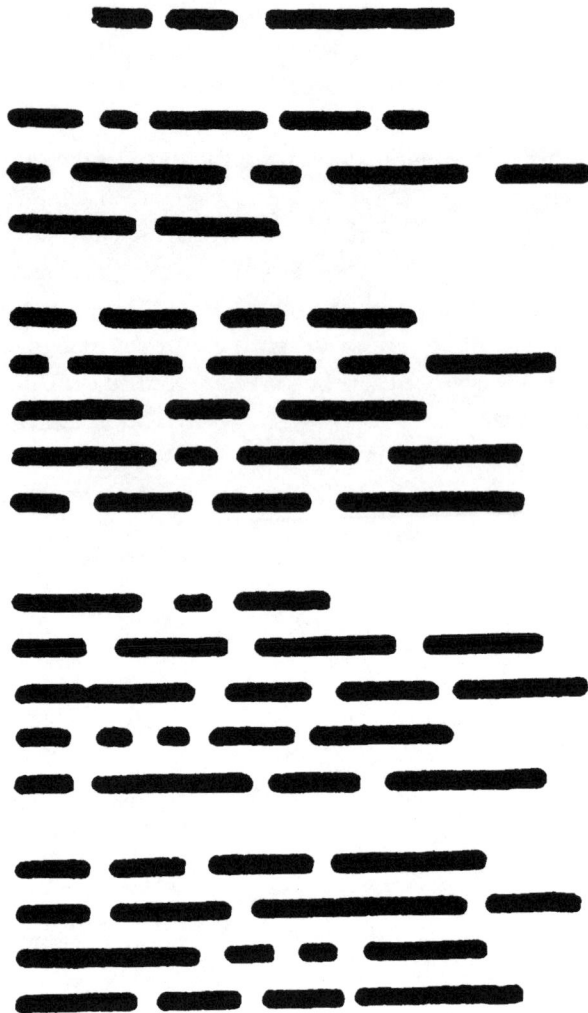

Figure 8. Man Ray, "Lautgedicht" (1924)

by both Waldrop and Man Ray are obviously closed and carefully measured forms. From the quick and uneven opening of its tercet first stanza,
"Lautgedicht" balances with two longer stanzas at its center and then con-
veys a strong "sense of an ending" with the sturdy, neatly four-square final
stanza, wherein the line lengths, which have varied somewhat throughout
the poem, settle to a much greater uniformity. The force of the quatrains
in Waldrop's poem, where the regularity of line length further suggests a
metrical regulation, is even more pronounced.[6]

The meanings which attend these details of visual prosody interact with the syntactic and denotative meanings of textual reference, and their information can underscore those references (as in most concrete poetry, for instance) or contradict them (as some dada poets discovered). Beyond such meanings, the visual text also encodes more specific information about the material production of its language. As the textual history of Susan Howe's work has made clear—with the "same" poem altering its appearance slightly as it migrates from chapbook to journal to one anthology or another—the range of a text's visual prosody depends to a large extent on the mechanics of reproduction. Certain effects, and this is particularly true of overprinting, can be obtained only by letterpress, others by offset lithography, others by Quark and a laser printer, and so on. Part of the information carried by the visual form of *Camp Printing* is the possibilities and constraints of its medial technologies.[7] The text, for instance, informs the reader that it was composed on a machine which permitted the same sheet to be *re*printed with some precision; similarly, regardless of the look of its letterforms, the text announces that it was not produced on a typewriter, where the carriage space would restrict the rotation of the paper. One could deduce further specifics, but the point is that the material exigencies of the text, in these ways, always hint at the allegory of its mode of production, and it is in this sense that the printing of Waldrop's book—while not being particularly funny (the overprinting is too meticulous and beautiful to avoid seeming serious)—is indeed actually *campy:* self-ironic and always drawing attention to its artifice.

So while the physical opacity of a text prevents communication from ever being perfect, meaning is always being communicated by that very materiality. Those excesses of signification provided by the physical properties of a poem complicate any simple understanding of concepts like "meaning" and "information." More clearly than most works, *Veil* and *Camp Printing* serve as reminders of the conceptual limitations of restricting such terms to denotative reference. In their refusal to convey denotative information, the texts I have been considering would seem at first to be the ultimate fulfillment of a definition of "poetry" which has echoed through this century as a mainstay of formalist poetics. In Jan Mukařovsky's familiar version, "poetry" is that language which "is not used in the services of communication," and Wittgenstein offers a similar caveat: "Do not forget that a poem, although it is composed in the language of information, is not used in the language game of giving information." The text, however, has already been picked for the team and cannot help but play along; it can never escape from the services of communication or decline to give information in any but the narrowest sense. As reminders of the non-denotative aspects of language, statements like these are important, but even in their rejections they still operate on the terms of normative, implicitly conservative, models of communication, and they too quickly foreclose possibilities for a wider understanding of the very concepts they employ.

Similarly, in the terms of information theory, obstacles to "giving information"—the overinking, doubled printing, or smudge which blots out a word, to give just a few relevant instances among a wide range of potential impediments—would usually be considered as "noise." By explicitly introducing noise *as* message, these poems briefly short-circuit the parasitic economy; they remind readers that the distinction between "message" and "noise" ultimately deconstructs itself (in the most technical sense of the phrase). I have addressed the political aspects of these issues at some length in chapter 2, and here I want to recall Michel Serres's torus as a model for understanding the precarious limnal space where these poems balance in other (though ultimately, perhaps, equivalent) terms. In their most extreme instances, the works I have been discussing occupy a privileged position between what we might name "meaning" and "signification," or "language" and "writing," or "writing" and "inscription."

So far, all of the examples I have mentioned of information being communicated by the material text still operate referentially; that is, they convey some arbitrary, culturally determined "meaning." While form must mean, it need not necessarily correspond to any particular, a priori meaning. The materiality of written language, however, opens up yet further possibilities for formally encoded signification which would generate meaning by radically different protocols.[8] However naturalized they seem, the strategies we normally use to activate written language as signs (what we usually think of simply as "reading": what you are doing now in following this sentence to its end) might be substituted with other techniques of engaging a text. These alternatives, moreover, would not necessarily be perverse, to the degree that the writing itself does not mandate the conventional (in all the relevant senses) modes of processing its data. The material form of language, by definition, permits those conventional modes of reading, but they cannot be extrapolated back out of the material form in any requisite way. By deploying language vertically and disrupting the horizontal spacing of words and letters, overprinting explicitly presents codes other than the pursuit of words spread out in sequential, horizontal lines meant to be followed repetitively left to right, top to bottom.[9]

Perhaps the most infamous example of an alternative protocol comes from Ferdinand de Saussure's notebooks on *paragrammes*.[10] The story by now is familiar, but worth recalling. In brief, de Saussure suspected that classical verse contained the names of otherwise unmentioned dedicatory figures, whose monikers were disseminated through the text in disarticulated phonemes. "Apollo," for instance, might appear distributed as "<u>a</u>d mea temp<u>la</u> <u>p</u>ortat<u>o.</u>" With a chilling meticulousness—"we are not forgetting the patience of the mad, their love of detail," as Lyn Hejinian might put it—de Saussure labored to enumerate the intricate and unfailingly consistent rules he saw governing the *paragrammes*. But then he wasn't so sure after all. Not only could a single couplet supply an almost endless number of names, but the *paragrammes* were not limited to classical verse—one might start reading them out of any text and seeing them everywhere. From this vantage, the material signifier thus comes to be seen as not simply an unfortunate precondition for communicating some intended linguistic meaning, but also as the matrix for the generation of multiple, uncontrollable, and unhierarchized meanings. Faced with *la folie du langue,* this "uncontrollable power of the letter as inscription," de Saussure suppressed his work and backed away from the project with a caution that "supports the assumption of a terror glimpsed."[11] That terror was the inhumanness of language.[12]

I borrow this term from Paul de Man, who provides a succinct and tellingly emphatic definition:

> the inhuman is: linguistic structures, the play of linguistic tensions, linguistic events that occur, possibilities which are inherent in language—independently of any intent or any drive or any wish or any desire we might have.[13]

De Man here contrasts the linguistic (language as a material structure) with the discursive (language as meaning).[14] Given the articulating system of alphabetic writing, with its grammar of spacing, lettering, and recombination, a material signification—as de Saussure's *paragrammes* demonstrate—is always excessive and indiscreet. The multiplicity of potential meanings in such a system can sometimes be exploited, or recuperated, but it can never be entirely circumscribed or controlled; the materiality of language always escapes *semantics,* in the sense of any totalizing reading that could claim coherent closure. That is to say, one could of course write paragrammatically, bringing its model within the circle of intention and control, but then other possibilities would have to be overlooked, and even if all of those alternatives could be recognized, they could never be simultaneously engaged; to pursue some would mean that still other models would slip away in turn. Nor is this to make any arguments about the origin of alphabetic language, or its obvious use as a human tool: only to recognize that once the system is in place it keeps working beyond its mandate.

For just one illustration of the way in which language "is totally indifferent in relation to the human" in this way, notice that whenever you write "slaughter" you write—necessarily and inescapably—"laughter" as well.[15] I should be quick to emphasize that this is not a claim about the cleverness of the writer or the ingenuity of the reader; stop reading, and it continues. Look away; it's still happening. Close the book. It's still going on. Try to forget it. It goes on. It doesn't care. It continues. Language is relentless in its excesses, and those inevitable excesses are precisely that "nonhuman aspect of language . . . from which we cannot escape, because language does things which are so radically out of our control that they cannot be assimilated to the human at all, against which one fights constantly."[16] Part of that fight is taken up by the way certain reading habits condition us to ignore the material effects of language, just as we are conditioned to regard the eye as transparent. But the wolf is always at the door; from the moment of inscription writing introduces

> the materiality of the letter, the independence, or the way in which the letter can disrupt the ostensibly stable meaning of a sentence and introduce in it a slippage by means of which that meaning disappears, evanesces, and by means of which all control over that meaning is lost.[17]

"Matter asks no questions, expects no answers of us. It ignores us. It made us the way it made all bodies—by chance and according to its laws," as Jean-François Lyotard puts it in his own essay on the "inhuman."[18] Or again, as George Oppen writes: "Words cannot be wholly transparent. And that is the 'heartlessness' of words."[19] The indifference (in *différance*) of language can be felt in the "laughter" that always emerges from "slaughter," but that laughter is never mocking, because—like the opacities of vision that the eye, beyond the range of willful bodily control, produces independently of picturing any external images—the inhuman of language has no regard for its meaning effects; "a pure language (*reine Sprache*) . . . would be entirely freed of the illusion of meaning."[20] In the slaughter of semantics, that laughter "n'éclate que depuis le renoncement absolu au sens [bursts out only on the basis of an absolute renunciation of meaning]."[21]

If the description of the "inhuman" has the feel of *dèjá lu*, that is because it has taken many incarnations in recent theoretical writings, of which I want to single out just one particularly resonant version, which also takes de Saussure's *paragrammes* as its cue.[22] In Jean Baudrillard's account, the display of illegibly overprinted texts, "purement graphiques et indéchiffrables [purely graphic and undecipherable]," where the message has ceased to exist under the imposition of the medium—a writing where there is nothing to read, like "une image où il n'y a rien à voir [an image where there is nothing to see]"—achieves "l'extase de la communication [the ecstasy of communication]."[23] Under that swoon of language,

> ce n'est plus nous qui lui donnons un sens ou non en le [monde] transcendant ou en le réfléchissant. Merveilleuse est l'indifférence du monde à cet égard, merveilleuse l'indifférence des choses à notre égard, et leurs passion pourtant de se dérouler et de mêler leurs apparences.

> *it is no longer we who give or withhold meaning in transcending or reflecting upon the world. The indifference of the world in this respect is marvelous; the indifference of things with regard to us is marvelous—and still they spread out before us, in their promiscuous poses, with such passion.*[24]

In this gleeful version of de Saussure's terror, Baudrillard recognizes that "le malin génie du langage consiste à se faire objet, là où on attend du sujet et du sens [the evil demon of language consists in its ability to render itself as an object, where one had instead expected to find subject and meaning]."[25] In Baudrillard's idiosyncratic vocabulary, the indifference of that ecstatic demon (an incarnation of Serres's: ex-static) is *fatal*—"Tout ce qui s'enchaîne hors du sujet, donc du côté de sa disparition, est fatal. Tout ce qui n'est plus une stratégie humaine devient par là même une stratégie fatale [Everything linked up beyond the subject, and therefore on the side of its disappearance, is fatal. All that which is no longer a human strategy becomes, by definition, a fatal strategy]"—as well as *seductive*: "si l'objet nous séduit, c'est d'abord par son indifférence [if the object seduces us, it does so first by its indifference]."[26] And as we shall see next, "La séduction est maudite (mais ce n'est pas là son moindre charme) [Seduction is damned (but that's not the least of its charms)]."[27]

To conceptualize language in these ways is to understand it as operating in a general economy.[28] In contrast to restricted economies, which are predicated on scarcity, general economies are driven by surplus and excess. Georges Bataille develops the concept at length over several volumes, but he provides a concise definition of such systems, as well as the related idea of "sovereignty," in a footnote from *L'expérience intérieure*:[29]

L'économie générale met en évidence en primier lieu que des excédents d'énergie se produisent qui, par définition, ne peuvent être utilisés. L'énergie excédante ne peut être que perdue sans le moindre but, en conséquence sans aucun sens. C'est cette perte inutile, insensée, qu'*est* la souveraineté.

General economy *evinces, firstly, that excesses of energy are produced which, by definition, cannot be utilized. That excessive energy cannot but be lost without the least goal, and hence without any meaning. It is this useless, meaningless loss, which is sovereignty.*[30]

"Dans la souveraineté, l'autonomie procède . . . d'un refus de conserver, d'une prodigalité sans mesure . . . . La souveraineté ne diffère en rien d'une dissipation sans limite [In sovereignty, autonomy proceeds . . . from a refusal to conserve, from an infinite prodigality . . . . Sovereignty does not differ in the least from a limitless dissipation]."[31] We have already met Bataille's "sovereignty" in the queenly (*Reine*) indifference of "pure" (*reine*) language, which one can do absolutely nothing (*rien de rien*) to rein in completely or deny (*nier*) its ultimately elusive margin of material signification. Recalling all those "demons" which have haunted systems (from Clerk Maxwell's entropic to Baudrillard's ecstatic to Serres's prosopopoeia of noise), as well as Blake's repeated assertion that "the limit of Opakeness is named Satan," that material excess of the textual (general) economy, the "inhuman" measure of language, is—in Bataille's lexicon—*le part maudite:* the devil's lot, the accursèd share. *Le part maudite* is that portion given up to waste in potlatch or "sacrifice," which in Bataille's argument compensates for the abuse something suffers in its role as an object of utile servitude by restoring it to subjecthood. Accordingly, by ostentatiously celebrating language's indifference (in both the narrow sense of erasing articulation beneath an undifferentiated inscription, and the broader sense of its disinterested sovereignty) at the expense of its role as an uncomplicatedly servile object of utilitarian communication (servile utility, one will recall, was precisely and not coincidentally the goal of the new traditionalists' typographic transparency), poems like those in *Camp Printing* become that mode of sacrifice in which the victims are words.[32]

The point is worth repeating; this understanding of language does not imply that some of the ineluctable excesses of the linguistic system could not be recuperated, by either a resourceful writer or reader, as part of a restricted economy of semantic meaning. Indeed, even to view the inevitable loss of meaning in a (general) textual economy as tragic or nostalgic is to lose one's grip on the *general* as it slides irrevocably into a restricted economy in which that apparently profitless loss has thus been salvaged — if only partially — as affect, and so recycled for the benefit of the reader.[33] Rather than think of a general or restricted economy as being a fixed characteristic of some object, one would do better to conceive of them as shifting frames of reference, or as the point of view from which a given system is understood. General and restricted economies are not, however, easily separable alternatives which one might simply choose between; they ceaselessly irrupt within one another according to the same dynamic that defines the relationship between opacity and transparence. In ways that constantly destabilize the very categories of "general" and "restricted," every text threatens to sacrifice itself in an ecstatic loss of meaning, at the same time that its meaninglessness can always be accounted for (even if only as the meaning of "meaninglessness"). If there is no language perfectly subservient to the communication of exophoric reference, neither is there "souveraineté *elle-même* [sovereignty *itself*]."[34]

To put this another way, let me be explicit about the converse of a proposition I have taken up in some detail; a purely opaque materiality would be as untenable as a perfectly transparent language. Faced with language in its sheer materiality, one would no longer be able to recognize it *as language*.[35] Paradoxically, Warde's ideal of the "crystal goblet" is achieved at the price of its inversion; only in its complete opacity, and not in some imagined transparency, does writing become invisible, does it disappear as writing. "Le cristal," as Baudrillard sums up, "se venge [the crystal takes its revenge]."[36] "We all secretly venerate the ideal of a language which in the last analysis would deliver us from language by delivering us to things," according to Maurice Merleau-Ponty, but even if that "thing" is the material of language itself, deliverance is always ultimately withheld. Even to recognize a single disarticulated letter *as a letter* already incorporates the rest of the alphabet which it presupposes, or — as with an unknown script — to imagine the possibility of an alphabet. That moment of recognition accounts for the giddy thrill of encountering a foreign language written in a script one does not understand, and it has intrigued the many writers who have attempted, as Wittgenstein proposed, to "imagine some arbitrary cipher."[37] Henri Michaux's anthropomorphized "characters," Christian Dotremont's logogrammes, Decio Pignatari's semiotic poems, Dieter Rot's 4⁴ variations, B. P. Nichol's *26 Alphabets,* the graphism of *les lettristes,* as well as much graffiti art, all experiment with that alphabetic threshold. Even more pertinent are Hansjörg Mayer's overprinted alphabets, some of which recall the blurred motion of Waldrop's poems or the lattices of Bernstein's "veils."

Both *Camp Printing* and *Veil*, in fact, might be thought of as participating in this intergenre tradition, because like invented scripts they provide a glimpse of the moment—fleeting and almost imperceptible—when writing shifts between a general and a restricted economy as "the materiality of the letter" passes from the unrecognizable opacity of "pure . . . datum" into readable, if not intelligible, "language."[38] One catches that glimpse not through Alberti's transparent window out on the world, but from the other side of the screen from which language looks back with its "stony gaze." Even if it could never achieve a *reine Sprache* that would be identifiable as such, the illegible poem offers a rare view as it balances on the cusp of Serres's torus: displaying the material precondition of language in all its nonreferential opacity while—momentarily—staying the illimitable movement of the *gram* which might induce *la folie de Saussure*.[39] "The unreadable text is an outer limit for poetry," Bernstein has written, and by inhabiting the threshold at which writing passes between the field of human language and the inhumanness of sheer materiality, the illegible text is a literalization of Wittgenstein's proposition that "dass die Grenzen der Sprache (der Sprache, die allein ich verstehe) die Grenzen m e i n e r Welt bedeuten [the limits of language (*the* language which I understand) mean the limits of *my* world]."[40] Approaching the limit (*sub limn*) of an "opake immeasurable," in fact, is all to the point.[41] As they negotiate that unstable middle ground in the field of inscription, the most extreme poems in *Veil* and *Camp Printing* open onto vistas of the textual sublime.

De Saussure's reaction to the *paragramme*'s infinite proliferation of recombinatory possibilities "in a manner analogous to terror," indeed, suggests nothing so much as the experience of the "mathematical sublime."[42] Moreover, to arrive at a recognition of the inhumanness of language through texts like *Veil* or *Camp Printing*—with their "obscurity," "privations such as darkness," "silence," and "difficulty"—would seem to correspond perfectly, if rather literally, to Burke's description of the sublime object, which intervenes against habit and familiarity to make things strange, and which works to "create particular problems for the sensations—by presenting themselves as too powerful or too vast or too obscure or too much of a deprivation for the senses to process them comfortably."[43] The discourse on the sublime (not to be confused with sublime discourse) has done brisk business recently, and this is not the place for yet another critical reading of the tradition which has developed under its name.[44] I do, however, want to draw attention to how suggestively the rhetoric of the sublime reads in relation to illegible writing, as well as how neatly it dovetails with descriptions of the "inhumanness" of language, further emphasizing the striking affinities between those descriptions and related theorizations of language.

In his study of the "sublime as text," Vincent A. De Luca posits the project of approaching a *reine Sprache* and "liberating the signifier from the signified" as the very definition of the textual sublime. As an exemplary case, he examines the most densely scripted and difficult-to-read pages from Blake's illuminated books, which he describes in terms that could be applied equally, if not better, to an overprinted work like *Veil*. As Blake "increases the density of inscription to the point of visual strain," "fatigue," and "vertigo," those inscriptions "tend to withdraw from referential function altogether" so that "the text becomes iconic, a physical *Ding an sich*, not a transparent medium through which meaning is easily disseminated."[45] This opacity "inevitably irritates those who come to texts for smooth communication[;] the effect of this impediment to the reading eye is precisely to reify the signifier and so provoke the tension necessary for the sublime experience."[46] The constant movement of words in and out of readability which we saw in *Veil* thus becomes, for De Luca, the very grounds of the textual sublime:[47]

> The barrier seems to flicker before the eyes, now opaque, now translucent, at once forbidding and yielding. The sublime object presents a towering face and yet offers a conspicuous invitation to ascent, or it holds back and teases with the promise of penetration, or it hints at ineffable possibilities of Presence and then defers them.[48]

As with Waldrop's printing or Bernstein's poems, the "attention of the reader is diverted from a sequential pursuit of words and lines to a visual contemplation of the whole block of text as a single unit, a panel," which De Luca names "a wall of words."[49] Or, as *Veil* itself announces, "WALL OF WORDS WHICH MEANS LOOK YOU LOOK."[50]

Given the concentration and visual strain demanded by a work like *Veil*, or the double vision so perfectly replicated by many of the poems in *Camp Printing*, looking at that "wall of words" for any length of time can be quite literally dizzying, and De Luca's description of "fatigue" and "vertigo" should not necessarily be taken as figurative hyperbole. In fact, the most striking precedent to Waldrop's overprinting is a nineteenth-century warning against precisely such dangers. (See figure 9.) Taken from James

xiv *Introduction:*

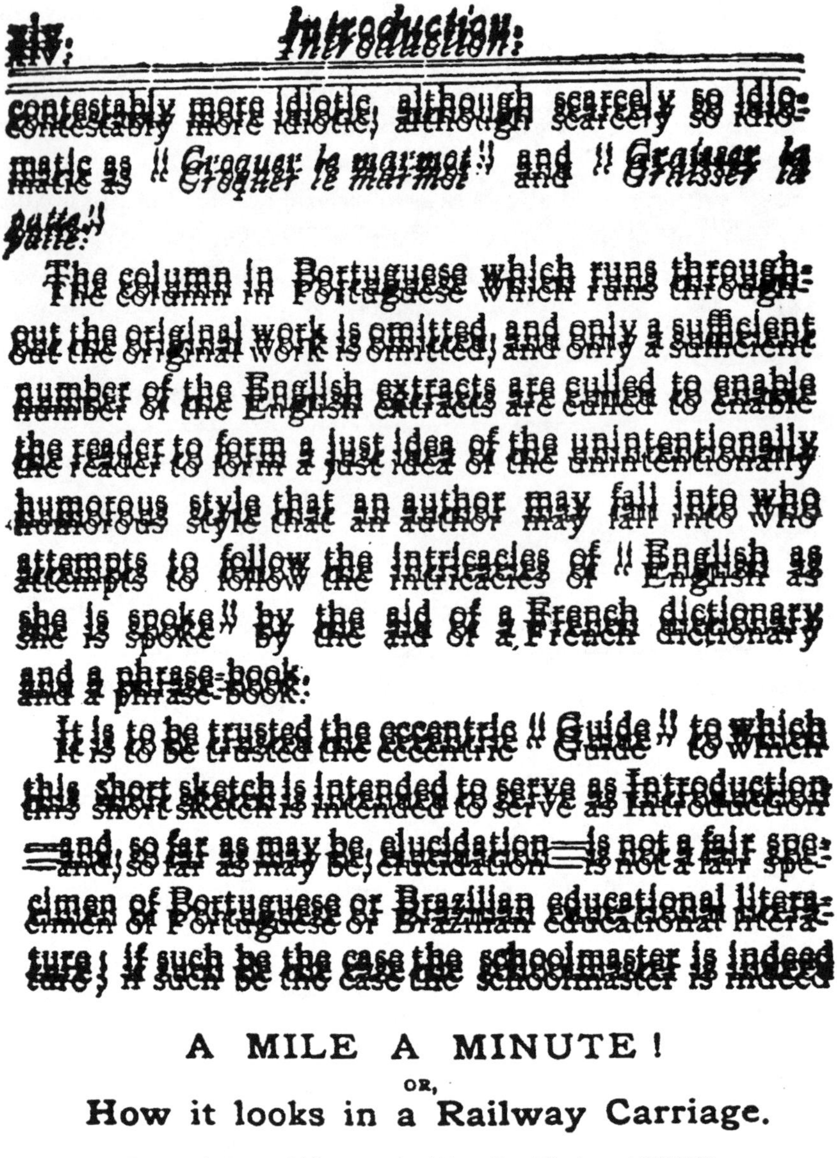

contestably more idiotic, although scarcely so idio-matic as " *Croquer le marmot*" and " *Graisser la patte.*"

The column in Portuguese which runs through-out the original work is omitted, and only a sufficient number of the English extracts are culled to enable the reader to form a just idea of the unintentionally humorous style that an author may fall into who attempts to follow the intricacies of " English as she is spoke" by the aid of a French dictionary and a phrase-book.

It is to be trusted the eccentric " Guide" to which this short sketch is intended to serve as Introduction —and, so far as may be, elucidation—is not a fair spe-cimen of Portuguese or Brazilian educational litera-ture; if such be the case the schoolmaster is indeed

A MILE A MINUTE !
OR,
How it looks in a Railway Carriage.

Figure 9. James Millington, *Are We to Read Backwards?* (1883)

Millington's 1883 *Are We to Read Backwards?*, this page was meant to illus-trate the dangers of reading on the "metropolitan railways." The simula-tion of vibration in Millington's text is assumed to be so self-evident that the appearance of "train cars," in conjunction with a visual vocabulary ("window," "imagery," "watching," "mirrors," "tears," and so on), in James Camp's "The Iron Year" may not have been incidental in Waldrop's choice to treat it with an almost identical technique.[51] Appropriate to a scene in which the speaker imagines the hallucinatory illusion of actually experiencing the "clanging" of the rails, Waldrop's tremulous printing becomes a complex and witty inscription of that experiential illusion back into the monologue itself. The synesthesaic translation from the vibrations of sound in the "ear" to the visual tremors of a vibrating railcar would indeed be the irony ("The [Iron Y]*ear*") of the text. (See figure 10.)

As with all of the poems in *Camp Printing,* as well as those in *Veil,* the text read on a trembling railway calls "for a continual adjustment of the focus of vision" which, when "added to the muscular tension necessitated by the vibration of the carriage," would, in Millington's opinion, "sufficiently account for much of the nervous malaise felt by some habitual travellers on these lines." Those are "lines" of rails and not of writing, but while dizzying textual effects may not be responsible for the stress of commuting, they do seem to be commensurate with the experience of communicating when that communication disappears into the textual sublime. De Luca notes that the prototypically sublime moment is "usually described as *vertigo* or blockage or bafflement," and Steve McCaffery accordingly explains that de Saussure, in his investigations of the *paragrammes,* "hit upon the vertiginous nature of textuality"—echoing Starobinski's description of de Saussure's "vertige de erreur [vertigo of error]," as well as de Man's characterization of the paragrammatic project as "vertiginously speculative" and Baudrillard's repeated description of the "vertige [giddiness]" of de Saussure's anagrammatic texts.[52] "Il y a," Baudrillard announces, "un état propre de fascination et de vertige lié à ce délire de la communication. Une forme de plaisir singulier peut-être, mais aléatoire et vertigineux. [There is a state of fascination and giddiness which attends that delirium of communication. A singular form of pleasure perhaps, but aleatory and vertiginous.]"[53] This is the pleasure of the illegible. *Le délire de lire.*

Once again, as we saw with all those theories which consider writing as a "general economy," the particular details of the material text, when engaged with the attention and patience of a truly radical formalism, figure the most abstract theoretical constructs. At the fundamental level of concrete, physiological response to specific textual demands, works like *Veil* and *Camp Printing* produce equivalents to theoretical positions even before any given "message about" such theories might be conveyed. However, any such "content"—no matter how comfortingly familiar or easy it would seem when compared with the demands of an "obstinate physicality"— would have been redundant, if not paradoxically contradictory. Which is

THE IRON YEAR

"...now submerges an iron year."

"...now submerges an iron year."

Positions of pigeons on train cars

but surely

remain

winter

into an undersea sound.

Figure 10. Rosmarie Waldrop, *Camp Printing* (1970)

to refuse to posit these works as mere illustrations; they *enact* the very condition of the theoretical claims which might be made on their behalf.[54] For this reason, it is perhaps no coincidence that the designers of the journal *Visible Language* chose overprint as the emblematic typographic technique with which to represent "instant theory." As Blake understood in his own profound attention to bibliographic detail, "Minute Discrimination is Not Accidental," because "Singular & particular Detail is the foundation of the Sublime."

Someone says to me: "Shew the children a game." I teach them gaming with dice, and the other says "I didn't mean that sort of game."

—Ludwig Wittgenstein

I have scarcely begun to make you understand that I don't intend to play the game.

—Guy Debord

5. Gamble and Sharp

Cheating at Language Games

Early in Charles Dickens's *Great Expectations* (chapter 7), Joe Gargery testifies to his "oncommon" fondness of reading:

> Give me . . . a good book, or a good newspaper, and sit me down afore a good fire, and I ask no better. Lord!" he continued, after rubbing his knees a little, "when you do come to a J and a O, and says you 'Here, at last, is a J-O, Joe,' how interesting reading is!"

Like de Saussure "deciphering" Saturnian verse, the implications of which I explored in the previous chapter, Joe here performs a "paragrammatic" reading, and he provides a surprising precedent for the procedural "writing-through" techniques of John Cage and Jackson Mac Low.[1] In the early 1980s, with apparent inscience of one another's projects, both Cage and Mac Low—who had studied together in Cage's classes in experimental composition at the New School for Social Research in the late 1950s—were simultaneously writing-through Ezra Pound's *Cantos,* and a comparison of the results is instructive. Cage refers to his strategy of writing-through as "mesostic," because it spells out a name or theme-word down the middle (meso) of a verse line (stich), just as an acrostic spells down the beginning of the lines, or a telestich down the termini. The mesostich is an ancient verse form, of course, but Cage adds a twist to his version; in its strictest mode, first proposed by Louis Mink, Cage's mesostics follow the rule that between any two letters of the key-word those letters may not appear. So in

"Writing Through *The Cantos*," for instance, Cage chose the index "Ezra Pound" and proceeded through Pound's source text until he came to the first word containing an "e" but not followed by a "z," then continued until he came to a word with a "z" neither preceded by an "e" nor followed by an "r," and so on in succession through the text, repeating the index and allowing himself to include as many words on either side of the index-letter as he wanted so long as they fit within the standard 86-character spread of the page and did not violate the exclusionary index-letter rule.[2]

Jackson Mac Low refers to his own writings-through, appropriately enough, as "diastic" methods (a term I will adopt in this chapter to cover Cage's mesostic operations as well), and he has used several variations of the procedure on a wide variety of source texts. For *Words nd Ends from Ez* he read through *The Cantos* much as Cage did, replacing the exclusionary rule with the constraint that each index-letter had to occupy the same position in the excerpted source text as it does in the index-word. The letter "e," for instance, begins a string that continues to the end of whatever word contains it; the letter "z" holds the second place in the following string; "r" occurs as the third letter in the next string, and so on. This rule both obviates the inclusion of extra words between index-letters, a degree of intervention that Cage permits himself, and also frequently requires Mac Low to truncate words or back up in the source text, disrupting the word boundaries that Cage always maintains.

So given this passage from "Canto I,"

> And then went down to the ship,
> . . . .
> Men many, mauled with bronze lance heads,
> Battle spoil, bearing yet dreory arms,
> These many crowded about me; with shouting,
> Pallor upon me, cried to my men for more beasts;
> Slaughtered the herds, sheep slain of bronze;
> Poured ointment, cried to the gods,
> To Pluto the strong, and praised Proserpine

Cage extracts

> and thEn with bronZe lance heads beaRing yet Arms
> sheeP slain Of plUto stroNg praiseD

and Mac Low derives

En nZe eaRing ory Arms,
Pallor pOn laUghtered laiN oureD Ent[.]

Of all the paragrammatic strategies examined in this book, Cage and Mac Low's are clearly the most systematic, and while many of the works discussed in previous chapters have rendered their illegibility visible, inking words over words, these poems depend on the implicit absence of a partially erased text; after working through the eight hundred or so pages of Pound's text in these ways, Mac Low reduces the epic poem to fewer than eighty pages, while Cage's version extends to only eight. I will examine the most immediately obvious aspect of these poems, "the sudden spluttered petulance of some capItallsed mIddle," later in this chapter, but for now let me briefly call attention to the less salient accidentals.[3] Cage's poem omits any punctuation, while Mac Low's incorporates what amounts to an extrapolation of Pound's prosody; he includes any punctuation or line break found at the end of a letter string—as well as any hyphens found within the string—and he organizes his long poem into sections corresponding with the sections of the New Directions edition of the collected *Cantos.* Additionally, it perhaps needs to be stressed that for all of their calculation and unfamiliarity these poems are often quite beautiful.[4] Mac Low's "ecRetary fex," to cite just one instance, has the vocal frisson one expects from a poem by Peter Inman or Clark Coolidge, either of whom might have intentionally authored this unintentionally generated line.[5] Similarly, the Joycean music of lines like "ShUn timNal un unDer Elody" in Mac Low's poem are matched by Cage with the melos of lines like "gonE glaZe gReen feAthers," which picks up on a network of words ("graze," "glaze," "gaze") that structure the larger movements of Cage's poem much as Stein organized her most carefully constructed texts.[6]

In Dickens's novel, Joe's oncommon encomium on the swell pleasures of reading is prompted by one of Pip's writing exercises. With its word fragments, unexpected letter combinations, and irruptions of capital letters, Pip's halting epistle looks, at first glance, not unlike a passage from Mac Low's. Dickens reproduces the smudge-pipped epistle as

mI deEer JO i opE U r krWitE wEll i opE i shAl soN B haBelL 4 2 teeDge U JO aN theN wE shOrl b sO glOdd aN wEn i M preNgtD 2 u JO woT larX an blEvE ME inF xn PiP.

The initial appearance of this text aside, however, the episode from *Great Expectations* might also evoke one of the many pedagogic vignettes from the first part of Ludwig Wittgenstein's *Philosophical Investigations*. Not coincidentally, both Mac Low and Cage have written-through Wittgenstein's work as well. Among the source texts used by Cage in his notorious Charles Eliot Norton lecture (published in 1990 as *I–IV*), Wittgenstein accounts for the single largest number of quotations; Mac Low's first "purely acrostic-stanzaic chance poem" was composed around 1960 using Wittgenstein's *Blue and Brown Books* as its source, and he has more recently used the *Investigations* as part of his computer-assisted "DIASTEX" poetry.[7] With a striking accord, Wittgenstein's text addresses precisely the same nexus of themes brought to the fore not only by Pip's scene of writing, but also by the mesostic and diastic poems: proper names, rule-following, and what activities can properly be said to constitute "reading" and "writing." Before returning to a closer examination of Cage and Mac Low's poetry, I want to briefly consider the conjunction of these topics in the *Investigations*. I should be quick to note that I do not intend to advance anything like a standard philosophical interpretation of this notoriously hermetic work. I do, however, want to propose that Cage and Mac Low—like Kosuth and Johns in the visual arts—have engaged in a kind of "applied Investigation."[8] At the very least, I want to forestall a common reaction to their compositions and suggest that such writings-through should not be too quickly dismissed as mere gimmicks, but may in fact constitute works which get at the heart of some of the most vexing and fundamental topics of modern philosophy.

In the larger scope of Dickens's story, Pip's letter appears in a chapter illustrating his early education, a training by which he learns to "read write and cipher." With "cipher" understood as encryption rather than arithmetic, these three terms might all stand in apposition. Pip composes his letter, significantly, with an alphabet at his feet "for reference." Like Joe selecting and rearranging from the source text before him, Pip—or Dickens himself, or any other writer, for that matter—is doing much the same. Similarly, by "making writing use of / something thought to be for reaDing," as Cage puts it in his own response to Mac Low's *Words nd Ends,* the procedure of writing-through underscores, by rendering literal, the way in which readers always participate to some degree as writers: selecting certain material from a text while ignoring other aspects, activating particular codes of signification at the expense of other strategies, and adhering to given protocols of linguistic recombination as they necessarily violate alternative procedures.[9]

Whether or not rule-determined procedures can be said to properly constitute poetic "writing," one might still ask, as Dickens does, to what degree they count as "reading." The joke, though it's a serious one and always on us, is at least as old as Shakespeare; when Polonius asks Hamlet "What do you read, my lord?" the Prince famously responds: "Words, words, words."[10] The difference between a physiological scanning process and a comprehensive assessment—"the understanding of what is read"—is one of the key distinctions Wittgenstein teases out in his investigation of the grammar of "reading."[11] Within the argument of the *Investigations,* the language games of "reading" are intimately related to those of "speaking" ("we do not say it of a parrot; nor of a gramophone"), and the same sort of analysis is famously applied to "seeing" in the 1948 addendum.[12] The grammar of "writing," in this context, would certainly be equivalent: the distance, for example, between how the pen in the seismograph might be said to be "writing" its seismogram and the way that I might be said to be "writing" this book. The diastics are a record of particular performances of functions of "reading," even if the sort of reading they execute—disarticulated letters rather than semantic units—is not what we usually mean by the word. In Wittgensteinian terms, then, Cage and Mac Low might be seen as reading machines set to different idling speeds.[13]

Another way of posing these distinctions is to cast them in the terms of a material medium over and against a referential meaning. Wittgenstein suggests precisely such a framework in the vocabulary of §102 in the *Investigations,* where the philosophical content, or "understanding," of a proposition is simultaneously embodied, hidden, and revealed "through a medium." A few sections later he clarifies: "We are talking about the spatial and temporal phenomenon of language, not about some non-spatial, non-temporal phantasm."[14] In more familiar poststructuralist terms, this contrast would be posed as the cleaving of material signifier (the spatial and temporal distribution of letters on a page, or vibrations in the air) and signified meaning. Although his vocabulary is instead one of "words" versus "meaning," Wittgenstein returns to this Sé/Sa split throughout the *Investigations,* a semiotics made particularly clear when he employs the analogy of "money, and its uses":

> You say: the point isn't the word, but its meaning, and you think of the meaning as a thing of the same kind as the word, though also different from the word. Here the word, there the meaning.[15]

Starting from the word rather than the meaning, paragrammatic readings, as I argued in the previous chapter, are implicit in the materiality of writing and are a logical extension of that materiality's implications. Accordingly, the possibility of paragrammatic strategies — "whether or not you read according to some generally recognized alphabetical rule" — plays a central role in Wittgenstein's investigation of the grammar of "reading" (and hence in his general exploration into rules and rule-following).[16] In a marginal note, Wittgenstein reminds himself that "it is possible to be interested in a phenomenon in a variety of ways"; which is to say that one might approach language from the other side of the sign and pursue the signifier through its unfamiliar "labyrinth of paths" rather than through the more familiar and heavily traveled routes of the signified.[17] "This would seem to abolish logic but does not do so"; it merely substitutes one logic for another.[18] For an illustration of such alternative paths, Wittgenstein employs palindromes and mirror images: generating "EVOBA" from "ABOVE," and — with a certain pathos — scripting "Pleasure" in reverse (in a book replete with analyses of the grammar of "pain" there is a touchingly understated literalness, a litotes of sorts, in remarking that a mirror image of that script "is the reverse of pleasure").[19] Moreover, the strange schemata introduced at §86 — first a set of long arrows stretching across the page from left to right, and then the same set, with one arrow skewed diagonally across the others — might be understood not just as "different ways of reading a table" but as different ways of reading any prose text, including the *Investigations* itself, which are usually read from top to bottom and left to right, but might be read at another time in some other way.[20]

In fact, the problem of how to move through a text is particularly vexed in Wittgenstein's disjunctively segmented work. The connections between many of the sections in the *Investigations* are radically paratactic and discontinuous, as Wittgenstein abruptly introduces topics or picks up those he had suddenly abandoned pages earlier — all without comment or note. Moreover, other sections bear remnants of transitions from their original notebook contexts, so that they actually suggest a false hypotaxis when they appear, unedited, in the collage that makes up the *Investigations*. In such a work, the repeated example of the student who does not know "how to go on" is not merely a hypothetical illustration, but a section-to-section dilemma for Wittgenstein's own reader. In addition to the self-reflexive tenor of those passages, Wittgenstein's conspicuous numbering of the sections further adds to the metatextual resonance of the student's mathematical rule-following.

In the larger argument of the *Investigations*, the exposition of unconventional reading habits rhymes with Wittgenstein's repeated insistence on multiplicities. We may habitually read in only one way, for instance, but that does not preclude the many other decoding processes that might also legitimately constitute "reading." This insistence on multiple alternatives is an attempt to counter the rigid atomism and absolutes towards which Wittgenstein felt the *Tractatus* had previously erred by giving in to that essentializing "dogmatism into which we fall so easily . . . when we are dazzled by the ideal."[21] In the *Investigations,* by contrast, Wittgenstein underscores again and again "the fact that there are other processes, besides the one we originally thought of."[22] With reference to mathematics, for instance, the "point is, we can think of more than *one* application of an algebraic formula"; just as a sentence might be read in nonhabitual ways (as the phonetic encryption of a proper name, for instance), so a mathematical formula might be read in other ways as well.[23] Dispelling the illusion of a single logical necessity for decoding the formula (the *must* which seems to attend a mathematic computation) then leads Wittgenstein to the figure of the machine. The utility associated with machines—like the communicative utility of conventional reading and writing—induces us to forget that they might equally perform other functions. The point is not just that we might be *bricoleurs,* but that even the conventional, utile operation of the machine contains the latent potential for other functions and activities; we talk about a machine as if its parts could move only in one way, "as if they could not do anything else," while we "forget the possibility of their bending, breaking off, melting, and so on."[24] That machine, of course, is not just a symbol for the modal grammar of mathematics; it is the new model of the "reading machine" Wittgenstein had earlier proposed.

Unlike Jean Tinguély, or the Survival Research Labs, however, Wittgenstein is more the conscientious mechanic than the prurient spectator of a self-destructing machine. Marking the distance between himself and writers like Mac Low and Cage, Wittgenstein asserts that "it is not our aim to refine or complete the system of rules for the use of our words in unheard-of ways."[25] To this extent, and despite its affinities with so many of the twentieth century's avant-gardes, the *Investigations* is a deeply conservative text. Like the purgative argument of the *Tractatus,* in which one category after another is excluded from the realm of the propositionally meaningful, the *Investigations* acknowledges transgressions in order to ultimately exclude them from the purview of its project. However attentive Wittgenstein becomes to moments when the system goes awry, his concern with those moments is still always with avoiding such episodes in order to keep his investigations on track. Whatever his metaphysics, the serious investigation of the exception would be a 'pataphysical enterprise that Wittgenstein declines to undertake. He never allows himself to experiment, for instance, with what happens when only one aspect of the system "goes on holiday" while the rest remain at home, hard at work—or when the engine idles *in order* to stay in gear. By picking up on elements of the *Investigations* that Wittgenstein invokes but does not pursue, Cage and Mac Low provide examples not only of what it would mean to take seriously the idea of a Wittgensteinian poetics, but also what the next stage of those investigations might look like: a specific philosophical praxis to follow from the general theory.

Within the *Investigations*, for example, the "name" is another of the categories into which Wittgenstein attempts to introduce some play as he worries its Augustinian status as "a simple" into the warp and multiplicity of a complex family resemblance. As with the concept of reading, the name plays in a variety of very different language games, a condition manifested in a sentence like "Mr Scot is a Scot" or "Ms White is a white White." [26] Where Wittgenstein analyzes the grammar of proper names, however, Cage and Mac Low use proper names *as a grammar* by which to generate and articulate their texts, in which the rigid designator forms the ridged design of raised letters running through and structuring the poem. [27] With this onomastic metrics, what Cage and Mac Low "have primarily discovered is a new way of looking at things. As if you had invented a new way of painting; or, again, a new metre, or a new kind of song." [28] Having learned the lesson of Wittgenstein's insistence that there are always unthought-of uses for a name, Cage and Mac Low return to test the Augustinian position with the literalness and intentional misunderstanding of the most serious joke: what if names *were* in fact used as a strict calculus? What if the name actually did become a fixed invariant at the base of linguistic production?

This reliance on the proper name by Cage and Mac Low exposes one of the many sites of radical contradiction within their writing-through. Both poets studied with Daisetz T. Suzuki at Columbia University in the 1950s, and they both explicitly describe their algorithmic procedures as a way to follow the Buddhist and Taoist goal of working towards a dissolution of the ego: what Mac Low has glossed as "taste, constitutional predilections, opinions, current or chronic emotions." [29] To this end, they take part in the long avant-garde tradition of attempting to eliminate the "lyrical interference of the ego," a goal which has variously occupied writers as diverse as Henry Adams and Hugo Ball, F. T. Marinetti and André

Breton, Gertrude Stein and Charles Olson, Marcel Duchamp and Andy Warhol.[30] The contradiction is not a new one, as even a brief reflection on the ego*mania* of each of these figures immediately suggests, and while neither poet chooses his own name for an index in writing-through others' work, the most salient aspect of these supposedly anti-ego works is still the authorial proper name, the very sign of the ego.[31] Mac Low and Cage capitalize (on) that name, which not only makes it readable in the first place—one can easily imagine an alternate version of the writing-through which did not advertise its index at all—but also establishes an automatic hierarchy between the index-name and the rest of the derived text. This process also reifies that name, as the diastic poem obsessively repeats it like a fetish, and this effect is all the more forceful because of the degree to which the author's name is uncritically assumed to be a natural choice of index. Furthermore, the display of the author's name in Mac Low's project for writing-through *The Cantos* extends beyond the index-word; in the context of that insistent indexical inscription, the process of fragmentation in *Words nd Ends* creates a flurry of additional words that can only be read, as in the title, as Pound's nickname: "Ez" and "Es." Like the pun on the pundit "Pound" in "Pund," or Bob Brown's quip "Well, what guy cant write a canto, Ez?," this effect is frequently amusing.[32] Pound's anxious paranoia is thus glossed as "eZ / Nerveux," and his exceedingly bizarre physiological equation of sperm with spinal fluid is summed up by "glanD et eZ," a phrase which might well serve as an alternate title to Gaudier-Brzeska's 1914 sculptural portrait of Pound, the *Hieratic Head*.[33] Darker political commentary emerges from combinations like "eZ muRdered" and—as I will examine in the second half of this chapter—"eZ erRed." In the end, however, these spurious namings all work to emphasize the author's name as such. One occurrence in particular emblematically underscores Pound's presence in the pantheon of modernist writers ("cummings," "Binyon," and "Lewis") by contracting sixty-eight lines of the original *Cantos* and half of "Velazquez" to leave "eZ" among "the greats."[34]

Were this effect—an unmotivated result of the rules of English letter combination—not to have occurred, and even had Cage and Mac Low chosen alternate, non-onomastic indices, the status of the ego in the diastic poems would still be vexed. On the one hand, rule-governed procedures sufficiently distance the conventional, romantic conception of the artistic ego from the production of the poem to provoke skeptical, if not indignant, responses from many readers; on the other hand, the recourse to rules never seems to surrender agency completely enough. Cage's technique, of course, insists on the poet's willful intervention around the fixed core of mesostic-determined words.[35] Mac Low's "words nd ends" variation of his diastic method, in contrast, suggests an answer to Wittgenstein's question: "But what does a game look like that is everywhere bounded by rules? whose rules never let a doubt creep in, but stop up all the cracks where it might?"[36] Mac Low's strict procedure proposes one solution, in other words, to the problem of what it would mean to imagine a mode of writing that was in fact like the calculus we often take it to be and not like the game model for which Wittgenstein convincingly argues.[37] Even in Mac Low's version, however, the individual choice of the poet plays an indispensable role: the agreement to follow a particular rule, the selection of a source text, and the decision to keep and publish the results.[38] In order to abdicate choice, Cage and Mac Low—paradoxically—make a series of choices which are all the more willful and capricious; they try "to / avoid taking chances / by / taking chances," as Mac Low puts it in his "Seventh Light Poem" (dedicated, not incidentally, to John Cage). The ideals of the diastic poem repeatedly appear to be compromised by the very procedures intended to effect their achievement. Consider, for another example of this bind, the analogously troubled attempt by Mac Low and Cage to use rules in order to engage in an explicitly anarchist poetics: productive and progressive consensus based on the coproduction of meaning between reader and writer, diastic and source text. Yet in many ways, their work is far more proscriptive than contingent or negotiated. One could easily point out further discrepancies, but that very state of "discrepant engagement," to appropriate Nathaniel Mackey's superb phrase, is worth considering in itself.

The most simple and straightforward sentence, of course, displays a great number of complex, fully internalized rules; it also attests to the years of disciplining by which such grammars are learned, and by which, moreover, they come to appear so simple and natural that they disappear to the writer *as rules*. Indeed, as Wittgenstein demonstrates, "every course of action can be made out to accord with a rule" (or in Cage's own version: "one thing always follows another").[39] By preventing the possibility of following conventional rules—including those of which they might not even be aware—and instead adhering to baldly artificial rules, Mac Low and Cage escape the carceral structure of standard, fully internalized grammars while simultaneously highlighting how extensive and deeply entrenched such rules are: not just sentence grammar, but capitalization, punctuation, morphemic construction, letter combination, and so on. The diastic poem, that is, works indirectly and efficiently as a *приём остраннения* (device of making strange); by committing itself to an ostentatious surface of openly acknowledged rules, it obliquely "lays bare" the networks of compulsion that have been internalized in more standard grammars and become invisible by disappearing into a horizon of ideological naturalness. Cage and Mac Low exaggerate rules until they turn against themselves, collapsing beneath the weight of their own totalizing tendency. Part of the significance of capitalizing the index-letters, in fact, is that they do not permit readers to grow accustomed to the new set of rules, or to forget that they are in force. By maintaining an awareness of rules in these ways, the diastic poem succeeds in engaging what Mac Low has suggested could be called "the political side of Dharma."[40]

The same argument also suggests a solution to the paradox of making an emphatically deliberate set of choices all in the interest of surrendering choice. The most important issue, however, may be less the resolution of a specific problematic than the way in which the diastic poem repeatedly insists on the structure of paradox in general. In this sense, writing-through is like the enactment of a zen koan. Wittgenstein might have been describing the diastic poem when he wrote:

> The fundamental fact here is that we lay down rules, a technique, for a game, and that then when we follow the rules, things do not turn out as we had assumed. That we are therefore as it were entangled in our own rules.[41]

To accept that entanglement is precisely the ethical dimension of poetry for Cage. In the specific terms of reading his own work, this means accepting the results of rule-governed operations even if they go against personal taste and aesthetic judgment: resisting the urge to tweak a line, or to overlook the rule in just one instance because the diastic has come close, but not quite, to an even better phrase that it suggests. Or in Mac Low's words, the challenge is to avoid the errors "made / by following instructions exactly / some / times."[42] The diastics' ethics of acceptance, moreover, is farther reaching than the question of taste. By flaunting its paradoxes, the diastic poem tries to teach its reader to accept the difficulties presented by unstable and reversible terms as they move through a dynamic of indeterminate relations. To eliminate the ego completely, for instance, would simply reverse polarities and insist on a new set of absolutes, as well as a new hierarchy (the aleatory over and above the intentional); by simply damping, or "toning down" the role of the artistic ego instead,

Cage and Mac Low draw attention to its workings while also offering the more important lesson of how to negotiate a contradictory world without easy absolutes. Through the erection of structures which check the fluid operation of binaristic or dialectic thinking, the diastic poems continually warn against that "dogmatism into which we fall so easily . . . when we are dazzled by the ideal."[43]

By eliciting and then blocking such dogmatism, the diastics extend beyond mere caveats; they also work as litmus tests of the strength of our desires to make judgments on an all-or-nothing basis, and our tendency to hold the poet to an ideal, at whatever pole of the spectrum.[44] These poems also do more than merely register the impulse and then frustrate our desires for an absolute, or sabotage our attempts to fix them as exempla by refusing to hold to one extreme or the other. Through these processes the diastic poem also reveals that concepts like "totality" and "the absolute" are themselves far less totalizing and absolute than we might like—whether we seek to uphold or oppose them—but rather fold into and out of their opposites with a slippery and complex dynamic. As we will see, this is a lesson particularly apposite for those who would look to counter the totalitarian aspirations of Pound's ostensibly fascist epic. In the context of the thematics of Pound's politically appalling text, the diastic poems' ability to engage overt rule-following, while simultaneously nudging the reader away from settling into too facile a judgment, or from slipping into a dangerously easy binarism, becomes fraught with particular import. Because the "totalitarian" is always far more subtle, supple, and complicated than its bulkhead would have it appear, to be too quick to accept it on its own terms and take it as monolithic—even in defense against it—is already to have given over and handed it a victory from within. With these stakes in mind, I want to return to the diastic poems for a closer reading of their language, and try to apply the lessons of their koan structure not only to *The Cantos,* but to the writings-through themselves.

As they submit their source text to algorithmic procedures, the diastic and mesostic methods not only dismantle the obvious references of the source text; they also paragrammatically (re)construct significations latent in the works they write-through. For all of the genuinely restive disjunctions in these poems, many of the lines can be read as only slightly modified or eccentric versions of standard sentences: "DOwn e oUt," for example, or the humorously irreverent "singing to Zeus[:]down heRe fAtty."[45] Such mundane meanings are even more striking when one keeps in mind the randomness of their conjunction. Consider, for example, the "yes, no, yes" which stutters from "ays No oke" once Mac Low's method has erased most of the lines "he that holdeth by castle-guard / pays no scutage / And speaking of clarity / Milite, Coke, Edwardus."[46] The coupling of "Cardinal" and "porphyry" is similarly uncanny; in their original context in "Canto IX" these words refer, respectively, to an ecclesiastic officer and a feldspar stone, but Mac Low's poem collapses their initial distance of three lines and twenty-one words to create a new context that colors what is read and emphasizes the happenstance of their shared denotation of shades of red.

The most interesting meaning effects, however, result from the way in which the irruptive capitalization of the index-letters, like the fragmentation of Mac Low's diastic method, disrupts lexical integrity to pack and unpack signification below the level of the word. For instance, the emphasis of a single letter in a word can muffle a "muttering" into a "mutte" "Ring": precisely the sort of Joycean paradox—like "laughtears"—that so delighted Cage.[47] The capital "R" in "heR ichArd," to give another example, restores the truncated capital from the proper name to shift genders and suggest the appositive "he, Richard."[48] Similarly, while the spacings within a line like "sOme d oUt us" cannot cancel the evocation of "some doubt us," the internal capitalization of the "O" introduces further segmentations to bring out the pronominal play between "us" and the latent "me."[49] In the unfamiliar territory of the diastic text, the slightest hint of reference can orient its deliriously resonant language. As fragments of the words "shelved (shored)" from the opening of "Canto VIII" are collected into "elveD Ed)." for instance, the period after "Ed" suggests the abbreviation for "education," which in turn works backward in the line to coax out the possibility of an impish pedagogic reference in "el[e]ve": a French student, or *élève*.[50]

As I discussed in the previous chapter, these linguistic effects would have been recognized by the Russian formalists as сдвиги (shifts). The examples I have already noted from Susan Howe's carefully crafted poetry reappear in the fault lines that fracture Mac Low's arbitrarily generated poem, where the violent cutting of words appears as a " 's worD," and the frequently humorous revision of Pound's militaristic "slaughter" appears as "laughter."[51] The "P rOof" of the unstable and indiscreet significations which threaten language at its slightest disruption can also be seen in the indeterminacy brought out in lines like "tO y oUr," which toys with the play of paragogic ambivalence that a line like "f lanD Eveloped" develops more fully by suggesting not only the subdivision of real estate ("of land developed"), but also the enveloping folds of custard which make flan.[52] Further possibilities emerge from a line like "And Plant sO t rUe," in which the verbal mass of "rue" competes with the "so" to attract the "t" suspended halfway between them, pitting the straight reading of "so true" against the foolish play of inebriated street language that would constitute "sot rue," or even tobacco ("sot-weed" being one of the original terms for the plant), given the horticultural context of the passage ("rue," "plant") and the shimmer of "sew" (to plant) behind "so."[53] Examples could be multiplied almost endlessly, but the point is that Mac Low's poem repeatedly surprises; the infinite and inhuman resourcefulness of language continually astounds, and *Words nd Ends* stands—with a work like *Finnegans Wake*—as a testament to the wonders of language itself.

Beyond illustrating the general economy of language in these ways, the diastic poems inevitably propose a specific commentary on their source texts, and so the poetry of Cage and Mac Low might productively be read as critical essays in its own right.[54] Part of the interest of the diastic poem lies in the tensions between its source text and the resultant writing-through: that chance "fit" which is sometimes conjunction and sometimes convulsion (the tics in diastics). For an instance of the latter, note that by submitting Pound's book to their algorithmic methods, Cage and Mac Low perform an ideological hijacking of sorts; they *détourne* Pound's text in ways that can only be taken, from Pound's perspective, as a challenging affront and indignity; their Buddhist- and Taoist-inspired processes rework what is surely the most virulently *anti*-Buddhist and *anti*-Taoist book in the Western literary canon.[55] The examples of Pound's rage are legion, as he devotes long stretches of the middle cantos to reiterating, ad nauseam, his claim that Confucian governments were advantageous and others iniquitous. A few of the most explicit passages from "Canto LIV" should jog the memory: "Goddam bhuddists" and "damn bhuddists" aside, Pound terms one age of Buddhist influence a "seepage of bhuddists," and he places the worst plagues in apposition: "lamas, foés, / shit and religion always stinking in concord," "war, taxes, oppression / backsheesh, taoists, bhuddists / wars, taxes, oppressions."[56] The diacritic aside, "Foés," in *The Cantos,* are clearly the enemy: always, also, simply "foes." Adding insult to injury, the capitalization of the index-words forces the source text to perjure itself and confess against its will. The "z" in his name makes Ezra quite literally responsible for bringing out the "zen" latent in his own writing: the repeated "citiZen," "citiZens," and "doZen" of Cage's text, for instance, all make words like "loZenges" and "Zenos" resonate as well.[57] Mac Low's procedure is somewhat less prone to produce this effect, but his poem also records a literal "seepage of Buddhists" through the letters of Pound's text until they can in fact be seen on the page. "Δίκη"—that divinely poetic justice—indeed.[58]

Moments of conjunction between the works also create a number of less pointed in-jokes for the reader familiar with Pound's poem. Does the ant in his dragon world, for example, become a "scent ar?"—a phrase that resonates strongly in Mac Low's poem despite the fact that it derives not from one of Pound's most famous lines ("The ant's a centaur in his dragon world"), but rather from a phrase in the previous canto: "how hast thou the crescent for car?"[59] As aspects are sent from one context to another, that fit between the two poems also works to highlight certain facets of the source text, and they can help to clarify a reader's understanding of its workings by establishing a textual version of parallax: the same element seen from two slightly different perspectives. Mac Low's fragmenting diastics, for instance, underscore the polyglot nature of *The Cantos*. "It can't," as Pound admits, "be all in one language," and while this component of the poem is central to its reputed difficulty and aggression ("I shall have to learn a little greek to keep up with this / but so will you, drratt you"), *The Cantos* have not figured prominently in discussions of bilingual or multicultural writing.[60] The multilingual cross-referencing between Mac Low and Pound can be most easily seen in the "e"s and "et"s which are so frequently mined and isolated from Pound's English; while this effect merely represents a statistical projection of letter frequency and the rules of letter combination in phonemic constructions in modern English, it also echoes these letters' appearance not as fragments but as legitimate words in Pound's use of Italian and the wide range of classical, medieval, and approximated Latin that recurs throughout the poem. Similarly, combinations such as "tz" mimic his transliteration of Chinese, which in Pound's orthography follows the French standard, although these particles in fact most often derive, in Mac Low's poem, from Pound's quotations of German or his imitation of Eastern European languages, dialects, and accents.

Linguistic promiscuity also plays a central role in the visual prosody of *The Cantos*. Passages in Greek appear against the Roman type "out of odd hollows and solids / . . . slanty," and all of the alphabetic writing in the poem—from whatever language—stands in marked contrast to the ideograms, hieroglyphs, and petroglyphs which become increasingly frequent and pronounced as the poem progresses.[61] Unlike Mac Low, Cage does scan the Greek, but neither accounts for the ideogrammatic Chinese. This omission not only confines the look of their poems to an alphabetic text, and continues the erasure of visual codings that has marked the publishing history of *The Cantos,* but also eliminates the reminder of writing systems which operate vertically, or—as Wittgenstein's schema of tables would have it—are predicated on very different ways of "going on."[62] These differences are particularly evident in Cage's poem, which is set with long lines flush right—a horizontal layout that stands in marked contrast with all of his other mesostic poems, which are arranged around the rigidly vertical axis of index-words like this:

and thEn

with bronZe lance heads

beaRing

yet Arms

sheeP slain

Of

plUto

stroNg

praiseD

By instead setting the poem in more strongly horizontal lines, Cage laterally redistributes the vertical, downward thrust of Pound's later poetry, and he calls attention to the role the ideograms play in organizing the space of the page. Cage's poem thus argues for the degree to which the Chinese characters—regardless of their referential meaning—signify within Pound's text.

This is not, I want to stress, an incidental remark about the poem's decorative stylistics. Despite Pound's faith in the ability of true artists to intuit the meaning of the ideograms, one might reasonably assume that many of his readers—whatever the likelihood that they actually know Latin, Greek, Italian, French, *and* German—do not initially understand the Chinese in referential terms, or that any but the most dedicated and pedantic of scholarly readers has the patience to continually cross-reference a dictionary or readers' guide.[63] Nonetheless, the ideograms still play an important part in constructing the poem's meaning. In the opening cantos of *Rock Drill,* for instance, the heavily weighted ideograms frequently provide a strong central axis, very much like the capitalized index-words of a typical Cage mesostic.[64] Jerome McGann has rightly suggested that such layouts, in *The Cantos,* can be read "as a phanopoeic allusion to Pound's idea of the unwobbling pivot."[65] The significance of these images, however, is broader still. Within a work that had been conceived of prior to *Rock Drill* as an explicitly fascist epic—a modern *speculum principis* written by the self-styled trouvère of the Salò Republic—the visual prosody of these pages is far from incidental.[66] As Bob Perelman argues, the ideogram also makes phanopoeic allusion to the fasces, and so they also always stand, to some degree, as visual emblems of authority in Pound's poem. Moreover, when strictly arranged down the center of the page these representations of authority take on an added charge. The thematics of the "unwobbling pivot" in *The Cantos* is directly related to the justification of authority and obedience: "Law of MOU is law of the just middle, the pivot."[67] That "Law of MOU," furthermore, evokes *The Cantos'* celebration of the law of Mu(ssolini), who plays both Aeneas and Octavius Augustus to Pound's epic, serving simultaneously as imagined patron and pivotal hero. In this context, the ideograms' *ordering* function, and their appearance in uniform, rigid, and hierarchized lines, takes on a rather chilling presence, especially for the reader complicit with following their structuring design and reading according to their rule (and who has not been well disciplined by graphic design conventions in the protocols for these codes of visual semiotics?). "The order does not end in the arts," Pound ominously writes in an early poem: "The order shall come and pass through them."[68] Or, as Bruce Andrews puts it: "The content gives orders to make order content."[69]

But as Robert Smithson knew, "there is no order outside the order of the material," and the dialogue between the diastic poem and its source text also takes place in even more complex ways. The significance of effects such as the irruption of "Zen" through the work, for instance, goes further than the humor of a practical joke, however well it works to deflate Pound's pontifical rage. The success of the writing-through is predicated on the ability of language to operate in a general economy. As I argued in the previous chapter, the excessive measure of language's signifying potential, *la part maudite*, always frustrates a writer's attempt either to control language completely or to direct strategies of reading, and that refusal of circumscription is an important resistance to the authoritarian imperialism with which Pound appropriates source texts and arrays them for his readers. One would not want to be too quick to imagine that linguistics, on this account, automatically saves us from the possibility of an authoritarian work (though a readership more attuned to such moments and less swayed by thematics alone might go a long way toward establishing a buffer against their efficacy). *The Cantos*, however, specifically highlights and encourages the disruptions of linguistic play. Richard Sieburth notes that Pound's "addiction to punning, so evident in his letters and in the late Cantos, provides a particularly obvious instance of the sheer productivity of the signifier in the generation of semantic surplus value."[70] Such moments are certainly not limited to the ecstatically resonant *Thrones,* or to Pound's quirky correspondence; *The Cantos* is replete with displays of the signifier's surplus productivity from the very beginning. A blatant example from the second canto should give a sense of the reading practices Pound invites throughout the poem: "Elanor, ἔλανδρος, and ἐλέπτολις!" repeated in "Canto VII" as "Ἑλέναυς, ἔλανδρος, ἐλέπτολις."[71] In Charles Bernstein's argument, such opaque slippages and refusals of coherence constitute the saving grace, rather than the failure, of Pound's writing; they keep it from becoming a "meRe ss nArration," as it were.[72] As the earliest record in the *Oxford English Dictionary (OED)* would have it (1598): "errata, or faults escaped." Or as Pound himself would confess: "my errors and wrecks lie about me," where "lie about" is taken not only in the sense of "fragments shored" but also in the sense of "speaking untruths in reference to."[73] Accordingly, Mac Low's poem is important for Bernstein because it "foregrounds much of the 'free play' that remains the most salient feature of *The Cantos.*"[74] "At an allegorical level," Bernstein thus proposes, "*Words nd Ends* exorcises the authoritarianism that underlies *The Cantos.*"[75]

The dynamics at work are important ones, and Bernstein does well to call attention to them, but the exorcism, unfortunately, is not quite so simple. Like McGann, Perelman, and Sieburth—as well as Christine Froula, Robert Casillo, and others—Bernstein is part of a recent tradition in Pound criticism that insists on unflinching readings of the politics of poetic form. The reception history of *The Cantos* attests to the dangers of allowing formalism to excuse content, but the naïveté of ignoring the signification of form is all the more dangerous when it permits the reinscription—at an even more entrenched and insidious level—of the very meanings it seeks to oppose. Such glosses surrender the subtleties and sophistications most desperately required by ethical and political complexities to a simplemindedness that is ultimately far more dangerous than the risks run by reading the most overtly fascist poetry. Hence the treacherousness of those communities—and I can think of several English departments where this is currently the case—that reward an uncritical dismissal of Pound by encouraging surface engagements, thematic readings, biographical and "historical" appeals to some ultimate grounding truth, and even the dismissive assertion that one need not read a work like *The Can-*

tos at all. Such approaches once again rob the reader of a prime tool in the service of the very politics they would advance. To the extent that indeterminacy provokes fear and helplessness, it is in the service of authoritarian regimes that would offer the reassurances of coherence in place of the anxieties of the unfamiliar. Presenting opportunities to face and work through the contradictory and indeterminate—to develop skills of effective engagement—is one of the chief virtues of avant-garde literature, regardless of its ostensible political affiliations.[76] In part, scholars such as Casillo remind us that we cannot afford to be lazy or gullible readers, because the price of admitting aspects of a poetics without thinking through their implications, or of accepting the authority of thematic claims without considering what the structure of those claims enacts, is far too dear.[77] The principled scrutiny Bernstein brings to his reading of *The Cantos* is precisely the mode by which we should continue the analysis of Cage and Mac Low's own texts.

To begin with, readers can hardly avoid the authoritative, repetitive, and controlling regime of rules in the composition of the diastic poem. As in Pound's idiosyncratic history of Chinese politics, the Buddhism in Cage and Mac Low's poetry is inextricably bound up with issues of governance. When Pound writes "And they worked out the Y-king or changes / to guess from," the inscription of political authority (the "king") within the means of "nonintentional" procedure (the *I Ching*) is emblematic. As chance would have it, both Cage and Mac Low have at times employed the *I Ching* as part of their attempt to enact a Buddhist poetics, and in the diastic poems the equivalent technique for surrendering intentionality takes the form of disciplined rule-following.[78] The coercion behind this technology of chance should not be minimized. "The only correlate in language to an intrinsic necessity," as Wittgenstein argues, "is an arbitrary rule."[79] In Wittgenstein's writing, the political implications of following such a rule, the grammar of which is fundamentally linked to that of obeying an order, is underscored by the slide from "rule" to "ruler" (the straightedge meter stick) to "ruler" (a sovereign). "What I have to do [in describing the nature of a rule]," Wittgenstein explains, "is as it were to describe the office of a king," and this move is related, at several levels, to his ruminations on the analogy of the chess piece (once again, not incidentally, the *king*) to the rule-governed uses of words in a sentence.[80] Given Bernstein's insights into the politics of poetic form, a formal procedure that is so obviously bound (rhetorically, if not in fact logically) to a totalitarian practice seems a dangerously weak point on which to posit resistance to Pound's totalitarian poetics—particularly when the diastic poems are so deeply implicated in the totalitarian structures of Pound's own textual strategies.

Pound explicitly announces his aspiration for many of the references in *The Cantos*: "Perhaps you will look up his verses." [81] For Pound, it seems, this ability to serve as a reference to "the Classics"—a students' guide to further study, essentially—grounds the utility of his epic poem. Marshaling, organizing, and directing a literary tradition, *The Cantos* would have functioned as an instructional tool in the service of fascism: the cornerstone of educational curricula and cultural policy for the Salò Republic. [82] In the first place, the choice of *The Cantos* as a source text for writing-through does little to subvert a sense of literary hierarchy; like it or not, it too is one of the modernist "classics." As Pound knew: "You respect a good book, contradicting it," and however much one might "Edit *rZa* teRms" ("edit Ezra's terms") by "pruNg nbriDge Er" ("pruning and abridging error"), the result remains, to some extent, for "Ever Ez." [83] In fact, throughout Cage's career (this is not true for Mac Low), the gallery of written-through subjects offers a glimpse of personal taste but no real surprises; they are drawn from a list of (exclusively male) masters: Joyce, Duchamp, Satie, Schoenberg, Emerson, Ginsberg, et al. [84] More important, however much the diastic poem works to disrupt and sabotage certain elements of Pound's text, for the reader familiar with *The Cantos,* Cage and Mac Low end up performing what is perhaps the primary function of the Poundian epic: excising, collaging, and recalling a source text with a tachygraphy of "gists and piths." [85] Just as Pound references other works, at times with only a single word, so a single "luminous detail" from *The Cantos* itself, reappearing in the diastic poem, works to remind the reader of the themes of Pound's own work. [86] A particular citation of Pound's diction can prompt the reader to recall, "that's from the part in 'Canto XVI' about the poets sent off to the First World War," or "oh yes, there are the verses about the leopard towards the end," or whatever. The specifics depend, of course, on the individual reader, but even if readers refuse to follow the lead of Pound's citations, or if the reader of the diastic poem has never read *The Cantos,* the structures of textual authority are even more deeply rooted in the diastic method.

As *The Cantos* progresses, its references become increasingly self-citational. As if under pressure from the "speed of communication," an excerpt from "the Classics" quoted in an earlier canto will be recalled in a subsequent canto with a shorthand phrase, and that phrase is later invoked with further truncation or ellipsis, perhaps even as a single talismanic word. By

"Canto CII," Pound is essentially "writing-through" his own text and composing exclusively with telegraphic fragments from previous cantos. For example:

> 'Eleven literates' wrote Senator Cutting,
>> 'and, I suppose, Dwight L. Morrow'

returns, with the aptly named Senator cut, as

> 'eleven literates and, I suppose,
>> Dwight L. Morrow'[87]

I could document the sources of the remaining lines, but even a cursory reading of the later cantos cannot help but catch the clamor of these echoes, and for now I simply want to note that Pound's mnemonic method inscribes a coercive protocol for reading across the larger-scale structure of the entire *Cantos*. For the references of Pound's increasingly abbreviated citations to make sense, *The Cantos* must be read from the beginning in a linear and sequential manner. "Thus the book of the mandates."[88] Correspondingly, the supposedly anarchic models of diastic reading demand a far more linear, uniform, fanatically disciplined, and rigidly unforgiving reading than even *The Cantos* induces: writing-through moves not just chapter to chapter, but letter to letter with unrelenting discipline. The diastics preclude the forward and backward skimming and skipping, the waxing and waning of attention, the assumption and guesswork of unread or half-read words that describe conventional reading. With yet another paradox, the paragrammatic diastics, that is, adhere to a strict prohibition against optical, lexical, or attentive *wandering*—and error (Latin *errare*), in these works, is all to the point.

The Reign of Error

> Jackson Mac Low can not type.
> —Amiri Baraka

> Genius is the error in the system.
> —Paul Klee

Jackson Mac Low explicitly thematizes the connection between wandering and error in his 1989 poem "Barnes 4," which enacts the very process of wandering and textual error that it describes. One of a series of works that write-through the texts of Djuna Barnes, the poem represents a more even balance of intentional and procedural practice than do works like *Words nd Ends*.[89] With distinct echoes of Gertrude Stein's "insistent" style (the lines frequently sound as though they were extracted whole from one of her poems, rather than reassembled from the prose of Barnes's novels), Mac Low's poem repeats and permutates both syntactic patterns and individual words. Moreover, a series of paragogic terms rambles through the poem: "around" and "ground," "well" and "wall," "ear" and "dear." "Wondered" and "wandered" are by far the most strongly emphasized pair of such words. They frequently occur side by side, and even when appearing independently they often seem to exchange places; the line "Wondered her back works" is followed by "Wandered back never moved," for example, and in one of the poem's refrains they alternate almost stroboscopically: "Told wondered wandered wondered wandered against." These conspicuous shifts charge the particles of the entire textual field of "Barnes 4," until a phrase such as "back works" immediately suggests "backwards," which in turn works back from "wards" to carry a whisper of "words." The poem is scarred in these ways by spectral traces of the nomadic signifiers' errant paths: "Matter that wondered wandered against the whisper" of alternate readings.[90] From the very first line of "Barnes 4," in which only eight letters form all of its seven words, "matter" really does "wander mysterious" as the eye or "ear moves" from word to word. The poem opens: "Now very never more never more no." Letters themselves seem to grow and retract descenders and minims as the proximity of w's and v's, v's and y's, n's and m's highlights their minimal differences. On a larger scale, the words themselves appear to merge and separate: "now" drops its final letter to form the final word ("no") rather than the syntactically expected "so"; the first two words of the line combine to form the paragrammatic third; the "o," "e," and "r" then reattach to a mutated "n" to form "more"—and indeed *more* of an "n" would in fact be an "m."

That minimal meaningful swerve of typographic matter—the coefficient of textual errancy which makes wonder wander—is of course familiar as the clinamen. By exploiting the clinamatic swoon of language, "Barnes 4" joins works like Christopher Dewdney's "Fractal Diffusion" and Steve McCaffery's "Zarathrustran 'Pataphysics," both of which (to borrow Stein's phrase) are brilliant examples of "composition by explanation," enacting the very structures they simultaneously address through conventionally discursive and thematically referential means. Dewdney's exponentially pro-

gressive and cumulative substitution of syllables for letters proceeds with
a decimal geometry that refracts the fall of syllables through the morphemes of his prose text's grid. The scatter pattern turns out "ave faraver /
farettcohetdio cooncolusion," as "only thet ococoavesionavel wordio or
somettimets phraveset stavendios intavecot" (and that after only the first
six letters of the alphabet have been replaced!). Because of its programmatic encryption, Dewdney's essay pits competing strata of referentiality
against one another; the *fractal* nature of the text, in fact, is its replication of referential patterns at multiple levels. At a submorphemic level,
the substituted syllables refer directly to the letters they replace, but by
doing so they simultaneously fracture and cripple the conventional referential capacity at the level of the word. Reference, when taken literally—
or at least letterally—suffocates itself. At the same time, language, in its
errance, occasionally—and to everyone's surprise—finds itself.

Without this "tightly regimented" "dispersion of mavethemaveticoal
hieravercohies," this conjunction of "er" and "orDer," McCaffery's essay
deploys a similar strategy with a somewhat different theoretical focus.[91]
It both argues for—and also inhabits—the 'pataphysics of Lucretius's famous analogy of atomic to lettristic clinamina. As in Dewdney's text, the
degree of deviation from standard orthography increases as the essay progresses. Without the calculated schedule of Dewdney's metric substitution,
however, the argument of McCaffery's essay is less for the nature of referentiality than for the dynamics of the alphabetic system as it permits   ·
of lexical reference. In bibliographic terminology, of course, the details
of that system are known as "accidentals"—a deliciously felicitous rubric
in the context of McCaffery's investigation of (and by) mistake. Far from
being incidental, such so-called accidentals follow the dangerous logic of
a Derridean supplement: establishing the ground for a signification which
they subtend but to which they cannot be assimilated. Like Wittgenstein,
McCaffery reminds his reader of "the possibility of a distortion" of the
parts in the textual machine, "of their bending, breaking off, melting, and
so on."[92] Unlike Wittgenstein, however, he also goes on to prove that the
machine continues to operate—if in unexpected or unintended ways (self-
destruction and short-circuits are still operations, after all), and he uses
the new device to measure the fragility and resiliency of that supple supplemental economy of writing with a 'pataphysical precision. Moreover,
McCaffery argues that when "the semiantic deviance, introduced unto
writing by the clincamin, is not ti be valuud as erronoeus, nor as inspiring
a desife to be cornected," it leads to "a peetics thal delibterately introducters

errop into linguistic dystens of constraint ti initiate the interplt og chauce ans neceddity."⁹³

In short, "in / Discourse / Ers . . . notation" and—conversely—the necessity of signification always "x seeDs Error" and the chance of mistake.⁹⁴ One site of the interplay between the two in Mac Low's diastics are the many morphemes that fragment from their source words to leave only a whispered "err." In the neighborhood of the sounds "ve<u>ry</u>" and "h<u>er</u>," "f<u>ir</u>st," "whisp<u>er</u>,"—the phonemic encryption of "error" in the lines "her very ear / First whisper" from "Barnes 4"—the ear moves that "ear" even closer to bleeding into "err," both aurally and graphically. To literally "err," in fact, is perhaps the most characteristic feature of the surface of *Words nd Ends*. From the opening stutter of "En nZe eaRing," Mac Low's writing-through *The Cantos* peals with the "Ring" of "ea[r]ring" echoes. Indeed, Mac Low's text is so overrun with "Er rs," "Er—s," "ero . . . s," "eers," "Eres," "ers," "ears," and similar permutations, that the reader's "eaRs er[r]" and hear the echo even in more distant versions ("erit," "ert," "Erum," "Erona," "euRs," "ours," "airs," "eirs," "eras," and so on)—not to mention the host of identical phonemes embedded within larger fragments. "Errare" itself, no less, makes its appearance in the reduction of Pound's two "Italian Cantos," though with a beautiful coincidence it has been mined from *afferrare*: both literally and figuratively "to grasp."⁹⁵ Given this arrant and ubiquitous "Ersation" of the source text, the valence of other "Drifting" sounds a resonant subject rhyme.⁹⁶ For instance, the veering of "veR ing" has "veR red" from the proper spelling one expects to have "re[a]d" there. Similarly, as "eiRs is mAde Paper," the connection between the cantos, or songs, is made clear: air and err.⁹⁷ To translate: *canti, chants,* chance. In fact, the "SUNG" nature of *The Cantos* is underscored in what might be taken as the diastic's own *ars poetica*:

> eriNg aw coDe
> Eliminated iZ
> weRe greAt Pire
> rOm e SUNG couNting
> stooD Er iZ ndRed[.]⁹⁸

The diastic ends up "eriNg" portions of the "Eliminated" source text by employing a "coDe" that hinges on the "rOte coUnt" of index letters: *The Cantos* not just as song (a word which recurs throughout this section of Mac Low's poem), but as Countos; where "couNting" once "stooD," there error shall be ("Er iZ"), and there be read ("nd Red").⁹⁹ With "eaRing lphAbets / Peaking"—which is to say "speaking" on their own in these ways— *Words nd Ends* works to "peRfect rer": itself a perfect printer's err.[100] Indeed, through its paragrammatic practice, Mac Low's poem reminds us that in the printer's lexicon, a "paragramme" is the term for a transpositional error in typesetting, and he pits the "Printers d Out" ("printers' doubt") against an incorrigible "rAscality Print."[101]

Following the death of Robert Lowell, *Time* magazine ran a cover article assessing the state of contemporary American "poetry in an age of prose," and among the notables in a "remarkable poetic pantheon" it misprinted the name of "the Zeus of that lofty company": "Erza" Pound.[102] While one would probably be wrong to take this as a slyly witty commentary on his work, print errors are themselves a central feature of *The Cantos*. Pound famously defined the epic as a "poem including history," and at one level, the history that Pound's own epic includes is the documental, textual history of its sources, errors and all.[103] In Pound's poem, preserving such clinamina in the "rain [reign] of factual atoms" is part of a larger ethic which also includes noting the aporia in the textual record.[104] Those lacunae come not just from a "day when the historians left blanks in their writing," but also from the fragility of the material support of that writing itself.[105] Such erasures are the very embodiment of history: "Time blacked out with the rubber."[106] So that: time signatures (where "signature" is a verb). Cage was taught by Schoenberg to write counterpoint with the eraser ("This end of the pencil is just as important as the other end," the maestro explained), but he might have learned such skiagraphy from Pound, whose blacking-out marks the errs of eras writ of *erit*. Pound incorporates those omissions and material reconfigurations in what is perhaps the most profoundly important moment in the entire *Cantos;* advertising his recognition of the textual condition, the opening of "Canto VIII" not only refers to "shelved" "fragments," it actually reproduces them:

> . . . hanni de
> . . . dicis
> . . . entia[107]

The missing letters, torn between the "two halves of a seal," are easy to supply: [Gio]hanni de [Me]dicis [Fior]entia, "equivalent to," as Pound notes, "Giohanni of the Medici, / Florence."[108] This stanza stands as the counterpart to Pound's translation, a few years earlier, of a Sapphic fragment.[109] The entirety of his exquisite poem "Papyrus" reads:

Spring . . . .
Too long . . . . .
Gongula . . . . . .

Underscoring his poem's elegiac mood, Pound registers the disintegrated papyrus with the same care that he reproduces the textual details of Malatesta's letter: the upper right of one, the upper left of another, what is left of what to write of fragments shorn. With a poetics of erasure that sets a precedent for Tom Phillips's *Humument,* which I will address in the following chapter, Pound is essentially "writing through" source texts to produce these poems. Indeed, the effect of the lines from "Canto VIII" chimes not only in those Clark Coolidge poems made up of lists of truncated words (*Space,* section IV), but also—not incidentally—in Mac Low's fragmenting diastics (ellipses in original):

iceNza

icteD

E . . . .

rror is central to *The Cantos* at other levels as well.[110] In her brilliantly entitled chapter "The Pound Error," Christine Froula argues that errors are integral both to the genre of the epic, with the wanderings (*errare*) and mistakes of its heros, and also to the particulars of Pound's modern epic.[111] Setting aside the question of how a reader might distinguish between Pound's intentional reworking of material and his unintentionally mistaken understanding or transcription of that material, scholars have documented the ways in which his composition introduces discrepancies that appear to be "errors of fact such as misremembered names and dates, misquotations, mistranscriptions, misspellings, and transliterations of Greek and Chinese produced by local or otherwise nonstandard principles."[112] Similarly, scholars have noted some of the divergences between the multiple versions of Pound's poems which accrued at the various stages of composition, copying, printing, and publication as the extraordinarily "long and complicated [textual] history" of *The Cantos* "provided frequent opportunities for errors of every description to enter the text."[113] Far more important than the complex state of the documents, or the introduction of mistakes, however, is the way in which Pound destabilizes the very category of "error" within those texts. "I refuse to accept ANY alphabetic display as final," Pound, the maverick, wrote to Lewis Maverick, and contrary to the intolerance of deviance and the insistence on absolute accuracy that one might expect from his totalitarian ambitions, Pound was notoriously capricious in his attitude toward errors.[114] At times predictably fanatical about "getting the facts rights," he was at other times surprisingly cavalier in his tolerance of imprecisions and mistakes, whether they were introduced by himself or by the copyists, secretaries, editors, and compositors who took part in publishing the cantos. In addition to Christine Froula, Jerome McGann and Hugh Kenner have documented and argued persuasively for the extent to which Pound, with his keen interest in bibliography, not only acknowledged errors of transmission but openly accepted them as fully authorized and genuine aspects of the poem.[115] Indeed, in James Laughlin's opinion, part of the intrinsic character of *The Cantos* itself is precisely those "so-called mistakes and inconsistencies" that Pound wanted to let stand as the received poem.[116]

On the one hand, Pound's recognition of the opaque mediation of the material text (the role of Andreas Divus, say, or of Aldus's die cutter Francesco da Bologna), like the scrupulous reproduction of textual particularities or the fidelity with which the ripped epistle is represented in "Canto VIII," all attest to Pound's interest in ever greater degrees of citational accuracy.[117] Pound understands that the meanings transmitted by texts extend to their bibliographic details, and at times he tries to pack as much information into his condensed lines as he can. On the other hand, he can be surprisingly sloppy. At the close of "Canto X," to give just one of many examples, Pound mistakes the diacritical marks in his source and writes "a quisti annutii" in place of "a questi aunnuntii."[118] Before automatically "correcting" the supposedly inconsequential misspellings, or making too fast a judgment, however, one might read moments like this as yet further examples of Pound's concern with textual accuracy: faithfully recording the history of his own note-taking and the poem's own material production in such a way that the horizon of error in *The Cantos* disappears within itself. Inscribing the clinamatic swerve into a confession of his habits, Pound admits to an "inclination to perseverance in error" once it has been made.[119] With error thus *mise en abîme,* the condition of the poem reaches a textual dilemma in which, as Anthony Braxton has famously remarked with reference to jazz improvisation, if you don't make a mistake, you're making a mistake.

Indeed, by so thoroughly incorporating error in all of these ways, Pound inoculates his text: *The Cantos* is a poem that cannot, in the final analysis, actually contain an error. For an illustration of this textual immunology, consider the line from "Canto CXVI": "Muss., wrecked for an error."[120] Given the unambiguous shortening of "Mussolini" to the familiar "Muss" elsewhere in *The Cantos* (as in the opening lines of "Canto CV," for instance), the subject of the line initially appears to be Il Duce of course. Those other appearances, however, also emphasize the erratic addition of punctuation in "Canto CXVI."[121] Given the bibliographic references in the lines that immediately follow ("But the record / the palimpsest"), one cannot be certain that the "error" in question is not the sort that would "wreck" manuscripts by making a "mess" of the abbreviation "Mss."; a few lines later, the word "mass" suggests both a possible correction—or yet another error—as well as the musical genre which would resonate with another candidate: the music of "Mus. viva voce" from "Canto LXXXVIII."[122] In both of these latter cases, moreover, the words appear proximate to "laws": a synecdoche for Mussolini's totalitarian rule (recall the coercive "must" implied by the "law of MU"), and a coincidence that further unsettles any attempt to fix the signification. Additionally, attentive readers will recall the sudden shift to Latin in "Canto LVI"; among the other signs of error wrecking the province, "muss" might be a witty rewriting of "mus ingens, ingens" ("a really large mouse"), quite literally a larger version of the simple "mus."[123] An actual mistake, in any of these cases, would be a (literal) shortcoming of the muses which inhabit Pound's epic—visible simply as muss. I should emphasize that this reading is neither to deflect the blatant references to Italian Fascism in *The Cantos*, nor to mitigate Pound's hagiography of Mussolini, but only to demonstrate the consequence of Pound's epic textual instability; there is a comedy of errors behind the tragedy. Or as Mac Low would have it: "uNder I finD Er—."[124] Like the missense left by the missing letters in Malatesta's missive, or the miscellaneous misspelled words in other cantos, the indeterminacy of words like "Muss." reduces the text, in the end, to an irreconcilable muss in which an error, if made, could not be recognized.

By James Joyce's measure, Pound thus establishes his genius. Before Stephen Daedalus delivers his Faustrollian proof of paternity in *Hamlet* ("He proves by algebra that Shakespeare's ghost is Hamlet's grandfather"), he proclaims: "A man of genius makes no mistakes. His errors are volitional and are the portals of discovery."[125] However facetiously Joyce presents the perverse logic of academic debate in this chapter on the "Acomedy of letters," he actually furnishes the proof himself in *Finnegans Wake*.[126] Even more than *The Cantos*, perhaps, the *Wake* is another text in which there cannot be an error, but the strategy of inoculation is precisely the same.[127]

By "calling unnecessary attention to errors, omissions, repetitions and misalignments," one of the central themes of Joyce's book becomes, in Fritz Senn's words (though he is referring to another aspect of "Joyce's misconducting universe"), linguistic "derailment, deviation, dislocation, omissions, chance delays and collisions, accidents—failure itself."[128] Moreover, Joyce pursues a polysemics in extremis; the errant particles of language in *Finnegans Wake* are charged to such a saturated state, and Joyce employs such a range of techniques to achieve its dream of linguistic delirium, that an error could not appear "in all its featureful perfection of imperferction"; it would be imperceptible against the background of "all the earrears and erroriboose" of the book's "fine artful disorder."[129] I want to emphasize that as with my claim for *The Cantos,* this is not an argument based on the work's notorious (if wildly overrated) difficulty. To judge what constituted "properer misakes" in the *Wake* would not just be difficult, as it is in the punning and pre-standardized language of Elizabethan texts, for instance, but that act of judgment itself would no longer be meaningful.[130] To try and discern a mistake does not make sense when standards of linguistic correctness—the very grounds on which error, as such, is predicated—no longer exist. The radical textual condition of the *Wake,* that is, obviates the category of error itself by canceling the criteria for defining an error and removing the necessary conditions for establishing its ontological status.

This is not the place to pursue a definitive analysis of Joyce's work, but I want to be clear about the conditions I have in mind. Like Pound, Joyce "did not always wish to correct an error once it had made its way into print," and one of the portals of discovery he opens lets in errors of transmission.[131] As Vicki Mahaffey provocatively argues *Finnegans Wake* explicitly "welcome[s] adulteration, chance, [and] the transmigration of written characters through time."[132] An illustrative parable comes from Samuel Beckett's brief service as Joyce's amanuensis: he was once taking dictation when someone knocked at the door;

> Joyce said 'Come in,' and Beckett wrote it down. Afterwards he read back what he had written and Joyce said, 'What's that "Come in"?' 'Yes, you said that,' said Beckett. Joyce thought for a while then said, 'let it stand.'[133]

Corroborating Joyce's claim that the book was not really being written by him, but by "you, and you, and you, and that man over there, and that girl at the next table . . . .," the *Wake* itself repeatedly argues against its writer as a guarantor of textual authority.[134] Joyce disperses the source of signification, that is, to language itself, but he does so without allowing language to ground even its own authority. "Après mot," as he put it, "le deluge."[135] At one level, the work removes further support on which the reader can anchor signification by refusing either sustained plot or characters against which to posit and test the interpretation of words.[136] Similarly, the *Wake* resists even an overall textual telos; the book not only repeats itself like a Möbius strip ("the lubricitous conjugation of the last with the first"), but individual words gesture freely and unpredictably forward and backwards through the text without regard for linear structures, thus "indicating that the words which follow may be taken in any order desired."[137] As these indicators of transmitted "message" decrease, so does the possibility of an error that could be posited against some larger fiction which would stand as arbiter. In other words, as the *Wake* moves from work to text its coefficient of error approaches zero. There are no errors at the level of inscription, only what—in Wittgensteinian terms—is *shown*. Or as Cage puts it: "A 'mistake' is beside the point" at the level of sheer textuality, "for once anything happens it authentically is."[138]

None of these points would be sufficient to eliminate mistakes as such, but within this already undependable context, Joyce places individual words beyond the measure of error. Those words are often comprised of different languages grafted and spliced at the level of the morpheme, so that Joyce's hybrid vocabulary constitutes an idiolect that ultimately moves beyond a deviance from "standard English" to create a language which cannot be confirmed by any single lexicon, and in which even the grammatical parts of speech are frequently miscegenated.[139] As "the traced words, run, march, halt, walk, stumble at doubtful points" through the difficult if decipherable syntax of the *Wake* (and note that the punctuation here indicates that "word" is the verb conjugated to agree with the nominative "traced"), even the indeterminacy of those words is unstable.[140] They continually shift models of reference from the more familiar uses of denotation, connotation, and allusion, to subtle metaphoric and allegorical patterns, to Joyce's trademark portmanteaux, etymological play, aural punning, graphic paronomasia, and a series of paragrammatic constructions (writing backwards, dislocations across word boundaries, anagrams, acrostics, and undoubtedly several devices that have not even been noticed). Since more than one of these models are often simultaneously combined in a single word, without definitively privileging any single strategy for reading, there is no base against which uncertain aspects of a word can be conclusively measured. The "verbivocovisual" terms of Joyce's text, in short, are "variously inflected, differently pronounced, otherwise spelled, changeably meaning vocal scriptsigns."[141] At its most neologistic extreme, the reader of this "idioglossary" no longer has recourse to positive terms against which deviation could be measured, only a series of hapax legomena, irreconcilable and unassimilable to one another to such a degree that none can claim precedence or priority.[142] Most important, one of the book's central lessons is that any "error" is itself a *felix culpa;* faced with what at times seems to be a "book composed entirely of misprints," or at least of "hides and hints and misses in prints," the reader must learn to treat the unfamiliar or unverifiable word not as an impediment to some "proper" or "correct" reading, but as the very site for pursuing multiple, ad hoc, and provisional strategies of reading.[143] "Strictly speaking," Juri Tynjanov remarks, "every deformation, every 'mistake,' every 'irregularity' of normative poetics is potentially a new construction principle."[144] Like the futurist texts from which Tynjanov learned his lesson, Joyce's own text is repeatedly "pointing to a fact that seems to be an error & showing it to be other than it seems," as Mac Low puts it in his first *Pronouns* dance, which carries the appropriately Poundian subtitle "making things new."[145]

The *Wake,* not incidentally, is the other major source of Cage's mesostics, providing him with five full poems. Starting in 1978 with the book-length *Writing Through Finnegans Wake,* then repeating the process with a more concise version, and moving to a stricter mesostic rule for the third writing-through, Cage subsequently produced an even shorter fourth version, which proceeds without permitting the reappearance of given syllable for a given letter of the [index] name"; the final writing-through, fourteen pages of closely set and frequently unspaced prose blocks, continues this exclusionary rule to achieve an even greater fragmentation: "no sentences, just phrases, words, syllables, and letters."[146] Cage's *Wake* texts ultimately match the level of disarticulation in Mac Low's *Words nd Ends,* and they both perform a successive "dismemberment of language, as meaning-producing tropes are replaced by the fragmentation of sentences and propositions into discrete words, or the fragmentation of words into syllables or finally letters."[147] This decomposition of linguistic structures is a perfect, if literal, example of Paul Bourget's definition of a "decadent" style, and one which Cage and Mac Low carry beyond its historical precedent:

> A decadent style is one where the unity of the book is broken down in favour of the independence of the page, where the page is broken down

to allow the in-dependence of the phrase, and [accordingly] the phrase in favour of the word.[148]

As this increasing degree of disarticulation favors the individual letter, it indicates the primary site for the possibility of error in the diastic poems, and even the least fragmented of Cage's mesostics gestures towards this location; the capitalization of the index-words, as we have seen, highlights the status of individual letters within the word.

Indeed, the status of those letters, when coupled with source texts like *Finnegans Wake* and *The Cantos,* sets in motion a series of striking reversals. Cage and Mac Low take texts replete with erratic orthography, but in which there cannot in fact be errors, and through rule-generated procedures they transform those sources into new texts which can indeed contain errors, but in which any mistake would be very difficult to notice; a reader would have to replicate the composition of the diastic poem, reading both the source text and the writing-through *en face.* Indeed, errors are not only possible in writings-through, they are actually quite probable given the difficulty of composing a diastic that accords with its rules to the letter, so to speak. To read through a book identifying and recording individual letters is more difficult than it might at first sound. As anyone who has composed a mesostic or worked as a textual editor or professional proofreader can attest, letters become all but invisible in the most familiar words, vowels smuggle themselves into the middle of words undetected, and ascenders masquerade as one another with equal cunning. A single mistake in the diastic, moreover, is rarely local; because the selected text is cumulative, a mistake almost always invalidates everything which follows. Aware of these difficulties, Cage adopts a practical approach; when he notices a mistake, he says: "If I can go back and correct it I do. If I can't (if, for instance, the printout used had already been thrown in the garbage which had already been collected) I accept what's happened and continue my work."[149] Continuing the series of reversals and diametric cancellations, the irruptive index-letters mark the transformation of intentionally composed texts, filled—as we have seen—with chance occurrences and interventions, into nonintentional compositions which are structured in such a way that they aspire to eliminate chance. Despite the frequent use of the term "chance procedure" to describe the poetry of Cage and Mac Low, the most rigid diastic poems—like *Words nd Ends*—are entirely determined. The author or reader may not know beforehand exactly how the poem will turn out, but once a source text, index, and set of rules are chosen that outcome is predetermined. Chance, in the diastic poem, occurs only with an error: only in an inadvertent violation of the rules or a mistake in transcription. Additionally, any error in the diastic poem actually becomes a sign of the individual human agent at work on an "unintentional" composition designed to deemphasize the ego.

These series of inversions, like the others I have enumerated in this chapter, lead to one final example, in which "inversion" is in fact all to the point. The erratic rewriting of *The Cantos* by Cage and Mac Low frequently results in what can only be termed an errotics. In Cage's writing-through, for instance, the blazón of an "upturned nipple" remarked from "Canto III" is followed by "As / sPeak," which contracts nine lines of Pound's poem to both cull the "ass" from his text and provide a peek of the "peak" of these body parts. This suggestive jocularity then continues in the miniature narrative that emerges around the joke syntax of "a whOre qUit the driNk saveD up / his pay monEy and ooZe scRupulously cleAn / Penis" and concludes with the punchline: "skin profiteers"—all of which then adds to the insinuations made by the sequence that follows a few lines later: "up to the beD-room / stubby fEllow cocky," and its hint of "fEl[ati]ow" foretold.[150] The import of such passages is less their scant locker-room humor than the rhetorical force of "deviation" when it couples the statistical register of the word (the diastic methods' recombinatory generation of text) with the social (the thematics of socially unsanctioned sexual activity). That crossing can be seen in Cage's reworking of Joyce's notoriously risqué prose, of course, but the effect is even more charged when the "openly closeted" Cage recuperates Pound's stridently homophobic text through the mesostic ellipsis which makes a "lipsus of some hetarousexual" poem.[151] These rewritings at times merely function as subtle censorings; guided by the statistical distributions of letter occurrence in English and medieval Italian, the mesostic passes over the lewd sailors' joke which closes "Canto XII" ("'I'm not your fader but your moder,' quod he, / 'Your fader was a rich merchant in Strambouli'"), as well as Malatesta's ugly quip at the end of "Canto X" ("They've got a bigger army, / but there are more men in this camp"), with an appropriately Cagean silence.[152] Intervening with similar understatement, Mac Low's poem wittily shortens "the man" to create "he mAn" out of the machismo of Malatesta's letters, rereading "what they found in the post-bag" as his mail bag, or rather: male bag.[153]

The proper distribution of that bag's contents—the *semen* of the scrotum and the σῆμα of the letters (alphabetic if not epistolary)—is thematically central to Pound's text, and structurally central to the diastic poems that cancel and redeliver his letters. When Pound visits Blake's "Printing house in hell" in Cantos XIV–XVI, he conflates a series of deviations *contra naturam*: "perverts,""inverts" (the figures are literally "reversed" and "head down," and those engaged in anal "intercourse" (in every sense of the word).[154] Even the names of the damned—erased from a time when publishers left blanks in their writings to protect themselves from libel—retain only their last letters: they are reduced to being nothing but (butt) ends. As in Alighieri's *Inferno*, Pound equates anal sex with bad economics because he imagines both to be at work "against Nature's increase."[155] Although Pound's text undoes itself in its ranting haste, accusing the hemorrhoidal landscape of England of being a place "devoid of interest" in the intellectual, but obviously not the financial, sense of the word, "Canto XLV" reiterates the logic which binds activities "without regard to productions; often without regard to the possibilities of production":

> Usura slayeth the child in the womb
> It stayeth the young man's courting
> It hath brought palsey to bed, lyeth
> between the young bride and her bridegroom
> CONTRA NATURAM[.][156]

Accordingly, the enemies in the so-called "hell cantos" are "obstructors of distribution"—whether of sperm, the Classics, or currency—and each of these moral mis-conceptions, improperly "distributing its productions," appears among examples of erroneous generation: the "foetor" of "foetid combustion" recalling the image of the unviably "swollen foetus," the parturition of "dung hatching," the excessive growth of the formicate "four-millionth tumour," and the "living pus" in which Pound imagines "dead maggots begetting live maggots."[157] These images rhyme with the thematics of "copies," "multiples," and mirrors in "Canto XV" to underscore the fact that appropriate *reproduction* is at stake.[158] Specifically, the "unsinkable shield" of efficacious reproduction—Perseus's improvised mirror—is implicitly contrasted with the emblem of Pound's condemnation of frustrated and unnatural reproduction: the "shield" or "condom filled with black beetles."[159] The phallic aggression of this repeated image is superbly overdetermined; not only is a "beetle" a tool for ramming (or *pounding*) something in, but a "black beetle" is another name for a *cock*roach—where "roach" denotes something having an upward curve and the insect itself is characterized by its hard "sheath" (yet another term for "condom").

These passages by no means exhaust the rhetoric of sexuality in *The*

Cantos, but they should be sufficient to establish the degree to which the diastic poems would be condemned by Pound's ethics. According to the logic of that ethics, writings-through enact an improper textual production by taking their usurious cut of the surplus of a source text's general economy; they produce poetry from poetry like "financiers" generating money from money.[160] Moreover, Cage and Mac Low may have taken up the golden thread and answered Pound's final question in *The Cantos*—"who will copy this palimpsest?"—but their act of reproduction is distorted in the very manner Pound abhors: blocking the circulation of his text and perverting the distribution of most of its letters, ending up "deepknee in error" among the "litterish fragments" of its subsequently "unreadable volumes."[161] Pound figures the anal focus of an inverted "eros" as "erosion" in the hell cantos, where "[type]faces" are "smeared" to feces, and the erosion of his text's own legibility by the diastic poem's writing-through replicates precisely that evil and "inchoate error" of perverted reproduction that we have seen Pound explicitly condemn.[162] A careful reading of the hell cantos, however, reveals that Pound also explicitly *enacts* that mode of perverse reproduction. In a passage where the Virgil figure explains, "This sort breeds by scission / . . . . In this *bolge*," Pound himself makes a scission of his source text, Dante's "*Malebolge* [evil ditch]"; he ditches the first half of the word to leave only the end, with the "male"—implicitly and wittily translated into English—understood.[163] The moment is emblematic; Pound's practice once again belies his rhetoric, and he anticipates the diastics' complex and paradoxical power not only to generate meaning through "breeding by scission," but also to present strong, and significant, formal arguments as they "WRite ert."[164] "To err," as Bruce Andrews says, is always "statemental."

The whole thing at once seemed to be artificial, and instead of interesting fact, to be very childish fictions.

    —W. H. Mallock

There is nothing we can say to the nineteenth century that wouldn't break its heart.

    —M. Remski

6. Cover-Up

The Archaeology of Knowledge/
The Knowledge of Archaeology

In 1965, IBM ran a full-page advertisement in *Art in America* appealing to the reader's interest in archaeology and the mystery of fragmentary texts. Beneath a photograph of the earthworks at Stonehenge, which IBM computers had helped to map, the copy featured Babylonian "books of clay" and the "tattered" Dead Sea Scrolls in which "words, even whole sentences, were missing." I am setting down these apparently aimless phrases so that the reader may have some sort of background, something less detailed than Umbrian clarity, some sort of retrospect, cloudy in itself, but from which the teeth and gnashing of the present, the mental incisions, can emerge and whereby they may have a chance of keeping some sort of proportion. At least that is how Ezra Pound might have put it; because despite the familiar story of science in the service of humanism, IBM was registering what Pound called the "tone of the time."[1]

The writers on Madison Avenue uncannily anticipated the fact that within the year a number of poets and artists would set independently to work on projects that replicated those fragmentary documents of antiquity and prehistory. Robert Smithson—who like other artists of his generation would soon visit Stonehenge—might well have taken that very issue of *Art in America* with him when he began the site-selection explorations that would bring his own "earthworks" indoors, mapping terrestrial displacements even without the aid of a computer; Tom Phillips was simultaneously out searching for the site that would yield *A Humument*, a text produced by tattering an old book so that "words, even whole sentences were missing"; and Armand Schwerner, with a comparable aesthetic, was beginning his *Tablets*, modeled on those very Babylonian "books of clay" the IBM computers had helped to date.[2] Such excavation, as Smithson noted in 1968—just a month before the Situationists would excavate the cobblestones of Parisian streets in search of the beach beneath—"is becoming more and more important to artists," and by decade's end Jonathan Williams, Ronald Johnson, Vito Acconci, and Alastair Johnston, to name only a few, would begin their own mining of source texts. Something was clearly in the air.[3] Or again, in Pound's appropriately geological words: "There was a strata . . . which mere criticism of books fails to get hold of, a strata that goes either into literature itself, I mean as its subject, or remains unrecorded."[4] This chapter will attempt to unearth those strata and sound out that tone of that time. Like the archaeologists who used an IBM computer to work backwards from the placement of cromlechs or cuneiform markings and correlate the network of planetary positions no longer visible to us, I want to look for "answers to literary puzzles" and gain "new perspectives on literary figures" by setting a series of artifacts in relation to one another and reconstructing the alignments and parallactic cancellations they may once have displayed.

I will begin in the winter of 1968, when Robert Smithson returned from a trip to the New Jersey Pine Barrens and constructed the first of his "nonsites." A hexagonal section cut from a topographic map of the Pine Barrens was reproduced and mounted on the wall; accompanying this photostat, a series of stepped aluminum containers were arranged on the floor in a correspondingly hexagonal array and filled with sand from the area indicated in the map. With an elegant simplicity, this "indoor earthwork" sets in motion an intriguing deictic network; the organization of aluminum bins refers viewers to the map, which references the absent site, where Smithson's prior excavations have displaced material, which leads one back to the bins, and so on in an endless concatenation. Moreover, the series of horizons *mise en abîme* by the installation—sand contained within bins, nonsite contained within a gallery, gallery within an outdoor plot that stretches to meet up with the area indicated on the map—are folded inside one another with the logic of a Klein bottle, so that the outside erupts at the interior.[5] Look to the site, and its significance—*as a site*—is instantiated in the gallery's stylized documentation, but the status of those materials in the gallery is underwritten by the absent site, which has nonetheless been incorporated at the very center of the interior nonsite. Each element, in short, directs the viewer to its own evasion. The nonsite can only be confirmed by recourse to the site itself, which comes into being only with the establishment of the *non*site, so that Smithson's new mode of sculptural mapping operates according to the dangerous logic of the supplement which Jacques Derrida, in 1967, was at that very moment explicating.[6] With the dynamic of their constantly switching dialectic deconstructing the two terms to generate a combined third, "both sid[/t]es are present and absent at the same time."[7] "No where," with the slightest shift of empty space, becomes "now here." For Lawrence Alloway, the accumulation of reference under these conditions constructs a relationship in which "the nonsite acts as the signifier of the absent site," and while this formulation misleadingly stabilizes the complexity of shifting relationships between the terms of Smithson's semiotics, the linguistic metaphor is entirely apropos.[8]

Smithson traces the development of the nonsite directly to his interest in cartography, which arose in turn from his study of crystallography and the mapping of crystalline structures.[9] Moreover, such crystalline, mineral structures are, for Smithson, equivalent to linguistic structures.[10]

> The names of minerals and the minerals themselves do not differ from each other, because at the bottom of both the material and print is the beginning of an abysmal number of fissures. Words and rocks contain a language that follows a syntax of splits and ruptures.[11]

"Embedded in the sediment," as Smithson saw, "is a text," and with a conflation nicely summarized in his coinage "earthwords," Smithson habitually figures language as chthonic and, correspondingly, casts geology in linguistic terms.[12] Language can bear the weight of this equation because it is an object with the same brute physicality as stone. Like Basil Bunting, who contemporaneously declared that one must "take a chisel to write," Smithson takes writing for granite.[13] Before the phrase "materiality of the signifier" became clichéd, Smithson was exploiting a decidedly poststructural understanding of language *avant la lettre*. Works such as the visual poem *A Heap of Language* (1966) and the "geophoto-graphic fiction" *Strata* (1970) embody his belief that "Language should find itself in the physical world and not end up locked in an idea in somebody's head . . . . Writing should generate ideas into matter and not the other way around."[14] Smithson's title for a 1967 press release, "Language to be looked at and/or things to be read," encapsulates his sense of language's accreted materiality, and in a postscript to that statement added five years later he explains: "My sense of language is that it is matter and not ideas—i.e. "printed matter."[15]

Smithson's affinity with a contemporaneous poetic avant-garde comes not so much from this shared emphasis on the materiality of writing, however, as from a common procedural practice and poetics. In his 1972 essay "The Spiral Jetty," Smithson quotes Thomas Clark and Colin Stern's *Geological Evolution of North America,* which had, significantly, been published in 1968: "The earth's history seems at times like a story recorded in a book each page of which is torn into small pieces. Many of the pages and some of the pieces of each page are missing."[16] Smithson's nonsites are one reconstruction of those fragments into new historical maps, but "all language," for Smithson, "becomes an alphabet of sites," and between the publication of *Geological Evolution* and Smithson's essay, several other writers had begun constructing books by displaying "pages torn into small pieces" and with "some of the pieces of each page . . . missing."[17] As with the diastic poems by Cage and Mac Low, these works were composed by writing-through a source text (or, in the case of Armand Schwerner's *Tablets,* creating a simulacrum of such fragmentation). Jonathan Williams selected case histories from the "Inversion" chapter of Havelock Ellis's turn-of-the-century *Studies in the Psychology of Sex;* as his site-specific source for *A Humument,* Tom Phillips used chance and predetermined rules to choose the single-volume reprint of William Hurrell Mallock's all but forgotten Victorian novel *A Human Document;* and Ronald Johnson derived his poem *Radi Os* from an edition of *Paradise Lost.*[18] Significantly, all of these writers echo Smithson and describe their literary projects in geological terms. Williams named his writings-through "excavations"; Phillips thought of his treatment as "an exhumation" (*ex humus:* "from the earth"), a word he felt resonated with the "earthy sound" of his book's title; and "mined" is perhaps the most frequent description of all these projects, including Johnson's text, which Guy Davenport characterizes as "sifted" like silt or soil.[19] As I will argue, these works are all nonsites, but for simplicity and clarity I will adopt Phillips's phrase and refer to them as "treated" texts.

For Smithson, "the material determined the choice of the site," and he emphasized the dependence of the nonsite on that source material: "I want to make clear the point that it's not preconceived. The things turn up as I go along. In other words, the piece is contingent on the availability of great amounts of homogeneous matter."[20] The texts by Williams, Phillips, and Johnson also depend on a suitable lode; this is why prose, or in the case of *Paradise Lost,* the relatively uniform layout of blank verse, works so well for these revisionist projects, and the way in which the resistance of that fixed and recalcitrant material inflects the resulting poem is one of the primary interests of their writing. Unlike the procedural and rule-guided diastics of Cage and Mac Low, these treatments are intentional and associationally free-form, but while they are not constrained by self-imposed rules, they are nevertheless bounded by the original typographic layout of the source text. Taking the page of that source text as a unit of composition, each of these treatments then erases or overprints to render most of the original text illegible, allowing the remaining clusters of words or fragmented parts of words to reforge new syntactic relationships. From the famous opening passage of Milton's *Paradise Lost,* for instance, Johnson deletes most of the words:

> ~~Of~~ Man's ~~first disobedience, and the fruit~~
> ~~Of that forbidden~~ tree ~~whose mortal taste~~
> ~~Brought death~~ into the World, ~~and all our woe,~~
> ~~With loss of Eden, till one greater~~ Man
> ~~Restore us, and regain the blissful seat;~~
> ~~Sing, Heavenly Muse, that on the secret top~~
> ~~Of Oreb, or of Sinai, didst inspire~~
> ~~That shepherd who first taught~~ the chosen ~~seed~~
> ~~In the beginning how the heavens and earth~~
> Rose out of Chaos: ~~or, if Sion hill~~
> ~~Delight thee more, and Siloa's brook that flowed~~
> ~~Fast by the oracle of God, I thence~~
> ~~Invoke thy aid to my adventurous~~ song,

and leaves, spaced across the first page of his book:

    O

              tree
          into the World,
                     Man

                   the chosen

   Rose out of Chaos:

              song,

Phillips's book follows the same procedure, and is equally constrained by the typographic disposition of the page of Mallock's novel.[21]

Part of the purpose of the nonsite was to defamiliarize the "physical, raw reality" of the site: "the earth or the ground that we are not really aware of."[22] The pun is exact, and all of the treated texts both depend on and underscore the perceptual ground of the page, even as their authors refer to its geological valence. Remapping the space of the dis-covered page, the treated texts rechart the contours of its layout with clusters of text like "landmasses that aren't following [the] preconceived boundaries" of the original, uniform print.[23] Phillips further emphasizes the original typesetting's gutter, those spaced and leaded gaps between type, which he isolates and uses like speech balloons to connect phrases; the meander and flow of those gaps, in fact, become an integral aspect of his treatment's aesthetic. He also extends the punning reversal of ground and figure whenever he pictures Bill Toge, the new protagonist he adds to Mallock's original two main characters; the "figure" of Phillips's "character" (itself, significantly, another typographic term) always appears with its contour shaped according to those " 'rivers' in the type of the original."[24] Moreover, if Toge's body and the connectors between words underscore the sinuous infiltration of ground that worms its way through the crannied plot of every prose-set type, Phillips is equally attentive to the rectilinear set of that block within the frame of the page. He uses the solidity of that shape both as an anchoring form against which to play the diverse visual styles of his pages, and also as a plane with which to create the effect of layered depth by allowing certain elements to float "over" the space of the central block. Phillips often underscores the inherent rigidity of justified type by adding hard outlines and multiple frames to the text block, creating pages within pages just as Smithson's nonsites established "rooms within rooms," and Phillips breaks with that given rectangle in only a handful of pages.[25] "In fact," as Johanna Drucker notes, "this respect for the margin is so strong throughout the work that in the few sites where it is broken through or bled into these read very clearly as gestures by contrast," and she adds with equal perspicacity that "part of Phillips' skill is his sensitivity to the existing structures of the page, as well as the complexities of the book form in its entirety."[26]

Williams also works with the structure of the page in his excavations; in "History XIX" the physical actions of reading the book—thumbing, handling, and releasing pages in their turning—are described with an uncanny anticipation of the reader's movements. Coming at the bottom of the page, just as readers are about to remove their hands and turn the leaf over, the text conflates the sexual activity of Ellis's case study and the reader's own manual, if not masturbatory, activity: "removed his hand / turned over." Johnson is equally attentive to the structure of the codex, and like Phillips and Williams he replicates his source text's run of title headers and its sequencing of books. Johnson, moreover, also incorporates the codexical structure metatextually into the thematic allusions of his poem. To begin with, the blank paper exposed by erasing so many of Milton's words rhymes with the "tree" that figures prominently in his poem. As we saw with Susan Howe's poetry, the book's link to the forest extended beyond its etymological ties when wood pulp replaced cotton rag as the chief material in the manufacture of paper at the end of the nineteenth century—that is, at precisely the moment when the volume used by Johnson was published.[27] "Books are my trees," Johnson might have said (although the line is quoted from R. B. Kitaj by Johnson's close friend Jonathan Williams), and when he writes "I return / turned / Through the wood," Johnson may well be referring to his own treatment of Milton's pages. Indeed, with the words spaced across the page in an imitation of open "field" poetics, a line like "amid the field / Of cross-barred / fold / into / the Tree" takes on a certain self-referentiality, suggesting the laid-lined ("cross-barred") paper that is bound into the gutter "fold" of the books where it "Forms / autumnal leaves" "gathered." In Johnson's treatment, the "shade" and "shadowed" "void" of that gutter-fold merges with the "shade" given by a tree's "leaves," and it ultimately becomes the figure of Milton's dark "Abyss."[28] The book's binding, that is, becomes the literal creation of an "utter darkness, / from the centre / whirlwind" of pages, the white paper of which stretches "on all sides round" like "bright arms": a body with "arms / From either end" revolving "out of . . . / darkness / an / unobscured / round." In fact, the essential structure of the codex, with its fixed spine around which pages can be turned in a cylindrical geometry of rotating segments, equates each page with a radius—or as Johnson's title would have it: books seen from the bottom are Os because their pages are Radi[i]. This figure of forms revolving and wheeling around a fixed center is a recurrent motif in Radi Os; occasionally imagined as the earth—"the O" or "new / globe" made from a "pole" and "circumference" of radii which turn to form "a globe / enclosed"—this image is most often cast as the sun: "Amid the Sun's bright circle / See / meridian / minded, / with corporeal bar / within the circuit of whatsoever shape." The sun's golden rays (Latin radii), moreover, rhyme with Johnson's mention of "golden ribs" and suggest another translation of Radi Os: the bones (Latin ossus) radiating from the spine.[29] Or again: the gilt-edged pages of an 1890s book radiating from their "spine." Which leads back, of course, to the figure of the tree: its root etymologically rooted in the Latin *radix,* and its ringed trunk and branches radiating out to "autumnal leaves" which have "turned" to become golden.

A Sedimental Journey

> Look at any word long enough and you will see it open up into a series of faults, into a terrain of particles each containing its own void.
> —Robert Smithson

> The closer you look at a word, the greater the distance from which it looks back.
> —Karl Krauss

The recurrent figures of elongated radial structures in *Radi Os,* with their play of horizontal and vertical, also include the horizontal layout of Milton's poem and the vertical reworking of Johnson's treatment. All of the treated texts, in fact, record a reading down the page, replacing the serial and linear horizontality of conventional reading with vectors that are not only vertical, but frequently oriented from right to left. This process of vertical reading and writing—constructing new syntaxes according to the formal possibilities inherent in the structure of language but against its conventions—should be familiar from previous chapters as a strategy of paragrammatic *détournement.* As we saw, *détournement* is the antithesis of quotation, and so even though they rely so absolutely on a source the treated texts are effectively "noncites." For all of their ostensible precision and documentation, Smithson's own noncites are also essentially paragrammatic, and he explicitly theorized them as the elaboration of new syntactic grammars.[30] If writers like Phillips and Johnson find alternate sentiments embedded in texts and accessed through methods of reading that evade the usual, rational order, Smithson—conversely—realized that "embedded in the sediment is a text that contains limits and boundaries which evade the rational order."[31] "From the linguistic point of view," he noted elsewhere, "one establishes rules of structure based on a change in the semantics of building."[32] From the engineering point of view, accordingly, the new semantic structures constructed by treating texts are themselves, in Smithson's vocabulary, the result of "site selection": "extracting from a site certain associations that have remained invisible within the old framework of rational language" so that "the aim is to re-construct a new type of 'building' into a whole that engenders new meanings."[33]

This radical architecture of Smithson's "new type of 'building'" aligns him with the Situationists' politicized geography, and one of Debord's first manifestos, in fact, calls for the sort of revolutionary mappings developed by the nonsite: "Entre divers moyens d'intervention plus difficiles, une cartographie rénovée parait propre à l'exploitation immédiate [Among various other means of intervention, a renovated cartography seems appropriate for immediate utilization]."[34] The nonsite of the treated page also shares an affinity with contemporaneous Situationist poetics; treated texts, like Debord's psychogeographical maps of Paris, construct a syntax of sites on the page irrespective of spatial contiguity but according to the *dérive* (drift) of the eye down the page as it finds new centers of attraction unhampered by the architecture of the original layout. With this same sense of contingency and play—a hallmark, as we have seen, of Situationist practice—Smithson's own constructions demonstrate his belief that "we have to fabricate our rules as we go along the avalanches of language and over the terraces of criticism."[35] Furthermore, working with "what form and / bounds prescribed" (Johnson), and like the treated text's maneuvers within the fixed and given dispensation of words in the space of the source text's page, Smithson's constructions repeatedly evince the Situationists' fundamental insight that interventions must always be made within preexisting structures. Gary Shapiro argues for the importance of this insight, and given the resonance of his vocabulary with material I have discussed elsewhere in this book, he is worth quoting at some length:

> Smithson's comments on the museum and, even more, his production of nonsites, earthworks, films, and other displacements ought to be seen as oblique or lateral interventions rather than as attempts at creating "new" institutions that could be reabsorbed into the museal culture. In this sense all of Smithson's activity is strategic rather than principled. That is, he is aware that there is no easy way out of the museum (which he often compares to a labyrinth) any more than (as Heidegger and Derrida show) there is any simple escape from metaphysics, for to claim that one is 'outside' or 'beyond' in these cases is to accept the horizon established by that from which one flees.[36]

In the nonsite, this examination of inside and outside takes the specific form of a play of circumscription and release; the nonsite "in a physical way contains the disruptions of the site."[37] As I argued in chapter 4, such terms correspond to the distinctions Georges Bataille drew between restricted and general economies, or between conventional and paragrammatic reading strategies. The paragrammatic procedure of treating texts, in fact, nicely illustrates the constantly switching dialectic I elaborated earlier; against the infinite instability and surplus of the source text, the treatment isolates and stabilizes one potential route for the outlet of its excessive significatory capacity. The treated page is thus a record of *la part maudite*, paradoxically canceling that measure in its very registration. By retaining and incorporating the trace of the source text in the form of the original page layout, like the nonsite's photostatic references to the site, the treated page constantly reminds its reader that the words still visible have been diverted from their intended function. "Here language 'covers' rather than 'discovers' its sites and situations. Here language 'closes' rather than 'discloses' doors to utilitarian interpretations and explanations."[38] As with the Situationists, Smithson frequently appeals to the utopian potential of an antifunctionalist perspective, and that sacrifice, one will recall, is the very condition of a general economy. Bataille's work on such economies, *La part maudite,* was published posthumously in 1967, precisely as Smithson was developing the nonsite, and Bataille's insistence on the ubiquity of inevitable, uncontrollable, and unrecuperable *dèpense* (expenditure) anticipates Smithson's fascination with entropy. Treated texts are obviously activities of such irreversible entropic loss, eliminating and erasing their source texts like the erosion and decomposition of mineral structures, and the insight of the artists I have been discussing is to recognize that such loss can itself always be productively exploited towards critical and aesthetic ends.

The theme of loss is of course central to Milton's postlapsarian epic, and in Johnson's treatment of the poem apparent references to the "fortunate fall" merge with phrases that inevitably read as metatextual references to the treatment's method of production from a "Dissolved" source. If, "In that dark durance. / The rest is / loss," there is nonetheless "fruition / from utter loss" because "high words" emerge "In loss itself." Like the negative ontology explicated by Smithson's nonsites, for which he adopted Carl Andre's formulation "A thing is a hole in a thing it is not," this paradox of productive loss is the "theory of sediment" posited by Steve McCaffery: "Sediment is a derivative from other material. Passing the way of words."[39] Making this connection between words and minerals even more explicit, McCaffery resurrects the geolinguistic vocabulary of the late 1960s and elaborates the metaphors we have already noted in the writing of Smithson, Clark, and Stern:

> Sedimentation is a process of denuding: the erosion of a land or text mass and its transportation to numerous environments of depositions; this leading to both stable and unstable forms. Reading provokes as a social act the release of turbid optical currents on a textual slope effecting both a lateral and vertical modification of the source texts.[40]

As we have seen, this ambivalent play of stable and unstable, lateral and vertical, is integral to the treated text, and several pages later McCaffery explains: "a more violent form of sedimentary transport is the treated text" in which "reading persists as an intervention into granular states," probing the ground between the latticework of type so that "the poems resulting are evaporites obtained from the closed basin of the page."[41] The degree to which such poems are "a drainage effected upon history" is nicely summarized by Schwerner's "Tablet X," which differentiates with ridiculous scholasticism between the unreadable (dots), the missing (pluses), and the confusing (crossed circles), and which ostensibly records the unlikely combination of a double article: "the the." The inevitable recollection of the conclusion of Wallace Stevens's "The Man on the Dump" is reinforced by the latter's conjunction of "stanza" and "stone," a conflation to which the pretense of Schwerner's *Tablets* aspires. While one might pursue a parallel reading of the two poems, or see Schwerner's as an explicit commentary on Stevens, I instead want to recall what may have been the source for Stevens's original stutter: Bertrand Russell's 1905 essay "On Denoting."[42] The only imaginable reading of those two legible words requires the first "the" to refer to the second, and although a logician might not be persuaded, for the casual linguist the definite article would seem to be the degree-zero mark of history. Unlike indefinite articles, "the" seems to presuppose an antecedent referent whose differentiable existence must implicitly precede the use of the article. By attesting to the facticity of that previous but absent state of affairs, the "the" thus inscribes history into its grammar. This condition of recorded loss, a "drainage effected upon history," is the condition of the treated page, which is analogous to a palimpsest, in which the destructive processes of time—the fading and eroding of the textual support—lead to the gain of earlier texts even as they destroy more recent writing. "In other words, it's one site superimposed over another site," as Smithson explained in describing the nonsite, and the treated page is itself a nonsite pitched at another degree of regress and located *at the site itself*.[43]

When the boundaries of that site-within-a-site are reduced to within the space of a single word, the treated text not only cuts across the syntax of the original work—shearing and cleaving along the planes built into the strata of its macrostructure—but also begins to disrupt its atomic structure and thus its status as a coherent language. Eroding "the old frameworks of rational language" to the point of generating entirely new vocabularies, Phillips has a score of pages that open onto such "nonce sites." These passages range from archaisms and Carrollesque portmanteaux to onomatopoeic vocalise and English-language versions of Russian futurist *zaum.*' Even his protagonist is a recurrent reminder of the degree to which Phillips's intervention veers from the intended trajectory of his source; Bill Toge can only appear, according to Phillips, "on pages which originally contained the words 'together' or 'altogether' (the only words from which his name can be extracted)."[44] Born from the literal breaking apart of what was once "together," the legendary source of this name adds a poignant emphasis to the jacket blurb's claim that Toge is "one of love's tragedies."[45] Since almost every critic or commentator on *A Humument* apodictically reiterates Phillips's claim about the requirements for his character's appearance, rarely citing him, I should mention that it is simply not true. "Photogenic" and "octogenarian" fit the bill, as do "protogenic" and "cystogenous," and I suspect some casual minutes spent with a good dictionary would reveal more, perhaps less common, possibilities. For that matter, "toge" is itself an English word derived from the late Latin for "toga," admittedly archaic and obsolete but not out of place in *A Humument* and right there in the *OED*— an authority that cites four of Mallock's books—for those who would care to check. "I am not against pedantry," and just to be precise, on at least one occasion Phillips forms the name from two adjacent lines.[46] Details aside, however, the point remains the same: regardless of its provenance, "toge" marks the generative possibilities of sedimentation even when it derives from the erosion of the morphemic structure of the source text.

As we saw with Cage and Mac Low's writings-through, such interventions do not just alter the source text, but can also critically comment on them. One of the key differences between these works, which might be further elaborated, arises from the differences in the status of their source texts; where Mallock signals a certain sense of high literary tradition, for instance, he certainly does not have the canonical status enjoyed by Milton. Phillips's work, in this respect, is closer to Smithson's; Mallock is the literary equivalent of the New Jersey Pine Barrens. This discrepancy in the cultural status of their source texts may account in part for why Phillips's treatment is more flippantly playful than Johnson's, which however much it "violates" the sacrosanct monument of English letters only ever does so towards serious, earnestly vatic ends. William Blake's audacious "corrections" of Milton, in fact, manifest the relative deference of Johnson's re-visions. My focus on the treated text's disruption of its source should not, however, overshadow the fact that such commentary is never unilateral. Rather than elaborate the treated texts' critique of their sources, I want to offer an example of the way in which the source text, in accord with the logic of the nonsite, makes reference to the treatment that it has always implicitly contained. Mallock's *A Human Document* opens with an announcement that might preface Phillips's own book: "the following work, though it has the form of a novel, yet for certain singular reasons hardly deserves the name."[47] Phillips not only reiterates the conventional love story of his source, but his treatment splinters Mallock's novel into avant-garde musical scores (Phillips began his artistic career as a composer), art criticism, manifestos on poetics, biographical confessions, philosophical epigrams, political commentary, lyrical poems, economic theory, passages of German and French, and so on. Mallock's novel in turn claims to be constructed from an intergenre source text: "a rough and experimental copy, interspersed with raw materials, of which as yet [the author] had used part only."[48] Part book, part photo album, "not entirely a journal, and . . . not entirely [an] imaginary" novella, this "scrap-book" "collection of manuscripts" contains, among other things, "descriptions, conversations, verses, philosophical and literary reflections, and pieces of self-analysis."[49] In this "volume compiled so strangely," a "single thread of narrative . . . ran through the whole volume; but this was broken by pages after pages of letters, by scraps of poetry, and various other documents" which intervene in the hand of another author.[50] Phillips's own "narrative was broken in many places by the insertion of various documents" as well, creating an equally allusive text in "crude and fragmentary" form: full of "broken" and "wounded" language, "baffled and crippled sentences . . . abrupt transitions, and odd lapses of grammar" that the reader "will have to pore and puzzle over."[51] In neither the text from which Mallock's novel ostensibly derives nor the treated text in which it ends do these fragments form "a story in any literary sense; though they enable us, or rather force us, to construct one out of them for ourselves."[52] Moreover, as with Phillips's treatment, part of the interest *A Human Document* claims for itself follows from its status as a writing-through and the way in which an "authentic" and invariable documentary source text is worked around to create a fiction from within its fixed parameters, leaving "a singular record, not only on account of its contents, but of the manner in which it seemed to have been composed."[53] In fact, even the physical character of Mallock's "source," unlike the close-set type and trade stock of the 1892 *Human Document,* is replicated by Phillips's *Humument:* printed on "thick cartridge-paper," of "varied . . . appearance" and "with a liberal allowance of margin."[54] Phillips, that is, renders visible and literal what the novel purports to be born from, returning the simulacral text an origin it never really had.

With "words so strange / double-formed, and / phantasm" (Johnson), the treated text thus haunts the source from which it comes, even when it is undifferentiated and invisible within an untreated copy, just as the unseen portions of the source itself ghost a continually evoked presence even after the obliterations of its most radical treatment. "The ambiguity thus arising in the referent produces a relief development of the text and pertains, of course, to the latter's sedimentary depth."[55] Phillips's Toge, once again, is the perfect emblem of this constantly shifting dynamic of presence and absence; whatever his associations with loss and rupture, Toge is also an index of supplementarity. If not, by itself, a familiar English word, "toge" is the conventional transliteration of the common Russian word тоже: "also," "as well," "too."[56] Like most of the works discussed in this book, that "also" is the hallmark of the treated text's appropriation. Keeping both source and derivative simultaneously in view, and making visible the traces of that doubled presence, the treated text is less a parasite on its source than a pair of sights. This binocular vision is explicitly thematized in Johnson's *Radi Os,* where "Both / eyes, / At once" and "eyes in opposition" see what the "Divided / eye beheld:" "all things at one view." We should, by now, expect both the pun and the paradox: the blur of that double vision also leads to a "nonsight"; the same palimpsest that keeps both texts simultaneously in view also ensures the zones of their mutual illegibility. The paronomasia is already implicit in Smithson's descriptions of the nonsites; like his evacuated and viewless spaces without vanishing points, the enantiamorphic chamber, or the anti-spectacular mirrors of the displacements, the nonsites are brought "to a low level of perception" and constitute a "loss of focus."[57] The hemianoptics of the treated text is thematized by Johnson's visionary treatment of the blind Milton: "in the dark / to gaze / Undazzled / sight no obstacle."[58] Johnson's mysticism ultimately equates the eyes with the orbs of both moon and sun, but the "optic glass" of that moon becomes an "ecliptic," blinding the sun which in turn stares back at the reader like the light of the page through the horizontal lines of type: "the sun / Looks through the horizontal / behind the moon, / eclipse."[59] Indeed, like the paper ground of the treated text, that glare of the sun's light is both the prerequisite for vision and its risk, permitting the sight which cannot encompass it.[60] The eye is the nonsite of the sun.

Which may, in the end, have had nothing to do with the earthworks at Stonehenge. Despite the success with which IBM promoted the self-publicizing theory that the megaliths were an ancient "astronomical computer," sighting the sun through its motions like the pipes of Nancy Holt's *Sun Tunnels,* their purpose remains a mystery and point of contention among archaeologists.[61] By the same token, the connections I have suggested in this chapter should not eclipse the more obvious lineage of the treated text. Taking up the challenge of Tristan Tzara and Marcel Duchamp's dadaist provocations, Bob Cobbing, Brion Gysin, John Ashbery, and William Burroughs were all cutting up source texts in the 1950s. The force of those physical manipulations, combined with the randomizing procedures pioneered by Cage and Mac Low, proved a potent mix for the poetic imagination of the postwar Anglo-American avant-garde.[62] My intention has not been to ignore such evidence, but to insist on remembering—even at the risk of relying on a state of affairs that was not *in fact* the case—that there are always unrecorded nexuses, unacknowledged affiliations, and unspoken conversations nevertheless at echo "in the air."[63] And they operate like the blank page of the treated text, exerting a pressure despite their absence. Even if the "tone of the time" is lost to us, the whilom existence of that tone should not be forgotten. It is the secret language of this century's avant-garde, "la belle langue de mon siècle," and its message is always the same: the most abstract and philosophical poetry is never a case of mind over matter, but always an example of mined-over matter. Or as *A Humument* puts it: "a little white / opening out of / thought."[64]

For writing to be manifest in its truth (and not in its instrumentality), it
must be illegible.

—Roland Barthes

Read the blank.

—Edmond Jabès

7. The Aesthetics of Censorship

Techniques of Remembrance

As with so many of the works I have discussed, the textual excavations
of the treated page draw much of their interest and power from having appropriated and then manipulated a source text. While I have emphasized
the utopian aspirations of these tactics of "writing-through" and the constructive potential for the misuse of given structures, the spaces of erasure
that result from those manipulations can be quite dark. The affective power
of textual illegibility derives in part from its ability to simultaneously motivate and threaten the authority of both the text and its reader. In this
final chapter, I want to consider the intersection of that drive and danger
as they come together in the visual text of censorship.

The twin valences of "repression"—as both an exercise of authoritarian
power and a psychological mechanism—are neatly grafted in the self-
censoring tactics of Ken Campbell's 1989 artists' book *Father's Garden*.[1]
Like the treated pages we saw in the previous chapter, Campbell's book
implicitly identifies the ground of the page as a place of *soil:* a fertile surface to till, a clean space to stain, and a site to mark the gain and loss of a
psychological spoil. Bound in a neo-Secessionist cover of green reptile skin
overstamped with Klimt-like motifs, the book's text is set in generous and
luxuriantly proportioned margins. On many of the pages the text is further framed within a border so that it appears like nothing so much as the
bird's eye-view architectural plan for a medieval garden: the lines of text
ranked like planting rows in a *hortus inclusus*. In both the narrative and

geographic senses of the word, the work, in short, is plotted. The crop of this garden, however, is never rotated; each page reprints the same twenty-line poem. This poem emphasizes its verse genre with strongly accented iambic and trochaic feet arranged, with the occasional expected substitutions, in a mixture of pentameter and tetrameter lines. The language of the poem navigates between the Victorian bombast of lines such as "no waves outraged his railing walls" and a subtle play of puns and implicit lexical echoes; the unspoken words "keel" and "kneel," for instance, haunt Campbell's narrative of submission and nautical adventure as they ghost between the nexus of "feet" and "kill" and "knew." The result of these clashing styles is a poem simultaneously embarrassing in its bald proclamations of heavy-handed symbolism ("our father's juice flows everywhere") and deliciously supple and slippery in its cleverly indeterminate and enjambed syntax.

On its own terms, the poem itself would not seem to warrant its lavish presentation and the attentiveness with which its richly inked pages are printed. The apparatus of Campbell's artists' book is justified, however, by the way in which the poem is presented. Or rather, is not presented; to thicken the plot, as it were, only portions of the poem are visible on any given page. The entire book, in fact, might be read as an illustration of Freud's figure of the unconscious as a partially illegible text, and the cumulative impression of Campbell's scotomizing cancellations is that the text is too painful for the author to face in its entirety. On the first page, all of the lines are canceled, save for the eponymous opening words "Father's garden." The poem then emerges bit by bit over the course of the book, as the gaps in those overprinted cancellations shuffle unpredictably and non-sequentially from page to page. As the reader moves through the book, the obscuring geometric bars appear to move up and down the page, revealing and re-veiling lines with each turning. With "the poem silenced" in this way, "everything becomes suspense, fragmentary disposition with alternation and face-to-face, concurring in the total rhythm . . . in the blanks."[2] Indeed, the irregular pattern with which that scrim of overprinting shifts through *Father's Garden* adds a rhythm to the book as such, making each turning of a page a moment of revelation and repression. Moreover, because the slats of these blinds—or blinders—allow only a glimpse of discrete portions of the poem at a time, they obviate any gestalt apprehension of the poem as a whole, so that the poem's illegibilities necessitate its reconstruction in the reader's mind. As readers engage in those acts of covered and re-covered memory they approximate, to some degree, an analogous position to the poem's narrator, who negotiates the recollection of a psychologically fraught relationship with the Father. "I don't remember," the poem seems to protest, "I was *blacked out.*" This parallel between the emotions at once described and elicited by the poem is further underscored by the text's hedging hide-and-seek, which cultivates a play of readerly desire and frustration. Even those readers who might want to distance themselves from the poem's rather overwrought sentiment are implicated in the psychological drama of *Father's Garden,* as they find themselves — in the act of merely accessing the melodrama — complicitous with the very psychological mechanisms it so mawkishly displays. Readers must, in this garden, be constantly *en garde.*

If *Father's Garden* as a whole presents a visual analogue for a psychological mechanism, its censored pages, when taken individually, evoke the aesthetics of texts repressed by external, regulatory censorship. The history of censorship no doubt extends as far back as the history of writing itself. Plato, to take only one particularly famous example, would have the politically dangerous passages from Homer erased.[3] Even an account restricted to the censorship of modern or contemporary literature would lie well beyond the scope of this chapter, but I do want to recall that the look of the censor's pen has at least a cameo appearance in one of the founding documents of the very avant-garde tradition I have been tracing throughout this book. In the first issue of the vorticist journal *BLAST* (1914), Ezra Pound's poem "Fratres Minores" appeared with the first and final two lines blacked out with the hasty swipe of a marker:

████████████████████████████████

Certain poets here and in France
Still sigh over established and natural fact
Long since fully discussed by Ovid.
They howl. They complain in delicate and exhausted meters

████████████████████████████

Although it is hardly the sort of "masterly pornography" blessed by Pound and the other vorticists who signed the "Manifesto" that also appeared in the first issue of *BLAST,* the complete text of Pound's poem, for those who are curious, is easily available in the *Collected Early Poems.* The poem does not improve with the lines' elucidation. One assumes, however, that the last-minute revision of "Fratres Minores" was not made on aesthetic grounds. Bodley Head editor John Lane, who had witnessed the publishing scandals of the Yellow '90s firsthand, was presumably willing to take only so many risks with a new journal whose raison d'être was to offend sensibilities.

Even before the lines of "Fratres" were canceled, however, censorship was a noticeable part of the journal. In their "Manifesto" the vorticists invoke a rhetoric of violent silencing and threaten to "wring the neck" of their enemies.[4] Moreover, Pound's own contributions to *BLAST* begin with a discussion of censorship. "Salutation the Third," a tame version of the rant that would later expand to become the "hell cantos," denounces the de facto censorship implicit in the conventions of mainstream writing and publishing. Pound announces the fate of all the "obstructionist" and "gagged reviewers" of the establishment press: "a little black BOX contains them." That figure of the little black box conflates the image of a coffin (Pound mentions their "TOMB-STONES" two lines earlier) with the blocky cancellation that will contain his own words just a few pages later. Moreover, when "Salutation" ends in a particularly ugly instance of Pound's protofascism—"Here is the taste of my boot / caress it, lick off the blacking"—the authoritarianism that would command such an action is in fact near at hand: the blacking pen of the censor which will literally cover the poet's figurative tongue. With a distinct irony, "Salutation" anticipates the graphic editing of "Fratres," which in turn serves as the perfect illustration for the claims of the former. Even without the context of these explicit references, however, the three black lines over "Fratres Minores" mark an important moment of disjunction in the text of *BLAST.* As a whole, the journal is poorly printed and shoddily typeset. Nevertheless, the cancellation of the lines in Pound's poem is particularly hasty and so unevenly inked that much of the original text can still be made out. The imprecise, uneven, handwritten swerve of that marker stands out all the more against the geometric precision and hard-edged aesthetic of vorticist design, underscoring the distance between the bellicose bravado of their futurist-fueled blasting and the banal violence of even the most petty, actual censorship: a "vulgarity in revolt."[5] Serving as a check on the excesses of the vorticists' aggressive rhetoric by presenting an instance of actual oppositional aggression, the censorship of Pound's poem reminds the reader of the consequences that can follow when such rhetoric is put into practice.

I do not want to make too much of the cancellation of a few lines from a poem which—even by Pound's standards—is scarcely remarkable even in its vituperatude; far more extensive acts of censorship and editing have certainly taken place, even within Pound's own oeuvre, and to greater effect. Nor is "Fratres Minores" interesting merely as an unintended instance of Pound's recognition, as we saw in chapter 5, that the most fragmented texts can be quite poetic. Instead, I want to recall the censorship of "Fratres Minores" because it is an instance of censorship made legible, and a moment in which it enters the graphic record of twentieth-century poetry. The visual apparatus of censorship would return when Duchamp's wartime postcard to André Breton left the genre of "correspondence" and entered that of "poetry" with its publication in *View* in 1941. Duchamp's missive was constructed by writing between and canceling certain preprinted words on one of the official cards supplied by the Axis occupation forces in France. Presenting interpolated civilian writers with a template, the card forced correspondents to write-through the found text of a suggested, and rather bleak vocabulary. For example, after a space for supplying the subject of the sentence, one of the lines concludes: "légèrement, gravement, malade, blessé [lightly, seriously, ill, wounded]." The instructions on the postcard read:

> Après avoir complété cette carte strictement réservée à la correspondance d'ordre familial, biffer les indications inutiles. — Ne rien écrire en dehors des lignes.
> ATTENTION. — Toute carte dont le libelié ne sera pas uniquement d'ordre familial ne sera pas acheminée set sera probablement détruite.

> *After having completed this card which is strictly limited to correspondence of a personal nature, delete unnecessary indications. — Write nothing outside of the lines.*
> *NOTICE. — Any card whose text is not exclusively of a personal nature will not be forwarded and will probably be destroyed.*

In the second decade of the twentieth century, Duchamp had created a series of texts of a "personal," if not hermetic "nature" through precisely the sort of deletions and strategic illegibilities suggested by the card: replacing each instance of the definite article with an asterisk in the poem "The," substituting periods for letters in the punning and multilingual inscription on "With Hidden Noise," and *détourning* the advertising copy of a Sapolin Enamel advertisement to create the title and caption of "Apolinère Enameled." With the "treated text" of his 1939 poem "SURcenSURE," Duchamp explicitly aligns such manipulation with censorship (*censure*). Like a page from Ronald Johnson's *Tablets,* most of the text of "SURcen-

SURE" has been replaced by ellipses, leaving only discrete and discontinuous phrases to remain legible. With its spoof of commercial language and its references to Jarry, Duchamp's essay "on censorship" is characteristically good humored, but those same references also recall the dictatorship of Ubu Roi, and the piece's title, like the occupation government's threat to destroy letters, hints at the serious stakes of his tactics of *détournement*.

As we saw in chapter 1, *détournement*, by definition, instigates a dialogue where authority would rather speak alone. But authority also knows how to hold up its end of a conversation, and it does so with what is perhaps the most familiar strategy of nonliterary illegibility: text canceled by a censor. And if the commonplaces about censorship are all true—that it merely draws attention to what it would seek to repress, that it spurs rather than quiets the prurient interest—its mechanisms, however predictable, can still be interesting and instructive.

Michael Camille, in a discussion of censorship and obscenity in medieval manuscripts, speculates that the erasures and obfuscations of censorship might best be seen as a version of gloss: accreted commentary that adds to the meanings of a text even as it takes away, quite literally, from its surface.[6] Not only do such tactics tend to draw attention to what they have censored, but—as the poets and artists discussed in the previous chapters have repeatedly shown—even the most illegible marks are positive contributions to the content of a text. Rather than decrease the signifying ability of the text by making portions of the print illegible, such erasures merely replace one set of signs with another, equally significant set. Indeed, those interventions actually increase the information carried by the text because they mark the absence of an anterior work which they can never completely silence or obliterate. "Censorship," as Dirk Hohnsträter writes, "is a technique of remembrance."[7] The censor's inability to intervene in a text without augmenting it, without increasing its semantic content, is another instance of what Bataille would recognize as a general economy. In the mathematics of the text there is no subtraction, and all the additions expand geometrically. "Subtraction," in this textual calculation, "leaves a mark of erasure, a *remainder* which is added to the subsequent text and which cannot be completely summed up within it."[8] Leaving a trace of the text that has been replaced—the shadowy outline of its body, the faint echo of its words, all those ghosts which haunt the space of their violent removal—censoring marks keep open a space in which the work cleaves between two moments of composition, and they establish a second system of signification, a competing semiotic regime, within the field of the text.

The erasures and cancellations of a censored text, in short, operate with the logic of a scar.

But scars, of course, can be quite beautiful, and the marks of the censor can always be aestheticized.[9] In the 1970s, for instance, the Italian visual poet Emilio Isgró created a series of *cancellature,* in which each word in a source text is written over by hand with a thick marker, so that entire books, including a complete edition of the *Enciclopedia Italiana,* are rendered almost completely illegible. Occasionally, a few words remain readable. For reasons discussed in chapter 3, those words often carry a self-referential charge, as when "baratro [abyss]" and "buco [hole]" appear on an otherwise overwritten page. Such moments of legibility, however, are not the focus of Isgró's treated texts, which at times seem to be the result of the destructive project proposed by the professors from the school of languages in Swift's Lagoda Academy: "a scheme for entirely abolishing all words whatsoever."[10] Indeed, much of the interest of his cancellations comes from the tension between his meticulous and obsessive process of methodically covering word after word, and the casual irregularity of the individual, hastily inked marks. The end result of these cancellations is visually similar to Man Ray's "Lautgedicht."

Unlike Man Ray's poem, however, the focus of attention of Isgró's *poesia cancellata* is extended from the length of a lyric to the level of the book as a whole; the scope of his treatments, sometimes sustained for hundreds of pages, shifts the emphasis from the visual structure of verse to the forms that organize individual units, like a single poem, within the architecture of a book. The technique of cancellation emphasizes the visual structure of the source by reducing it to an almost schematic form in which the elements of the codex and its design supplant the words to which they are usually thought to be subservient. After Isgró's treatment, the layout of the original document and its generic conventions can be read with a new clarity: the structuring power of headers and columns, the placement of page numbers and titles, the proportions of text blocks to margins and founts to leading, and the many subtle rhythms of paragraph, sentence, and word length. The elegance and visual ordering of these layouts and the cultured tradition of book design to which they belong contrasts with the *arte povera* aesthetic of Isgró's practice. Requiring only a pen and a found text, *i cancellature* were conceived of as part of a democratic poetics that would realize Lautréamont's dream of a poetry "made by all." Indeed, some of the cancellations were staged as happenings in which an audience was provided with markers and books and invited to compose along with Isgró.

"La poesia," as he announced in the title of a catalogue essay, "è facile farla e appartiene al popolo [poetry is easy to make and belongs to everyone]."

Moreover, the populism of Isgró's egalitarian process is given an added political edge by the sources he has chosen to cancel: encyclopedias and atlases. Not only do these works present themselves with all the authority of references—texts which one consults and defers to—but they are also emblems of the power consolidated around institutions of specialized knowledge. Although their assumptions are often tacit, such works implicitly contain traces of the ideologies of the commercial and national interests that underwrote their creation. By submitting such works to cancellation, Isgró symbolically reopens the space of authoritative discourse on its own ground and suggests that the words of its apodictic monologue might be replaced, or even abandoned. The black forms on Isgró's canceled pages are spaces in which readers can imagine new possibilities. Moreover, the aesthetics of his particular tactic appropriates the power of censorship, both as it inheres implicitly in any regulation and standardization of knowledge and also as it is at times explicitly exercised by institutional powers. If censorship is essentially propaganda by other means, Isgró's *cancellature* short-circuits the equation by preemptively censoring the censor.

"Such an operation thus appears contradictory, and the same is true of the interest one takes in it."[11] The "Inside Intelligence" issue of the quarterly *Granta* is a case in point. In 1988, after Anthony Cavendish circulated a few hundred privately printed copies of a memoir of his life in the British secret service, the British government—in the immediate wake of its futile and stubborn attempts to stop the publication of Peter Wright's *Spycatcher*—sought an injunction against the further publication of Cavendish's book. After a series of rulings, serials in the United Kingdom were permitted to print those extracts that were unrelated to the secret service, and the American magazine *Harper's* published some of the disputed passages, although its distribution in the United Kingdom was ostensibly prohibited. *Granta,* in both its North American and British editions, published a bowdlerized selection of material that the British government had previously approved, prefacing it with an aggrandizing and rather self-righteous editorial commensurate with Cavendish's own posturing about the gentlemanly and honorable reasons for publishing his book.[12] In addition, *Granta* dressed up its complicitous and compliant text with a garishly melodramatic layout. Occasional words and phrases, presumably those objected to by the government, are replaced by a studied handwritten scribble, underscoring the act of intervention in the text. Additionally, the layout as a whole presents a simulacrum of censorship: several of the pages have their text blocks framed by deliberately awkward, ugly, and exaggerated margins of thick-set black, and the text as a whole is punctuated with similarly blacked-out blocks replacing the text field altogether, or framing only the single word "censored," which recurs on several pages luridly printed in a 48-point bold sanserif display face.

The protest of these pages, and their advertisement of outrage, are of course well taken, but their ostentatious fields of black do not so much obscure Cavendish's secrets as they camouflage and distract from the fact of *Granta*'s acquiescence—rather than any real defiance—to the British censors. Moreover, the design and layout corroborate and supplement the intrigue of a work whose interest hinges on its status as a true account that will reveal "secrets" of the author's service. Ultimately, the inventiveness of the layout is far more interesting than even the unexpurgated text, which was eventually published in 1990, following a series of Law Lords appeals. Publicity over the *Spycatcher* case helped turn that book into a best-seller, and in *Granta*'s treatment of "Inside Intelligence," the graphic announcement of legal actions, or what amounts to the restaged visual display of legislation, works essentially as packaging and marketing hype, piquing interest in an otherwise wholly unremarkable work.

To quote a passage as evidence of the book's banality would be uncharitable and gratuitous, but the *Granta* publication reminds readers of the degree to which such selective censorship itself operates at the most banal level of the text: reference. Regardless of their ultimate effectiveness, those tactics familiar from the editors of mass media—silencing certain words with an electric beep, or replacing the letters of a supposedly objectionable word with dashes—is symptomatic of a theoretically unsophisticated relation to a language. Ignoring form entirely, such editing reifies the signified and treats it as an uncontextualized fetish. Perhaps a more sophisticated strategy of censorship would result in the type of work we saw in the previous chapter, or in the sort of vandal *détournements* recorded in chapter 1. Indeed, at the level of their tactics, the censor and the Situationist are indistinguishable; what differentiates censorship, as such, is the position of power from which it operates. But one should be vigilant to remember that a *détournement* can itself always be détourned.

That potential for a censor's productive, rather than restrictive, intervention is precisely the focus of *Gems: A Censored Anthology*, Robert "Bob" (Carleton) Brown's send-up of the logic of censorship.[13] Brown's book includes the gems of official verse culture and popular children's culture—romantic lyrics, Victorian chestnuts, and Mother Goose nursery rhymes—with portions of their text selectively canceled, so that familiar and innocuous phrases are replaced with suggestive innuendo. In general, Brown's clever technique produces surprisingly bland results; the poems in *Gems* are less transgressions than illustrations of the degree to which censorship combines outrage with banality. After Brown's treatment, for instance, Marlowe's Passionate Shepherd proclaims:

> Come live with me and be my love,
> And we will all the pleasures prove
> That ▮▮ and ▮▮▮▮, ▮▮▮▮ and ▮▮▮▮,
> And all the craggy ▮▮▮▮▮ yield.

If there is a certain endearing charm to the unembarrassed silliness of Brown's schoolboy graffiti and the clear delight he takes in these puerile winks and nudges, no reader should be surprised that the language of Marlowe's poem, the centerpiece of a courtly tradition of pastoral lyric, is fraught with erotic undertones and sexual symbolism. But Brown's cancellations could on occasion be inspired, and in the case of the Passionate Shepherd, his stroke of genius comes, as it were, in the end:

> There will we sit upon the rocks
> And see the shepherds ▮▮▮▮▮ their flocks.

"Pleasure in poetry," as Brown himself notes, "comes largely from reading between the lines." As we have seen again and again, all of those spaces between—whether intended or the result of erasures and cancellations—are instances of what we might term "veiling": a simultaneous concealment and revelation. Their concealments are obvious, but we need to remember that such blanks are revelations about hidden aspects of the rest of the text, which remains illuminated in a new legibility around their lacunae.

The effect is commonplace enough, and one we recognize from the logic of the schoolyard joke, but we might consider for a moment why we assume a certain kind of content when we read between the lines of Brown's censored poems; why, for instance, his erasures carry an erotic charge rather than suggesting material with a political valence, say. Like the schoolyard or sitcom innuendo, the effect of Brown's gems depends on the success of a formal logical fallacy. Because material with a sexual or scatological theme is so often censored in some way—with evasion, elision, indirection, gesture, or outright repression replacing explicit denotation with allusive and elusive connotations—the impulse is to infer that those sorts of illegibilities mark sexual or scatological content when they appear in other contexts as well.

Brown was one of the twentieth century's most vocal champions of visual poetry, and he strove for "a visual Literary Language sharply separated from the Speaking Tongue" because "literature," as Brown repeatedly insisted, "is essentially Optical———not Vocal."[14] Accordingly, his distinctively past-oral graphic cancellations are immediately recognizable. His *détourned* nursery rhymes and Mother Goose (liver) *epater* do, however, have a precedent, which, although it comes from a quite different technique, is also fully grounded in a visual poetics. In the second number of his dada 'zine *Merz* (1923), Kurt Schwitters published "PPPPPPPPP," a "pornographic i poem" which takes as its source "an innocuous poem in a children's picture book." Anticipating the textual folds and cuts of Burroughs and Gysin, Schwitters abbreviates the original poem by cutting vertically into its quatrain, dividing the poem in half:

P P P P P P P PP

pornographisches **i**—Gedicht

Die Zie **l**

Diese Mech ist **l**

Lieb und friedlich **l**

Und sie wird sich **l**

Mit den Hörnern **l**

Der Strich zeigt, wo ich das harmlose Gedichtchen aus
einem Kinderbilderbuch durchgeschnitten habe, der Länge
nach. Aus der Ziege ist so die Zie geworden.

Und sie wird sich **l** nicht erboßen,

Mit den Hörnern **l** Euch ze Stoßen.

P P P P P P P P

p o r n o g r a p h i c **i**—p o e m

The go **l**

Its bleating is **l**

Sweet & peaceful **l**

And it will not **l**

With its horns **l**

The line indicates where I cut lengthwise through
an innocuous poem from a children's picture book. From
the goat came a go.

And it will not **I** become provoked
With its horns **I** to shove & poke.

I have included the entire text, with its explanation of poetic technique, because the specifics of the poem's composition seem to come less from a typical dadaist mockery of the domesticated propriety of bourgeois ideology exemplified by the children's picture book, or even from a more subtle and pointed critique of the authority inherent in the pedagogy of the alphabet book from which this poem probably came (with "ziege" illustrating the final entry), than from the design aesthetic of Bauhaus typography. With its bold segmenting line intersecting an asymmetrical, constructivist layout, and the clean-edged tensions of interruption and continuation produced by the collage-like layering of geometrical blocks of text and white space, "PPPPPPPPP" echoes many of the designs from Schwitters and other contemporaneous practitioners of the new typography.

In addition to its visual affinities with other aspects of Schwitters's oeuvre from the 1920s, "PPPPPPPPP" also rhymes with his overall stylistic interests. Like his collages, much of Schwitters's poetry consists of found or appropriated material modified from a common public source; his poems frequently rewrite the language of commercial advertising and government proclamation to underscore the absurdity and banality of the originals—or perhaps to suggest the value of a genuinely nonsensical dadaist alternative. "Banalities," in fact, figures in the titles of several of Schwitters's poems, and in the case of "PPPPPPPPP," the banality is once again found not so much in the "lieb und friedlich" kindergarten verse of its source as in the mechanisms of censorship itself. The product of Schwitters's writing-through is, like most of Brown's gems, hardly exceptional. One might, with sufficient effort and imagination, pair the historical association of the goat with lechery and the iconography of horns to construct a suggestive narrative, but if the pornographic nature of Schwitters's "i poem" is not immediately evident, that disjunction between title and text may well be the point. As with Brown's gems, the poem is less the creation of an erotic text than a reminder that without censorship, there is no pornography.

The Critical Obscene

I have been concerned, throughout this book, with how we read works that are quite literally illegible, but the works I have focused on have themselves been largely unreadable in a more figurative sense as well. That I am able to read these works at all—*as poetry*—is not a historical accident. Equally contingent are all of the particular interpretations I have proposed. For example, regardless of its persuasiveness, the ability to seriously advance a reading of "PPPPPPPPP" as an avant-garde poetic composition rather than having it remain sheer nonsense should not seem natural, or be taken for granted. The complex mechanisms which make a work generically legible are neither obvious nor direct, but their operation is worth considering even if it cannot be explicitly traced—even if its processes remain, to some degree, entirely illegible.

Perhaps the most famous artistic work to evoke the chillingly beautiful aesthetics of censorship is Marcel Broodthaers's "edition" of Stéphane Mallarmé's *Un coup de dés* ("A Throw of the Dice"), to which the conceptual artist adds the subtitle "(image)." Broodthaers replaces the lines of Mallarmé's poem with black rectangular blocks positioned and sized according to the instructions Mallarmé left for the layout and font of his poem. The result is a geometric, constructivist design in which the calm expanse of Mallarmé's oversized page is interrupted by the hard-edged precision of fixed forms that punctuate it. With this thorough illegibility, Broodthaers thus establishes what Jacques Derrida would call "a text, that is, a readability without a signified."[15] Like the mocked-up pages of commercial layouts or the sketches Mallarmé made in preparation for the realization of his late work, *(image)* emphasizes the spatial dimensions of language while eliminating its reference. With one variable removed, the effects of another can be more easily considered, and *(image)* is certainly not without interest for readers of Mallarmé's poetry. But as with the idiosyncratic renditions of verse in Peter Walkden Fogg's late eighteenth-century grammatical treatise *Elementa Anglicana,* in which schematic figures of straight lines replace sequences of words so that the reader can better analyze a poem's phrasal, rather than syllabic, metrics, it would not be adequate to consider Broodthaers's diagrammatic measurement as a mere reduction. Rather, *(image)* is more a logical extension of Mallarmé's poetics, recognizing not just the obvious fact that *Un coup de dés* is a visually marked poem with a uniquely significant layout, but that Mallarmé's work was predicated—even in its most transcendently spiritual aspirations—on the materiality of the letter.

Broodthaers produced at least two, quite different versions of *(image)*. In one, the conventionally bound pages are made of transparent paper, so that the black rectangles of print appear to float through the depth of the book, their edges increasingly softened with each layer of paper scrim. In contradistinction, the other version of *(image)* eliminates, rather than underscores, those aspects of the book, as such, that are literally and conceptually the center of Mallarmé's last projects: the signatures and dimensions of the codex. This edition replaces the white, pliable, transparent pages of the bound book with a series of rigid aluminum plates sized as openings and with no indication of the bookbinding's center fold. In both versions, *(image)* comments with perceptive critical acuity on the conceptual concerns of *Un coup de dés,* and they are able to access that critical reading by recognizing, as Ernest Fraenkel has put it, that "un *texte plastique* reste caché dans les couches extraconscientes du psychisme du poète, parallèle au *texte verbal* du poème [a *plastic text* remains hidden in the extraconscious layers of the psychism of the poet, parallel to the *verbal text* of the poem]."[16] Fraenkel himself, in fact, produced a version of *Un coup de dés* that also replaces Mallarmé's words with black shapes. However, unlike the cool, geometric clinicism of *(image),* which emphasizes the arrangement of lines as distinct units on the field of the page, Fraenkel links each line; he impressionistically suggests Mallarmé's verse with thickly blotted forms made by never lifting his pen from the page. Fraenkel's erratic handwritten scrawl gives the impression of a readout from a machine set up to record the eye's scan, linger, and return sweep while reading Mallarmé's poem. However, because it forgoes the precision with which Mallarmé distributed fonts through *Un coup de dés,* or the dimension of the book as a poetic unit in itself, Fraenkel's version of the poem fails to retain the way in which its landmark source actually redirects and disrupts the linear scanning of the reader's eye. As Mallarmé wrote in "The Book: A Spiritual Instrument": "Let us have no more of those successive, incessant, back and forth motions of our eyes, tracking from one line to the next and beginning all over again."[17] Whatever its shortcomings as a critical reading of its source text, Fraenkel's work, like Broodthaers's *(image),* captures the visual excitement of *Un coup de dés.*

Although it would of course be inaccurate to reify it as some sort of singular originary moment, Mallarmé's book did in many ways inaugurate and help to instigate a century in which readers and writers would become increasingly attuned to visual poetics. The tradition of visual poetry which followed in the wake of *Un coup de dés* has led by indirect and circuitous routes, and joined along the way with the tributaries of other traditions and tendencies, to a moment in which we can now read a range of visually marked works from historically more prosaic genres *as poetry*—and in which we can now in fact return to Mallarmé and actually read portions of his work for the first time. Although I am speaking of a general trend in generic expansion, one can look specifically to Jerome Rothenberg and Pierre Joris's *Poems for the Millennium* for evidence of this paradigm shift. Rothenberg and Joris's monumental 1995 anthology opens, quite deliberately, with *Un coup de dés* as the initial poem in the section "A First Gallery." Their book, however, displaces and diffuses that inaugural move by including a section of "Forerunners," which itself concludes with a selection from Mallarmé's writing following the composition of *Un coup de dés*. This simultaneously anterior and subsequent text is drawn not from a conventionally poetic text, however, but from Mallarmé's manuscript notes toward his final unfinished project *Le livre*. These notes are filled less with drafts of poems, as such, than with numerical calculations, vocabulary lists, abbreviated schemata, and purely graphic sketches that seem to anticipate the sort of visual renditions that Broodthaers or Fraenkel might have made of the poems they would presumably have become. Rothenberg and Joris not only translate their selections from *Le livre* from French into English, but also translate from the conventions of the textual edition of Mallarmé's manuscripts into a visual approximation of how the original page appears. The entire text, the first page of the manuscript as it was assembled by Jacques Scherer, is, appropriately enough, canceled. As Scherer notes, "tous les mots de ce feuillet sont biffés [all the words on this sheet are crossed out]":

     finir

       conscience

          Et peines +

                +

             rue

        +

      enfance

     double

     leur

     foule +

        +   un—crime—égout

or in Joris's translation:

~~end~~

  ~~conscience~~

    ~~And sorrows~~ +

        +

    ~~street~~

   +

~~childhood~~

~~double~~

~~their~~

~~crowd~~ +

  +   ~~a crime sewer~~

The temporal short-circuiting of the anthology's structure, which makes this newly contextualized text a forerunner to the work that in fact predates it, is indicative of the strangely anticipatory prolepsis by which the innovations of Mallarmé's visual prosody have led, a century later, to a moment in which we can return to Mallarmé's work with a new poetic vision that permits us to read what he himself, perhaps, could never have read in his own writing. "Le livre," as another page from *Le livre* reads, "supprime [the book deletes, suppresses, censors]."[18]

This moment of newly permissive reading is perhaps best exemplified by the work of Susan Howe, whose visual poetics I examined in chapter 2 and which I want to recall here. Howe's work is symptomatic of the poetic climate, which it has also furthered, in which a page from Mallarmé's manuscript notes can appear as a full-fledged poem. Following in the tradition opened by Pound's groundbreaking realization that the visual specifics of the historical record could be incorporated as poetic material, Howe's visual attention has increasingly turned toward manuscript pages and textual editions to discover a rich poetry within the most minute particulars of their visual text. The first line of her "Scattering as Behavior toward Risk," for instance, quotes a line from a specialized textual edition of *Billy Budd:*

> "on a [p<suddenly . . . an a> was shot thro with a dyed—<dyed—>a soft]"[19]

The line itself is quite beautiful and, as Peter Quartermain has shown in a masterful explication, rich with meaning. Without pursuing a further close reading, or detailing the specifics of Howe's other citations from various critical and textual editions, I want to note that in its original context, this line's strange sequence of brackets and arrows and ellipses are diacritical markings, each of which serves an instrumental role in the conventions of the text constructed by Harrison Hayford and Merton Sealts in their 1962 "genetic text" edition of Melville's "inside narrative." Within the genetic text, those diacritics encode the illegibilities, cancellations, and erasures of Melville's various manuscripts and editions in a synthetic scholarly edition of *Billy Budd* that is intended neither for casual nor poetic reading.

Appropriating and misusing the supposedly legible decipherments of the genetic text, Howe opens the unreadable aspects of that new text — the mysterious interruptions and disruptions of its brackets and indices — to a new poetic legibility. Howe is not alone in employing this tactic, and she has already influenced a number of writers, such as Andrew Mossin, who has written-through the facsimile edition of the notebooks of William Blake edited by David Erdman to produce the chapbook *From Blake's Notebook*. The coincidental compositional methods of these books is not their only interest, and one might pursue productive readings of these texts in their own right and on their own terms, but for now I merely want to propose that the return to specialized, professional, critical editions by these poets is not accidental. Such editions are exaggerated and clearly marked instances of what is always the case in literary studies: an acceptance and manipulation of the unreadable. The facsimiles, transcriptions, and notations of critical textual editions make legible the illegibility at the heart of the traditional literary scholarship with which we are all familiar. Even the most partisan advocates of a conventional literature and conservative literary studies — those openly opposed to the poetics of Howe, much less that of Cage — traffic in appropriation and illegibility, and they take as their typical practice a kind of writing-through. Appropriating a source text to advance its argument, this scholarly mode then renders that source largely illegible, writing between selected quotations, which it highlights even as others are erased. The very book that you are now reading, in fact, has all along been engaging in practices analogous — at a certain remove — to those it was discussing.

In the final analysis, however, that remove is too distant to excuse the legibility of this book, and too close an alignment with the radical practices I have catalogued would be disingenuous. At most, I have been able to indicate a space which I have myself been unable, or unwilling, to occupy. But the lapse of a particular practice should not detract from the value of the theory which it fails to live up to, and I want to underscore the stakes that mark the borders of the textual practices I have not crossed. Nor, given this project, could have crossed. The very act of recognizing moments of illegibility cancels their status as such; reading the illegible nullifies its own account in the precise moment of its construction and obliterates the very object it would claim to have identified, creating a new space of erasure which cannot itself be read. In that moment of singularity the unreadable disappears within its own legibility, and that legibility simultaneously effaces the text it would seem to read. Those singular moments, as I hope to have shown throughout this book, mark sites of intersection between organizations of power and authority, including their resistance to, and permission of, the authority of their own critical description. Whether they constitute openings and invitations, or blockages and deferrals, these sites are orifices and scars on the surface of the textual body, marking both the histories and the possible futures for conflicting and competing and collaborating semantic interests. Whatever the value of the claims I have made in this book through particular readings and arguments, the mere fact of that hermeneutic activity, even in the necessary absence of the state it valorizes with its betrayal, should suggest an ethics of the illegible and remind us that the unreadable text is a temporary autonomous zone: one which refuses the permanence of its own constitution, and which calls on its readers to account for the semantic drives that they cannot, in the end, resist—and for which we must learn, as readers, to take responsibility.

Notes

Introduction

1. University of California at Berkeley, Graduate Division, "Guidelines for Submitting a Doctoral Dissertation or a Master's Thesis" (N.p.: November 1997), 10.

2. Ibid., 6, 10.

3. Ibid., 6.

4. Chapter 3 will examine the attendant ideologies and political alignments exhibited by the university "Guidelines," but it is worth noting here that their formal concerns are a manifestation of the pedagogical "intolerable" explicated by Jacques Derrida, who quite rightly accuses the university: "What this institution cannot bear, is for anyone to tamper with language . . . . It can bear more readily the most apparently revolutionary ideological sorts of 'content,' if only that content does not touch the borders of language and all of the juridico-political contracts that it guarantees" (Jacques Derrida, "Living On: Borderlines," trans. James Hulbert, in *Deconstruction and Criticism* [New York: Seabury, 1979], 95).

5. Robert Smithson, *Robert Smithson: The Collected Writings,* ed. Jack Flam (Berkeley: University of California Press, 1996), 107.

6. Gertrude Stein, *The Geographical History of America, or The Relation of Human Nature to the Human Mind* (New York: Random House, 1936), 155.

7. Smithson, *Collected Writings,* 19.

8. Although they have not actually served as models, related strategies of reading can be found in Nicolas Abraham and Maria Torok, *Cryptonomie: Le verbier de l'homme aux loups* (Paris: Éditions Aubier Flammarion, 1976); Tom Conley, *The Graphic Unconscious in Early Modern French Writing* (Cambridge: Cambridge University Press, 1992); Jacques Derrida, *Glas* (Paris: Galilée, 1974) and *Signéponge* (New York: Columbia University Press, 1984); those notebooks of Ferdinand de Saussure collected by Jean Starobinski in *Les mots sous les mots* (Paris: Éditions Gallimard, 1971); and Garrett Stewart, *Reading Voices: Literature and the Phonotext* (Berkeley: University of California Press, 1990) — not to mention the poetic examples of bp nichol, Francis Ponge, Gertrude Stein, and many others. Nonacademic writers, in fact, have more often than not served as my models; the operations of a radical formalism are analogous to filling prescriptions at Rimbaud's pharmacy, or playing craps with Max Jacob (even though you know he's using dice loaded and on loan from Mallarmé), or consulting a dictionary compiled by Jean-Pierre Brisset and Louis Wolfson — then alphabetized by Raymond Roussel and indexed by Unica Zürn.

9. Jan Tschichold, *The New Typography,* trans. Rauri McLean (Berkeley: University of California Press, 1995), 74.

10. Ibid., 73.

11. James Mosley, "The Nymph and the Grot: the revival of the sanserif letter," *Typographica* 12 (1965): 2. Mosley summarizes the historical bridge between these two revivals: "It would seem that the sanserif letter in use today originated in England at the end of the eighteenth century among a small group of men with classical tastes to whom its associations and rational structure were as attractive as the same qualities of the Imperial Roman letter had been in the fifteenth century . . . . The sanserif might well have remained an antiquarian curiosity if the English signwriters and typefounders had not exploited it for their own purposes with a complete disregard for classical propriety, and thus preserved it for its twentieth-century career" (19). Mosley does not pursue that career, and I would want to add that a vital strut in that bridge between the two revivals (at least in the Anglo-American context) was the adoption of sanserif by Edward Johnston for the enamel signs of the London Underground, which brought together the sign painters' lettering with the connotations of modern technological functionalism.

12. Ihab Hassan, "The Culture of Postmodernism," *Theory, Culture, and Society* 2, no. 3:123–24.

13. Quoted in Julia Kristeva, *Revolution in Poetic Language,* trans. Margaret Waller (New York: Columbia University Press, 1984), 256.

14. Tony Lopez, *False Memory* (Great Barrington: The Figures, 1996), n.p.

15. Sigmund Freud, *The Standard Edition of the Complete Psychological Works of Sigmund Freud,* ed. James Strachey, vol. 23 (London: Hogarth, 1959), 236.

16. John S. Weitzer, "The Partial Veto," *Marquette Law Review* 76 (spring 1993): 626–27.

17. For the text of the decision, see State ex. rel. *Wisconsin Senate* v. *Thompson,* 144 Wis. 2d 429, 437, 424, N.W.2d 385, 388 (1988). In his dissent to the ruling that initially permitted striking individual letters, Justice Bablitch objected that such procedures could create works that "strained the English language beyond the breaking point" (at 400). Justice Bablitch seems to remember his Eliot, more or less ("Words strain, / Crack and sometimes break"), but one can only speculate on the force that one proper education in the avant-garde might have had on the balance of power in Wisconsin.

18. Derrida, "Living On: Border Lines," 80.

19. Ludwig Wittgenstein, *Philosophical Investigations: The English Text of the Third Edition,* trans. G. E. M. Anscombe (New York: Macmillan, n.d.), §198.

Chapter I

1. Gilles Deleuze and Félix Guattari, *Capitalisme et schizophrenie* (Paris: Éditions de Minuit, 1972/1980); translated by Brian Massumi as *A Thousand Plateaus* (Minneapolis: University of Minnesota Press, 1987), 213.

2. Ibid., 222.

3. Bruce Andrews offers a more thorough criticism when he suggests that such readings not only miss the point, but actually entrench the status quo: "When everything is framed in terms of efficacy, the work that gets promoted as efficacious is work that simply, to me, reinforces the very blindnesses that I think are central to the way the system holds itself together" (*Paradise and Method: Poetics and Praxis* [Evanston: Northwestern University Press, 1996], 63–64; cf. seq.). I elaborate the nature of those blindnesses below.

4. Jed Rasula, "The Politics of, the Politics in," in *Politics and Poetic Value,* ed. Robert von Hallberg (Chicago: University of Chicago Press, 1987), 317.

5. Andrews, *Paradise,* 50. In response to Marjorie Perloff's question—which might have been asked of my own project here—"If language is . . . denied its 'transparency,' how will 'social dialogue' take place?", Andrews replied: " 'Social dialogue' suggests, then, not a direct or unmediated response to social referents (which too often in its 'straightforward' or 'literal' mentioning takes for granted the apparatus of reference). Instead, it intimates a dialogue *with* the social, with a less-than-positive totality, and with the way it is produced and negotiated, with its (changing) principles of order and organization" (*Paradise,* 81).

6. Andrews, *Paradise,* 51.

7. Arthur Rimbaud, *Une saison en enfer/Les illuminations* (London: Oxford University Press, 1973), 62.

8. For an account of the political climate of the Left in France at the time, see Richard Gombin, "French Leftism," *Journal of Contemporary History* 7 (1972): 27–50. For a related, though very different movement outside of France, consider the Dutch Provo group. I discuss Georges Bataille's influence on later theorists in chapter 4; his significance can quite simply not be underestimated.

9. Despite their denials, the 'pataphysical influence on the Situationists is clear, as lines such as "Il n'y a pas problèmes il ny'a que des solutions" attest (*Les lèvres nues,* no. 4 [January 1955]).

10. Jorn's brother Nash would later split from the IS to form a "Situationist Bauhaus," centered at Drakagygget and publishing an eponymous journal; the group was most famous for claiming to have decapitated the little mermaid statue in Copenhagen harbour. (One can only fantasize about what revisions the Situationist Bauhaus would have made to the recent Disney film *The Little Mermaid.*) Debord was sufficiently riled by the defection to coin the term *Nashistouse,* glossing it merely as "vulgar." With a crystalline ferocity, Debord raises the insult to the level of a literary genre, rendering imprecations with a brilliance that shames the meager vulgarities of *BLAST* by comparison.

For introductory information on the lettrists, see Stephen Foster, ed., *Lettrism: Into the Present,* a special issue of *Visible Language* (17, no.3).

11. The exact role of the IS in the streets of Paris that summer is contested, although the Situationists' formulation of anarchist concepts, at the very least, played an undeniable role in the course of events. In 1963 Debord prophesied:

"nous n'organisons que le détonateur [we are merely setting the detonator]" (I.S. 8:28). Whatever the facts behind the competing (though equally mythic) accounts, the occupation of the Sorbonne and the nationwide, ten million-strong, wildcat general strike were in perfect accord with IS doctrine; 1968, in short, was a Situationist revolution regardless of responsibility or intent.

12. Jonathan Crary argues against this assessment, claiming that we have effectively passed into an age in which new networks of power have eclipsed those of the spectacle both structurally and qualitatively. Where Crary sees eclipse I discern only an abstracted entrenchment, though I do not intend to pursue the issue here, and my registration of difference should not distract from Crary's excellent concluding analysis of physiological resistance and breakdown. See Jonathan Crary, "Eclipse of the Spectacle," in *Art After Modernism: Rethinking Representation,* ed. Brian Wallis (New York: Museum of Contemporary Art, 1984), 283–94.

13. Guy-Ernest Debord and Asger Jorn, *Mémoires* (Paris: Internationale Situationniste, 1959), n.p.; facsimile edition by Les Belles Lettres (Paris, 1993).

14. Jean Baudrillard, *Pour une critique de l'économie politique du signe* (Paris: Gallimard, 1972), 199, 163.

15. Guy-Ernest Debord, *La société du spectacle* (Paris: Buchet-Chastel, 1967); translated by Donald Nicholson-Smith as *The Society of the Spectacle* (New York: Zone Books, 1994), 71/35. Nicholson-Smith's once samizdat translation of *La société du spectacle* is now in print. However, I will reference Debord's text by thesis number rather than page number, because many other versions still circulate.

16. One should not forget that Debord was a filmmaker, nor should *spéculer* in its economic sense be overlooked. The pun is played out in Alfred Hitchcock's roughly contemporaneous film *Rear Window,* wherein the issue at stake in both the characters' voyeurism and their discussions of the stock market is illicit and risky *speculation.*

17. Debord, *Société,* 34, 158.

18. Ibid., 18, 24, 18, 187.

19. Ibid., 16, 216, 13; *Potlatch,* 29; Debord, *Société,* 30.

20. Leon Trotskii, of course, wrote on the condition of "everyday life," and the concept is an important element of Slavic culture (cf. Boym, *Common Places: Everyday Life in Russia*). The proximate influence for the Situationists, however, was Henri Lefebvre's critique of "la vie quotidienne [everyday life]." Lefebvre and Debord collaborated in the late 1950s and early '60s, although the intellectual property rights were subsequently debated with a ferocity surprising for the supposed advocates of plagiarism. Such analyses have since become somewhat more familiar; for instance, Michel de Certeau's arguments in works such as *Arts de faire* (translated as *The Practice of Everyday Life*) are indebted to Debord as well as Lefebvre; his famous *bricoleur* is the love child of Lévi-Strauss's structural anthropologist and a wayward Situationist. Less well known is the analysis undertaken by Boris Arvatov, who in 1925 turned his constructivist attention to the con-

sumer's engagement with objects in everyday life. Like Debord, Arvatov imagines a world transformed because rather than unthinkingly follow established habits, "the bourgeoisie entered into active, creative contact with the world of Things" (Boris Arvatov, "бут и култура вещи," in алъманах пролеткулъта [Moscow, 1925], 75–82; translated by Christina Kiaer as "Everyday Life and the Culture of the Thing [Toward the Formulation of the Question]," *October* 81 [summer 1997]: 123). Where Debord focuses on the progressive potential of active consumers, Arvatov shifts agency to objects; he distinguishes between the active (socialist) object and the passive (capitalist) object, which is "something completed, fixed, static, and, consequently, dead" (122). However similar the rhetoric and methodology, Arvatov ultimately stands in contrast to Debord; with a conclusion that would have horrified the Situationists, Arvatov looks to a totalizing and hierarchic world in which objects systematically impose a certain progressive order on the world. Moreover, his constructivism comes through even in the writing on everyday life—however much he values flexible objects with a multiplicity of uses (cf. 126), that use is still primary. Debord and Baudrillard react against such utilitarianism with thinking firmly grounded in Bataille.

In its focus on production, Baudrillard's argument in *La Société de consommation* (*Consumer Society*) is worth comparing to Debord's; in navigating the "system of objects," Baudrillard argues, modern consumption constitutes an act of labor like that formerly required only of production. Similarly, Debord writes: "Innovation is ever present in the process of the production of things. This is not true of consumption, which is never anything but more of the same" (*Société*, 156). As we shall see, Debord attempts to engage consumption in the terms of production's continual and ever present innovations. See Jean Baudrillard, *La Société de consommation: ses mythes, ses structures* (Paris: Editions Denoël, 1970); translated as *The Consumer Society: Myths and Structures* (London: Sage, 1998).

21. Debord, *Société*, 151.

22. Ibid., 120.

23. For the elaboration of the term *bricoleur*, one who traffics in tactics rather than strategies, see Michel de Certeau on "making do" (chapter 3 in *The Practice of Everyday Life*). Claude Lévi-Strauss describes the *bricoleur* as one who "uses devious means compared to those of a craftsman" (Lévi-Strauss, *The Savage Mind* [Chicago: University of Chicago Press, 1966], 16–17). Recognizing the given and inescapable nature of any situation, then ignoring the intended use or habitual instrumentality of elements and violating their ostensible rules of engagement, Strauss's *bricoleur* creatively, contingently, and provisionally misuses elements "to make do with 'whatever is at hand'" and "reach brilliant unforeseen results" (17). One can see the same impulse in Baudrillard's argument against the ideology of utility and the status of "use" value in Marxist thought, which "has contributed to the mythology . . . that allows the relation of the individual to objects conceived as use values to pass for a concrete and objective—in sum 'natural'—relation be-

tween man's needs and the function proper to the object" (Baudrillard, *Pour un critique*, 134).

Unlike Lévi-Strauss's *bricoleur*, however, the Situationist is more given to "the sway of extraneous contingencies, whether of occasion or purpose" (Lévi-Strauss, 29), and is in fact "always on the lookout for *that other message* which might be wrested from an interlocutor in spite of his [or her] reticence in pronouncing on questions whose answers have not been rehearsed" (Lévi-Strauss, 20). As a scientist of the exception and the uniquely concrete, the Situationist *bricoleur* is more of a 'pataphysician (and probably a licensed general economist to boot). The Situationist resonance of Lévi-Strauss's emphasis of the "dialogue" in which the bricoleur engages will become clear.

24. Debord, *Société*, 178.

25. *I. S.*, 8:38; Debord, *Société*, 116; cf. 62, 187, 178; 112; 115.

26. Mustapha Khayati, "Captive Words: Preface to a Situationist Dictionary," in Ken Knabb, ed. and trans., *Situationist International Anthology* (Berkeley: Bureau of Public Secrets, 1981), 175. One should not overlook the romantic metaphysics of presence suggested by Debord's frequent use of adjectives like "real," "true," "authentic," "genuine," "direct," "transparent," and so on. Indeed, there is obviously much in Situationist writing to attract criticism, not least of which is a dubious sexual politics. The best of Situationist work—the sharp-edged and unflinching analysis that refuses to spare an equally rigorous auto-critique—dulls and sags with its repeated tendency to veer toward elegiac nostalgia and sentimental romanticism. There's nothing worse, as Thomas Pynchon once wrote, than "a sentimental surrealist" (Thomas Pynchon, *Gravity's Rainbow* [New York: Penguin, 1973], 696).

However, one should not be confused by Debord's idiosyncratic use of certain words as *termes de métier*. As I will argue in the third chapter, for instance, "transparency" is an ideologically loaded metaphor. For Debord, I want to emphasize, "transparency" stands not so much in contrast to opacity or illegibility, but to the reflective—the *speculum* (Latin: "mirror") effect of the spectacle. His concerns, once again, are mimetic; his language continually values embodiment over and against re-presentation.

27. *IS* 4:37. From the point of view of the Situationist object (technically, of course, the fusion of aesthetic and revolutionary activities in everyday life obviates the possibility of Situationist "artworks"), this ideal rehearses the familiar dream of radical modernism: not spectacular *re*production, but production, not representation but direct enactment. "The poem should be, not mean"; or, in Stein's words: "composition as explanation." The catchphrases could proliferate, but cf. Debord, *Société*, 187: "The point is to take effective possession of the community of dialogue, and the playful relationship to time, which the works of the poets and artists have heretofore merely *represented*."

28. Andrews, *Paradise*, 54.

29. Jean-Marie Apostolidès, "Du Surréalisme à l'Internationale Situationniste: La question de l'image," *Modern Language Notes* 105 (1990): 729.

30. Guy-Ernest Debord, "All the King's Men," in Knabb, *Anthology*, 114. Debord makes the point more broadly in his film *on the passage of a few persons through a rather brief period of time*, where he says: "One never really contests an organization of existence without contesting all of that organization's forms of language" (Knabb, *Anthology*, 30). The basic argument underlying the belief that the revolution of the word precedes *and makes possible* the revolution of our ways of life is not only a cliché of the twentieth century's avant-gardes, but is also implicit in Wittgenstein's writing as well.

31. Debord, "All the King's Men," 114, 117, 114.

32. Ibid., 114.

33. Debord, *Société*, 121, 122, 131; cf. 200.

34. Quoted in Kristeva, *Revolution*, 256. The willfulness of paragrammatic practice—the stubborn naïveté with which the 'pataphysician puts tools to use—carries a whiff of Barthes's "obtuse": "opening into the infinity of language, it can come through as limited in the eyes of analytic reason; it belongs to the family of pun, buffoonery, useless expenditure . . . .it is on the side of the carnival" (Roland Barthes, *Image, Music, Text* [New York: Hill and Wang, 1977], 55).

35. On the figure of the Situationist maze, see Vincent Kaufman, "Angels of Purity," trans. John Goodman, *October* 79 (winter 1997): 62.

36. Debord, *Société*, 208; Comte de Lautréamont (Isidore Ducasse), *Poésies* (London: Allison and Busby, 1978), 68. Appropriation was, for the Situationists, one way out of the bind with which they set tradition and innovation as a Scylla and Charybdis equally to be avoided. Even beyond the Lautréamont-inspired plagiarism of content, however, the principle of *détournement* can be read at the level of Debord's chiasmic syntax: a grammatical structure repeated and then inversely altered, usually by reversing the logic of the genitive. With the mannered Hegelianism of this "insurrectional style," the grammar of Debord's very sentences, that is, *détourne* their own phrases. (Cf. Debord, *Société*, 206.)

37. With their grafts and disruptive reversals resolving into a productive third term, *détournements* bear more than a passing resemblance to Derrida's *déconstructions*. For more on collage and deconstruction, see Gregory Ulmer, "The Object of Post-Criticism," in *The Anti-Aesthetic: Essays on Postmodern Culture*, ed. Hal Foster (Seattle: Bay, 1983).

38. Groupe μ, "Collages," *Revue d'esthétique*, nos. 3–4 (Paris: Union Générale d'Éditions, 1978), 34–35.

39. Marjorie Perloff, *The Futurist Moment* (Chicago: University of Chicago Press, 1986), 75.

40. Viktor Shklovskii, "Art as Technique," in *Russian Formalist Criticism: Four Essays*, trans. Lee T. Lemon and Marion J. Reis (Lincoln: University of Nebraska Press, 1965), 12.

41. Or as it might have been *détourned* with a shift (*sdvig*) into the vocabulary of the Situationists: *soûler, épave, veillée, plagiat* (to souse, shipwreck, a night out, plagiarism).

42. The phrase is a commonplace, of course—the same year that Jorn *détourned* this painting, Jacques Robert published his *Paris la nuit*—but Brassaï's landmark 1933 book of the same title would have been an inescapable point of reference for Jorn.

43. Debord, *Société*, 53, 24.

44. Clair Gilman opens her article on Jorn with the same observation, although she minimizes the consequences. Her argument opposes my own readings on several points and is worth consulting for a very different assessment of Jorn's success. While I see no need to dispute it on particulars, the source of our disagreement should be clear from the arguments made throughout this chapter. A tangential observation: although Gilman casts her analysis in oddly sexual terms, reiterating Jorn's "impotence," she never makes explicit the ejaculatory nature of the stains on *Paris by Night*, which she beautifully describes as "thin, white dribbles that settle on the surface like milk skim"(Gilman, "Asger Jorn's Avant-Garde Archives," *October* 79 [winter 1997]: 37).

45. Guy-Ernest Debord and Gil J. Wolman, "Mode d'emploi du détournement," *Les lèvres nues* 8 (May 1956); reproduced in *Documents relatif à la fondation de l'Internationale Situationniste*, ed. Gerard Barreby (Paris: Allia, 1985), 302; translated as "Methods of Detournement" in Knabb, *Anthology*, 8.

46. For the problem of Jorn's titles, see Guy Atkins and Troels Andersen, *Asger Jorn: The Final Years (1965–1973)* (London: Lund Humphries, 1980), 66n.

47. Atkins, *Asger Jorn*, 143.

48. Greil Marcus claims that *Mémoires* was composed at the end of 1957 but not published until 1959 (Marcus, "Guy Debord's Mémoires," 126). The 1993 Belles Lettres facsimile dates the first edition to 1958, which Debord's preface to that edition seems to corroborate; both Crow and Atkins cite 1959 as the date of both composition *and* publication (Thomas Crow, *The Rise of the Sixties*, 52; Atkins and Andersen, *Asger Jorn*, 66). *Fin de Copenhague*, it seems, was indisputably composed and printed in May 1957. Whatever the case, the point is that these books emerge from the same moment of activity that also brought the nascent Internationale Situationniste into existence.

49. Debord, *Société*, 138.

50. Once again there is some discrepancy over details; Atkins records the period of composition as a day, and a notice in the *Architectural Review* trims that to "a single afternoon." Marcus, however, claims the time of realization was forty-eight rather than twenty-four hours (Marcus, *Lipstick Traces*, 455; although he fails to cite his authority), and Len Bracken clocks it judiciously at "a weekend" (Bracken, *Guy Debord: Revolutionary*, 76). In the event, it is surely not unimportant that the

"average duration of a dérive is one day" as well (Debord, "Theorie de la dérive," 51). For more on the Situationist concept of *la dérive,* see below.

51. Literally, "has a papier-mâché mein"; figuratively, "looks washed out."

52. Kaufman astutely notes that the Situationists emerged "at a moment when drifting at the mercy of the signifier was becoming ubiquitous" ("Angels of Purity," 60).

53. Guy-Ernest Debord, "Théorie de la dérive," *Les lèvres nues* 9 (November 1956); reproduced in Barreby, *Document,* 312; translated as "Theory of the Dérive" in Knabb, *Anthology,* 50.

54. Ibid.

55. Ibid.

56. The disheartening naïveté is not so much the Situationists' belief that wandering drunk for days through the streets was revolutionary—with *dérive* simply giving a sophisticated French flair to the weave and stagger of an inebriate along the sidewalk—but our forgetting that it might *not* be.

57. Greil Marcus, "Guy Debord's Mémoires: A Situationist Primer," in *on the passage of a few people through a rather brief moment in time: the Situationist International, 1957–1972,* ed. Elizabeth Sussman (Cambridge: MIT Press, 1989), 128.

58. Len Bracken, *Guy Debord: Revolutionary* (Venice, Calif.: Feral House, 1997), 29.

59. "You eat well there. And you meet a lot of good folks. Some writers, some artists, more or less impoverished and, all of them, full of illusions" (Debord and Jorn, *Mémoires*). "At the café terrace" is one of the fragments collaged into *Fin de Copenhague;* I have drawn my account of Situationist bar life from photographs as well as interviews and documents quoted in Marcus, Bracken, and Debord's autobiography (*Panegyrique*), as well as from Jean-Michel Mansion's *La Tribu* (Paris: Editions Allia, 1998) and the photographs of Ed van der Elsken.

60. Debord and Wolman, "Mode d'emploi." Jorn's drips might also recall the faux-drip gothic lettering of the shop sign for Le Tonneau d'Or, one of the bars frequented by Debord and his coterie.

61. Stewart Home, *The Assault on Culture: Utopian Currents from Lettrisme to Class War* (London: Aporia Press and Unpopular Books, 1988), 30.

62. Guy-Ernest Debord, *Panegyrique: Tome premier* (Paris: Éditions Gérard Lebovici, 1989), 46; translated by James Brook as *Panegyric* (New York: Verso, 1991), 35.

63. Ibid., 43/33.

64. Ibid., 44/34.

65. Quoted in Greil Marcus, *Lipstick Traces: A Secret History of the Twentieth Century* (Cambridge: Harvard University Press, 1989), 352.

66. One the one hand, as I have suggested, Situationist "paragrammatics" involves an anti-utilitarian "misuse" learned directly from Bataille. This tendency

can be seen at the theoretical level—the MIBI's repeated calls for antifunctionalism, for instance—as well as at the level of diction. When Jorn describes his modifications as "painting sacrificed" he alludes to Bataille, as does the reference to "The Northwest Passage" in *Mémoires*. That path is not just the mythical line of flight, the course of the ultimate *dérive*, but "northwest" also evokes "the great Indian totems of North America" and the Chinook, who gave Debord the title for his journal, *Potlatch*. In contrast to the restricted economy favored by surrealism, according to Apostolidès, the IS "participe également d'une économie générale des conduites basées davantages sur le modèle du don/contre don que sur l'échange marchand [participates just as much in a general economy of navigations based above all on the model of the gift/counter-gift as on market exchange]" (Apostolidès, "Surréalisme," 748). I will discuss the nature of Bataille's "general economy" at greater length in chapter 4, but for now I simply want to note, *pace* Apostolidès, that if the Situationists perform certain anti-utilitarian sacrifices as part of their *détournements*, it is always in the service of a restricted economy that recuperates their "misuse" for specific, productive goals. Jorn, for instance, conceives of his modifications in explicitly (restricted) economic terms: "devalued" works that have been "reinvested" rather than simply taken out of the system altogether to take part in a symbolic exchange.

67. Debord was personally unimpressed if not actually opposed to other drugs besides alcohol, but "éther," "absinthe," "marihuana," and laudanum all make their appearance in *Mémoires*—the latter explicitly related to "drinking": "Et Thomas de Quincey buvant / L'opium poison doux et chaste / A sa pauvre Anne allait rêvant [And Thomas de Quincey drinking / The opium poison sweet and chaste / To his poor Anne gone dreaming]."

68. Debord, *Panegyrique*, 49/37. In *Les chants de Maldoror*, the line comes at the end of the dung beetle section of Chant 5: "The beetle, lovely as the tremor of the hands in alcoholism, disappeared on the horizon" (Comte de Lautrèamont, *Lautréamont's Maldoror*, trans. Alexis Lykiard [New York: Crowell, 1973], 149).

69. Debord brings out the rhyme in *Mémoires* with the line "*La fin, on l'a devinée [The end, they had predicted it]*."

70. Cf. Debord, *Panegyrique*, 35–36.

71. In Situationist terms, this would be an unalienated, anti-spectacular time. Debord defines the spectacle itself, at one point, as "in effect a *false consciousness of time*"; in contrast, anarchic time must be permanently imminent (*Société*, 158, 94).

72. Debord, *Panegyrique*, 45/35.

73. "I am sure many readers will undoubtedly deem me too indulgent. 'You mystify drunkenness, you idealize debauchery.' I must admit that in the face of wine's powerful merits, I do not [often] have the courage to dwell on its faults" (Charles Baudelaire, *Artificial Paradise*, trans. Stacy Diamond [New York: Carol, 1996], 8). Alcoholism contradicts Debord's best political aspirations for a revolution of everyday life. In its repetitions and compulsions, addiction (and I include

here the academic's morning cup of coffee—which I am sipping now between sentences) is an essentially fascist regime (Deleuze and Guattari, *Capitalisme et schizophrenie*).

74. Gilles Deleuze, *The Logic of Sense,* trans. Mark Lester with Charles Stivale; ed. Constantin V. Boundas (New York: Columbia University Press, 1990), 158.

75. Ibid.

76. *I. S.* 3:106. That valorization, according to the Situationists, is also the doomed calendar of the historical avant-garde. By definition, an avant-garde worthy of the name cannot, orphic, afford to look back, but neither can its members falter and imagine surviving into the future: they are truly *les enfants perdus.* In short: "avant-gardes have only one time" (Debord, *In girum imus nocte,* 63).

77. Deleuze, *Logic,* 159; Malcolm Lowry, *Under the Volcano* (New York: New American Library, 1971), 364, 369 et passim.

78. Deleuze, *Logic,* 160.

79. Debord, *Société,* 87, 141.

80. Ibid., 163.

81. Ibid., 126, 149, 147, 145.

82. Rimbaud, *Saison,* 104.

Chapter 2

1. Susan Howe, *The Birth-Mark: Unsettling the Wilderness in American Literary History* (Hanover, N.H.: University Press of New England for Wesleyan University Press, 1993), 157.

2. See, for instance, *Birth-Mark* and *My Emily Dickinson.*

3. Howe, *Birth-Mark,* 157.

4. The bibliography on Howe is already extensive. For an introduction, in addition to the works by Quartermain and McGann cited in this chapter, see also Peter Middleton's essay "On Ice: Julia Kristeva, Susan Howe, and Avant-Garde Poetics," in *Contemporary Poetry Meets Modern Theory,* ed. Anthony Easthope and John O. Thompson (Toronto, 1991); Kornelia Freitag, "Writing Language Poetry as a Woman: Susan Howe's Feminist Project in *A Bibliography of the King's Book, or Eikon Basilike,*" *Amerikastudien/American Studies* 40, no. 1: 45–57; Paul Naylor, "Where Are We Now in Poetry?," *Sagatrieb* 10, nos. 1–2: 29–44; Peter Nicholls, "Unsettling the Wilderness: Susan Howe and American History," *Contemporary Literature* 37, no. 4: 586–602; and two superb essays by Ming-Qian Ma: "Poetry as History Revised: Susan Howe's "Scattering as Behavior toward Risk," *American Literary History* 6, no. 4: 716–37; and "Articulating the Inarticulate: Singularities and the Counter-method in Susan Howe," *Contemporary Literature* 36, no. 3: 466–90. In addition to Rachel Tzvia Back's *Led by Language: The Poetry and Poetics of Susan Howe* (Tuscaloosa: University of Alabama Press, 2002), there are also sub-

stantial and relevant chapters in Rachel Blau DuPlessis, *The Pink Guitar* (New York, 1990); Marjorie Perloff, *Poetic License: Essays on Modernist and Postmodernist Lyric* (Evanston, 1990); Linda Reinfeld, *Language Poetry: Writing as Rescue* (Baton Rouge, 1992); Michale Davidson, *Ghostlier Demarcations: Modern Poetry and the Material Word* (Berkeley: University of California Press, 1997); and Susan Vanderborg's *Paratextual Communities: American Avant-Garde Poetry Since 1950* (Carbondale: Souther Illinois University Press, 2001).

5. Susan Howe, *Singularities* (Hanover, N.H.: Wesleyan University Press, 1990), 45.

6. Susan Howe, *The Europe of Trusts* (Los Angeles: Sun and Moon, 1990), 163. According to John Stallworthy's definition, this would preclude Howe from being a poet at all; his narrow-minded essay for the third edition of *The Norton Anthology of Poetry* apodictically opens: "A poem is a composition written for performance by the human voice. What the eye sees on the page is the composer's verbal score . . ." (John Stallworthy, ed., *The Norton Anthology of Poetry* [New York, 1983], 1403).

7. The closest Howe comes to Mallarmé may well be the title of her poem "Scattering as Behavior toward Risk," which might be taken as a witty adaptation of *Un coup de dés jamais n'abolira le hasard,* with "risk" as a deadpan translation of the false cognate *hasard.* In fact, Howe's title alludes to Donald N. McCloskey's "English Open Fields as Behavior Towards Risk," in *Research in Economic History* vol. 1, ed. Paul J. Uselding (Greenwich, Conn.: JAI Press, 1976), 124–70; McCloskey's essay is a study of the "scattering" of farm plots and the economics of enclosure which proposes an agrarian geography shaped by risk rather than utopian communalism.

8. Susan Howe, "Melville's Marginalia," in *The Nonconformist's Memorial* (New York: New Directions, 1993), 197; Guillaume Apollinaire, "Il pleut," in *Calligrammes* (Berkeley: University of California Press, 1980), 100.

9. Howe, "Melville's Marginalia," 105.

10. Ibid., 106.

11. Ibid., 99, 100.

12. Howe, *Singularities,* 21.

13. One exception is the graffitied title page of the Paradigm Press edition of *A Bibliography of the King's Book, or Eikon Basilike* (Providence, 1989).

14. None of which is to deny the pressures of the various traditions that do register on Howe's writing in other ways. Howe's famous grids, mirrored lines, and permutated word lists, for instance, suggest the influence of artists such as Ian Hamilton Finlay. Moreover, the strong correspondences between Howe's poetry and the art of the Russian futurists is an area which, although it unfortunately lies beyond the scope of this chapter, might be productively pursued.

15. *Clarissa* is also referenced obliquely in *The Birth-Mark* (38), although Howe claims not to have read Richardson's book (private conversation).

16. Howe, *Singularities,* 54; Howe, *Nonconformist,* 60; Samuel Richardson, *Clarissa, or The History of a Young Lady* (Oxford, 1930), 5:327, 328, 327.

17. Howe, *Nonconformist,* 18.

18. Howe, *Europe,* 72.

19. Ibid., 67; Howe, *Nonconformist,* 149, 146.

20. Howe, *Europe,* 99; Howe, *Nonconformist,* 146.

21. Howe, *Singularities,* 65.

22. Howe, *Europe,* 58.

23. Howe, *Birth-Mark,* 165.

24. Ibid., 164.

25. Howe, *Singularities,* 28.

26. Susan Howe, "Statement for the New Poetics Colloquium, Vancouver, 1985," *Jimmy and Lucy's House of 'K'* 5 (1985): 17.

27. Howe, *Singularities,* 19, 49.

28. Ibid., 21; Howe, *Europe,* 68.

29. Howe, *Europe,* 9, 103.

30. Jacques Attali, *Bruits: Essai sur l'économie politique de la musique* (Paris: Vendôme, 1977), 59; translated by Brian Massumi as *Noise: The Political Economy of Music* (Minneapolis: University of Minnesota Press, 1987), 29.

31. Ibid., 53/26.

32. Ibid., 54/27.

33. Howe, *Nonconformist,* 112, 98.

34. Peter Quartermain, *Disjunctive Poetics: From Gertrude Stein and Louis Zukofsky to Susan Howe* (Cambridge: Cambridge University Press, 1992), 184.

35. John Cage, *Silence* (Middletown, Conn.: Wesleyan University Press, 1961), 8, 152, 191. Note that Cage's qualification, "Until I die there will be sounds" (*Silence,* 8), echoes the arguments of both Jacques Attali and Michel Serres, who claim that in medical and biological terms "noise" is an indication of life: movement, heat, the processes of the conversion of energy. In light of such arguments, one might shift the intended emphasis of Luigi Russolo's assertion that "Every manifestation of life is accompanied by noise" and recall that silence, to trope the trope, does indeed equal death (Russolo, *The Art of Noises,* 27). Just a few years after Cage's experience, Miles Davis wrapped up the recording session for *Sketches of Spain* by turning to his collaborator and predicting: "Gil [Evans], our next record date will be silence."

36. Susan Howe, "The Difficulties Interview," *The Difficulties* 3, no. 2: 42.

37. Howe, *Singularities,* 23.

38. Cage, *Silence,* 42.

39. Howe, *Singularities,* 25.

40. Howe, "Melville's Marginalia," 150, 147.

41. Quartermain, *Disjunctive Poetics,* 184. Although my essay focuses only on

written language, one might note that Howe's poems also recognize the material requisite of spoken language as well; in an audible "Language [which] ripples our lips" (*Europe*, 63), "Words . . . are vibrations of air" (*Nonconformist*, 38).

42. Howe, *Nonconformist*, 52.

43. Ibid., 58.

44. Ibid., 64.

45. Ibid., 36, 75.

46. Howe, "Melville's Marginalia," 127.

47. Howe, *Europe*, 72, 61; Howe, *Singularities*, 47, 53; Howe, *Europe*, 36.

48. Howe, *Nonconformist*, 17.

49. Howe, "Melville's Marginalia," 109, 115.

50. Ibid., 115.

51. Caroline Blyth, "Touch Wood: coming to terms with bibliography," *Word & Image* 9, no. 1 (1993): 68.

52. Howe appropriates this title from the last stanza of Wallace Stevens's "United Dames of America": "There are not leaves enough to crown, / To cover, to crown, to cover—let it go—/ The actor that will at last declaim our end."

53. Howe, *Europe*, 171.

54. Howe, *Nonconformist*, 69; Howe, *Europe*, 103; Jerome J. McGann, *Black Riders: The Visible Language of Modernism* (Princeton: Princeton University Press, 1993), 104.

55. Howe, *Europe*, 17.

56. Howe, *Singularities*, 49; Howe, *Nonconformist*, 37, 39.

57. Howe's poetry is uncannily proleptic in the way that earlier poems consistently describe the actual look of much later work. A section from "The Liberties," for example, seems to anticipate the garbled errors of this page: "bedevilled by a printer's error / the sight of a dead page filled her with terror / garbled version / page in her coffin" (*Europe*, 158). Additionally, while "Coffin the sea" recalls the title-page figure and nautical deaths of Howe's earlier poem "Scattering as Behavior toward Risk," a more literal evocation might be found in Ian Hamilton Finlay's sculpture "Fisherman's Cross," in which "sea" is repeatedly inscribed within a coffin-shaped block of concrete. Howe discusses this piece and reproduces an illustration in her essay "The End of Art," *Archives of American Art Journal* 14, no. 4 (1974): 6.

58. Howe, *Singularities*, 54. Howe's obsessive engagement with the essentially conservative medium of the book, like her fetishization of the historical text and the "presence" that she identifies with original manuscripts and editions, is a point from which a less positive account of her visual prosody might well proceed.

59. Howe, "Melville's Marginalia," 106, 104.

60. Howe, *Nonconformist*, 78.

61. Howe, *Singularities*, 36; John E. Bowlt, "Kazimir Malevich and the Energy

of Language," in *Kazimir Malevich: 1875–1935*, ed. Jeanne D'Andrea (Los Angeles, 1990), 183.

62. Suggesting precisely such links, Howe has written: "Often I hear Romans murmuring / I think of them lying dead in their graves" (*Europe*, 158). Much of her poetry, in fact, involves a consideration of etymology and the way in which language links the past and the present with so many subtle threads: "Etymology the this / present in the past now / so many thread" (*Singularities,* 43). This interest in "etymological fancies" is connected with an attention to the dictionary which Howe evinces through her careful readings of Webster and the lists of definitions that help to structure her lectures, essays, and poems (*Birth-Mark,* 38). Moreover, elements of her poetry occasionally seem specifically motivated by the dictionary. In "Thorow" (*Singularities,* 56–57), a poem that opens with a brief prose meditation on the significance of the origin of words, Howe distills and rewrites the very sentence from Thoreau's *The Maine Woods* with which the *Oxford English Dictionary* illustrates "drisk": "we mistook a little rocky islet seen through the 'drisk' . . . for the steamer." Similarly, the *OED* illustrates the word "eutrapelia" with an entry from a work entitled *J. Melvill's Diary,* where it had been noted from an earlier text, and the reappearance of the unusual word—incongruous and italicized—in a poem entitled "Melville's Marginalia" cannot be entirely coincidental.

63. Howe, *Nonconformist,* 149; Michel Serres, *Le parasite* (Paris: B. Grasset, 1980), 56; translated by Lawrence R. Schehr as *The Parasite* (Baltimore: Johns Hopkins University Press, 1982), 25.

64. Serres, *Parasite,* 54/26–27.

65. Howe, *Singularities,* 22.

66. Cage, *Silence,* 68.

67. Attali, *Noise,* 56/28. The references here are complicated: citing P. Daufoy and J.-P. Sarton (*Pop Music/Rock,* 1972) in this passage, Attali quotes Charlie Gillett's summary (*The Sounds of the City* [New York, 1970], 300) of Colin Fletcher's argument (*The New Society and the Pop Process* [London, 1970]).

68. Attali, *Noise,* 67/33.

69. McGann, *Black Riders,* 107.

Chapter 3

1. Charles Kenneth Williams, *Flesh and Blood* (New York: Farrar, Straus, and Giroux, 1987).

2. The texts in *Veil* were originally composed in 1976; in March of 1979 they were displayed at Ugo Carrega's Mercato del Sale gallery (Milan) in an exhibit cocurated by Bernstein and Susan Bee. "Freely composed" is Bernstein's own description (Brito, *A Suite of Poetic Voices*).

While *Veil* may be the most extreme case, Bernstein has engaged visual prosody at various points throughout his career. Most notably, the *Language of Boquets* (Hot Bird Mfg., 1991) is a sort of handwritten veil not unlike what one imagines as a page from Williams's critic. Although they do not engage illegibility, Bernstein's collaborations with Susan Bee, such as *The Nude Formalism* (20 Pages no. 3, Sun and Moon, 1989), are also attuned to visual prosody. Moreover the typewriter aesthetic of *Veil*, which I discuss below, links it to poems like "Lift Off" and "AZOOT D'Puund" (*Poetics Justice* [Baltimore: Pod Books, 1979], 35–36; 25–26), both of which are exercises in a different type of unintelligibility. These might in turn be read as companions to the symbolic mathematical language in "Erosion Control Area (2)," which replaces the scientific and medical diction Bernstein had used to similar distancing effects earlier in his career (*Prosodia* 6 [spring 1996]: 57–64). As it appears in *Prosodia*, "Erosion Control Area (2)" is printed twice in succession on transparent pages, creating a concrete version of the layered depth simulated in several of the "veils." The connotations of that transparent page—which we shall see again in Marcel Broodthaers's work—will become clear by the close of this chapter.

The italicized passages which follow in this paragraph and the conclusion of the next are drawn from *Veil,* not only as an illustration of its self-reflexivity, but also as proof of its readability.

3. Jean Starobinski, *Les mots sous les mots: Les anagrammes de Ferdinand de Saussure* (Paris: Éditions Gallimard, 1971), 30; Nathaniel Hawthorne, "The Minister's Black Veil," in *The Centenary Edition of the Works of Nathaniel Hawthorne*, vol. 9 (Columbus: Ohio State University Press, 1962). Hawthorne's story, introduced as "a parable," is not of course reducible to a single interpretation, but it does suggest that one understanding of the enigmatic "black veil" which always comes between people is language itself. This is not the place for a detailed reading of Hawthorne's work, but one might begin by noting how the vocabulary of printing accretes as soon as the minister's "plighted wife" Elizabeth declares "Your words are a mystery too . . . . Take away the veil from them at least" (880); in response, the minister asserts that "this veil is a type," and "type" and "typified," which recur in relation to the veil throughout the short text, are repeated within a few lines. Defending his "character," the minister claims that he is "bound" (like a book) to wear the "[en]grave[d]" "material" "medium" of the black veil which "covers" his "[type]face" and which everyone wants "drawn" (like letterforms) and "cast" (as in a typefoundry) aside (880–81 et passim). The black veil, just like black print, quite literally "threw its obscurity between him and the [white of the] holy page, as he read" (874).

While neither advances this particular reading, corroboration is offered by John Irwin, who establishes the strong association of veils and writing in Hawthorne's oeuvre (*American Hieroglyphics* [New Haven: Yale University Press, 1980], 267 et seq.), as well as by Norman German ("The Veil of Words in 'The Minister's Black

Veil,'" *Studies in Short Fiction* 25, no. 1 [December 1988]). Although he concentrates on "Hawthorne's penchant for etymological punning," German's attentive reading demonstrates that Hawthorne "painstakingly worked out his themes even on the most fundamental linguistic levels" of wordplay, paranomasia, and anagram (41). Additionally, one should note that Hawthorne's biblical precedent already suggests that Moses' "veil" is the veil of language (2 Corinthians 3:12–14). For a relevant examination of the motif of the veil as text, see chapter 7 of Nelson Hilton's brilliant lexical archaeology of Blake's illuminated texts, *Literal Imagination: Blake's Vision of Words* (Berkeley: University of California Press, 1983).

4. Brought to a focus by the printing "reform" movement, the most vehement proclamations of this doctrine arise in the second decade of the twentieth century and peak in the 1930s, when its "apparently invincible philosophy was bestowed on and accepted by all sectors of the printing world" (Robin Kinross, *Modern Typography: An Essay in Critical History* [London: Hyphen, 1992], 66). Given this "hegemonic influence over the printing trade" (Kinross, *Modern Typography,* 65), it is no surprise that the tenets of invisibility still hold strong sway and can be widely recognized today. The aesthetics of the reform movement had precedents, of course, and one might note in particular Theodore Low De Vinne's influential claims on behalf of what he termed "masculine" printing, which "succeeds perfectly when the reader finds it a pleasure to read [a printed] work, without thinking at all of the means by which this pleasure is had" (De Vinne, "Masculine Printing" [1892], 164). Moreover, even printers who had serious quarrels with the party line of the new reformation, such as Jan Van Krimpen (a contemporary of Morison and Warde and one of the central figures in continental typography), came to express the hope that the "reader might not notice the typographical design" at all (G. W. Ovink, "150 Years of Book Typography in the Netherlands," in *Book Typography 1815–1965,* ed. Kenneth Day [1966], 268).

A critical history of design theory lies beyond the scope of this book, but one might initially situate doctrines of transparence in response to the mannerism of aestheticist design on the one hand, as well as the aggressively hard-edged design of *die neue typographie* on the other; while the young Jan Tschichold and his colleagues also made strident arguments for "clarity," their work always *announced* itself (as "new," "modern," "machine industrial," and so on) in a way that obviated transparence. All of these ideals — "invisibility," "beauty," and "clarity" — were reacting in their own way against the clutter of Victorian design.

Moreover, although experiments in legibility date back to Anisson's 1790 duel between the styles of Didot and Garamond, which basically involved having readers back up until they noticed a difference between two texts set side by side (R. H. Wiggins, "Effects of Three Typographic Variables on Speed of Reading," *Journal of Typographic Research* 1, no. 1 [1967]: 5), the development of more scientific physio-psychologic research into legibility is exactly coeval with the modern "reform of printing," and surely not unrelated. (Garamond won, by the way.)

5. Stanley Morison, *First Principles of Typography*, 2nd ed. (London: Cambridge University Press, 1976), 5. To be precise, Morison would distinguish between the transparent imperative for book design and what he grudgingly saw as the necessarily more aggressive design of commercial or political ephemera.

Morison, considered by many to be "the world's leading authority on typography and its related arts" (as noted by Beatrice Warde, *The Crystal Goblet: Sixteen Essays on Typography*, ed. Henry Jacob [Cleveland: World Publishing, 1956]), was able to propagate his views through his position as both editorial advisor to the *Fleuron* and typographic advisor to the Monotype Corporation. Additionally, Robin Kinross documents that Morison's "dicta began to spread through the world of typography in Britain and abroad . . . through the work of associates and acolytes" (*Modern Typography*, 65).

6. Warde, *Crystal*, 11.

7. Ibid., 11, cf. 94–97; 13.

8. Ibid., 16.

9. Wittgenstein, *Investigations*, §97.

10. Andrews, *Paradise*, 51.

11. One might compare the sense of screen and texture in these poems with the overprinted sheets of B. P. Nichol's "Lament" and one of Heinz Gappmayr's "sind" poems. The force of the limits of opacity as a response to the limits of life and subjective "being" will be made clear in the second section of this chapter. While this chapter will focus on *Veil*, the prevalence of overprinting as one of the key strategies of contemporary visual poets should not be forgotten. Even as he rejects it, John Cage indicates the viability of overprinting as an option readily available to poets by at least the 1960s; in the note to "Where Are We Going? And What Are We Doing?" he explains (*Silence*, 194):

> The texts were written to be heard as four simultaneous lectures. But to print four lines of type simultaneously—that is, superimposed on one another—was a project unattractive in the present instance. The presentation here used has the effect of making the words legible—a dubious advantage, for I had wanted to say that our experiences, gotten as they are all at once, pass beyond our understanding.

Cage's aesthetics of illegibility will be addressed in depth later in this book; for now, compare his statement to Louis Zukofsky's from *"A"–B*: "Voice a voice blown: print / Must not overleap, but the notes of voices would" (*A* [Berkeley: University of California Press, 1978], 52–53).

12. A note on vocabulary: "palimpsest" (from the Greek *palin psao*, "I smooth over again") originally referred to the effacement of a text by washing or scraping papyrus or parchment, which was then written on again (Bernhard Bischoff, *Latin Paleography*, trans. Dáibhí Ó Cróinín and David Ganz [Cambridge, 1990], 11–12).

The erased text would sometimes reemerge to produce an overwritten page. Another practicioner of overprinting, Luciano Caruso, has explicitly figured his works as palimpsests. See, for example, his *Piccola teoria della citazione* (Bologna: Tau/ma 5, 1974), which organizes several veil-like palimpsests over each other in an alternating, constructive pattern across the canvas of the book opening. Caruso's work is worth considering in relation to Tom Phillips's *A Humument*, which I discuss in chapter 6, as well as to the work considered in chapter 5, since he has written over texts by Ezra Pound.

13. Charles Bernstein, *A Poetics* (Cambridge: Harvard University Press, 1992), 26, 34.

14. Warde, *Crystal*, 36.

15. Ron Silliman, *The New Sentence* (New York: Roof, 1989), 13.

16. Shklovskii, "Art as Technique," 11, 12.

17. Jean Cocteau, "Le secret professionel," in *Le rappel à l'ordre,* from vol. 7 of *Oeuvres complètes* (Geneva: Éditions Marguerat, 1946), 188, emphasis added. Note that Warde's typographic theory is explicitly anti-defamiliarizing: "In the making of pictures it pays a hundredfold to do something for the first time, to invent, *to shock the ordinary man's eyes into new awareness.* But in typography, that same effort can lead to all sorts of graphic monkeyishness . . ." (*Crystal,* 66, emphasis added).

18. In 1958, Dieter Rot had similarly emphasized an earlier generation of machines with an overprinted poem "advertising my typewriter," as he put it, in which the permutations of "oliveti" suggest a quite literal "~~oveilti~~." Recalling Aram Saroyan's claim that the "machine—an obsolete red-top Royal Portable—is the biggest influence on my work," Bernstein has acknowledged the importance of the particular model of his own typewriter, which he had acquired just prior to composing the veils (private correspondence).

19. Bernstein, *Poetics,* 76. Compare this quatrain with similar passages later in the essay: "The re- / di- / rection / of at- / ten- / tion- / al / focus / can / as use- / ful- / ly be / located / in the / shift / of at- / tention" (78–79), and "the power of / making aware, which necessarily involves a / disruption of a single plane of attention or / belief, results in hyperattentiveness / that has its own economy of engagement" (83). I will discuss the nature of that "economy" at some length later in this chapter.

20. Ibid., 78. Bernstein's quotation marks reference Nick Piombino.

21. Wittgenstein, *Investigations,* §645.

22. Such techniques have been frequently employed, to different ends, by many avant-garde filmmakers, including Stan Brakhage whom I discuss below. The extremes of "perceptual cinema" find modernist precedents in Marcel Duchamp's roto-reliefs and *Anemic Cinema,* Fernand Léger's *Ballet Mécanique,* and Hans Richter's *Rhytmus 21.* Following Peter Kubelka's 1960 *Arnulf Rainer,* which created a complex fugue of black or white frames and white noise or silence, the inaugural

works of "flicker films," as such, include Tony Conrad's 1966 *The Flicker*, a strobo-scopic montage of clear and black frames, and Paul Sharit's *Ray Gun Virus* (1966), which investigates similar effects with single frames of different colors.

Beyond exploring the limits and nature of human visual perception, or the grammar of the single frame, flicker films lay bare the mechanical devices normally used to mask the discontinuous articulation of those frames. Technically, as Malcolm Le Grice explains,

> Cinema, as a mechanism, is designed to project one separate picture every 1/24 second [in 16mm]. If the period during which the projection shutter is closed is taken into account, each image occupies the screen for approximately half that time, about 1/50 second, while the rate of image change in film is deliberately located just beyond the point where the eye can discern flicker (Malcolm Le Grice, *Abstract Film and Beyond* [London: Studio Vista, 1977], 106).

Flicker films can thus be read as allegories of the mechanisms of cinema itself. Similarly, one might compare Kubelka's interest in the discrete separation between each frame in a film and his design for viewing booths at the original Anthology Film Archive, which separated each viewer in partitioned three-walled booths. This theater transfers Kubelka's interest in the mechanics of the machine for projecting film to an architecture which he conceived of as "a machine for film viewing" (introduction to Stan Brakhage, *Metaphors on Vision*, ed. P. Adams Sitney, 2nd. ed [New York: Film Culture, 1976], vii).

23. Miles Tinker, in his review of research into legibility, classifies most of these factors under the rather chilling rubric "hygienic reading situation" (Miles A. Tinker, *Legibility of Print* [Ames: Iowa State University Press, 1963], 253 et seq.).

24. The gloss of some technical terms may be in order. *Hypnagogia* (which refers to that moment just before sleep) includes those cerebrally produced patterns and eidetic images which flash suddenly and briefly before the mind.

> Change in the dilation of the pupil "influences focusing and the perception of brightness and color saturation" (William C. Wees, *Light Moving in Time: Studies in the Visual Aesthetics of Avant-Garde Film* [Berkeley: University of California Press, 1992], 70).

> The eye's movement back to the left of the page after reaching the end of a line of print is known as the return sweep or backsweep, and the result of its failure is known as "doubling."

> The *ciliary* muscle helps change the shape of the lens.

> *Foevea* denotes that small rodless area of the retina which affords acute vision; beyond the narrow area governed by the foevea, the visual field flattens and becomes increasingly colorless.

> The *punctum caecum*, or "blind spot," is the tiny area of the optic disk where the optic nerve enters the eyeball and so is not sensitive to light.

The eye does not pan smoothly across a page when reading, but rather skips abruptly in fits and starts between momentary fixations, and *saccades* denotes those tiny, rapid jerks of "Brownian motion" during which no clear vision is possible.

Phosphenes, those patterns and flashes which originate from within the eye rather than by external light, are discussed below.

Entoptic "floaters" refer to the condition of seeing the shadows of minute debris in the vitreous fluid cast on the retina, so that small opacities appear to drift and flinch across the field of vision like the transparent bodies in water seen under a microscope.

These effects are obviously dependent on individual readers; not everyone experiences floaters, for instance, and the sensitivity to phosphenes varies widely (Gerald Oster, "Phosphenes," *Scientific American* 222, no. 2 [February 1980]: 83). Similarly, those with contact lenses or glasses will be familiar with different optical (and environmental) effects, as will those with perceptual disorders or any of a wide range of optical conditions from *strabismus* to *amblyopia* and worse.

25. The quote is from Charles Bernstein, *Content's Dream: Essays 1975–1984* (Los Angeles: Sun and Moon, 1986), 137.

26. The move from *le voile* to *la toile* is no less easy, and although Bernstein mentions Morris Louis's "veils" as an inspiration (Brito, *A Suite*), I want to propose a less obvious analogue from the realm of painting. Compare my reading of the veils' optical portraiture with the interpretation of J. M. W. Turner sketched by Jonathan Crary, whose *Techniques of the Observer* (Cambridge: MIT Press, 1990) provides a broad context in which to place *Veil* as part of the modernity of vision. Taking Goethe's meditations on optical phenomena like the afterimage as an exemplary moment, Crary charts the sea change in which the human body goes from being simply a neutral and "transparent subject-as-observer" of an external world to the "active producer of optical experience" (70, 69), so that "the subjective contents of vision are dissociated from an objective world" and "the body itself produces phenomena"—such as those I have just catalogued—"that have no external correlate" (71). As an illustration of the artistic implications of this paradigm shift from the neutral to the neural, Crary argues that Turner "made central in his work the retinal processes of vision . . . the carnal embodiment of sight" (139), and he reads Turner's late paintings of the 1840s as records of the eye itself: "Through the afterimage the sun is made to belong to the body, and the body in fact takes over as the source of its effects" (141).

This interpretation expands on that of Ronald Paulson in "Turner's Graffiti: The Sun and Its Glosses," in *Images of Romanticism: Verbal and Visual Affinities,* ed. Karl Kroeber and William Walling (New Haven: Yale University Press, 1978), which Crary literalizes and deromanticizes. Paulson suggests that "There is in the sun as the 'eye of God' the sense that when the artist paints the sun he is

painting himself, and Turner's sun centered landscapes may be . . . self-portraits"
(182). Paulson himself is advancing a more literalized formulation of Jack Lindsay's
romantic reading in *J. M. W. Turner: His Life and Work* (London: Cory, Adams,
and Mackay, 1966), which relates the image of the "angel standing in the sun" to
Ruskin's once-scandalous comparison of Turner himself with the Angel of the Sun
in the Apocalypse. While Lindsay scruples to note that the painting is not a self-
portrait in any narrowly personal sense, he does claim that Turner "was saying that
every true Artist is this sort of Angel" (213). Given such fine precedents, I propose
to follow suit and literalize Crary's reading one step further.

For a very different essay on the relationship between blindness and self-portrai-
ture specific to drawing, see Jacques Derrida, *Mémoires d'aveugle: L'autoportrait et
autres ruines* (Paris: Édition de la Réunion des Musées Nationaux, 1990). Additionally, the institutional display of many different visual art forms transforms them
into de facto portraits because even under carefully lit conditions the most transparent protective glass tends to reflect, so that however trained we are to ignore
the materiality of display, the experience of viewing cannot quite suppress the nar-
cissism of viewing one's own image in palimpsest over the art work.

27. William Blake, *Complete Writings,* ed. Geoffrey Keynes (Oxford: Oxford
University Press, 1966), 617.

28. Warde, *Crystal,* 97, 95, 15–16.

29. Quoted in Joseph Mascheck's superb and sobering "Alberti's 'Window': Art-
Historical Notes on an Antimodernist Misprision," *Art Journal* 50, no. 1 (March
1991): 36. Mascheck quotes from Braudel's *Capitalism and Material Life: 1400–1800*
(New York: Harper and Row, 1973), 121, 214. Cf. Braudel's *Civilisation matérielle,
économie, et capitalisme: xve–xviiie siècle* (Paris: A. Colin, 1979), 257–58; translated
as *The Structures of Everyday Life: The Limits of the Possible,* vol. 1 (New York:
Harper and Row, 1979), 296–97.

30. Mascheck, "Window," 37.

31. Louis Marin, *Détruire la peinture* (Paris: Éditions Galilée, 1977), 61. This
double sense of material grid and transparent window come together in the projection "screen," which Bernstein discusses in an argument sympathetic with those of
Marin and Silliman: "The movie screen becomes, through the magic of cinema, a
window onto a world behind it" (*Content's Dream,* 93). In an abbreviated and simplified account, Bernstein continues in terms that should resonate strongly with
several of the themes taken up in this chapter. I leave the metaphorical valence of
"Windows," as a name for computer software, to those who do not compose on a
Macintosh.

32. In addition to this "small glass," Duchamp's "Large Glass" (*La mariée mis à
nu par ses célibataires, même*) also pits the play of transparence and opacity against
the "window" of the painting.

33. Blake, *Complete Writings,* 130.

34. Ibid., 433. Without elaborating on his idealist or spiritual argument, I want

to emphasize the vocabulary of Blake's visionary optics; he derides the "Corporeal and Vegetative Eye" earlier in *A Vision of the Last Judgement* (*Complete Writings,* 614), and he repeats the prepositional distinction, explicitly in terms of transparency, in "The Everlasting Gospel": This Life's dim Windows of the Soul / Distorts the Heavens from Pole to Pole / And leads you to Believe a Lie / When you see with, not thro', the Eye" (753). The full couplet from the "Auguries of Innocence" reads: We are led to Believe a Lie. / When we see ~~With~~ not Thro' the Eye" (433). Had he known Russian, Blake would have no doubt been delighted by the false cognate глаз (*glaz*), which brings together the homophonic "glass" and the denotative "eye."

35. Ibid., 189.

36. "Scopic regimes" have nothing to do with keeping breath fresh; I take the term from Martin Jay, who takes it from Christian Metz's *The Imaginary Signifier*. Sounding a cautious and conservative note, Jay reminds us to always "ask what the costs of too uncritical an embrace of . . . alternatives may be" (Martin Jay, "Scopic Regimes of Modernity," in *Vision and Visuality,* ed. Hal Foster [Seattle: Bay, 1988], 20).

37. Bernstein, *Content's Dream,* 135; Ludwig Wittgenstein, *Preliminary Studies for the "Philosophical Investigations," Generally Known as the Blue and Brown Books* (Oxford: Blackwell, 1969), 63–64.

38. See, for example, Stan Brakhage, *Brakhage Scrapbook: Collected Writings 1964–1980,* ed. Robert A. Haller (New York: Documentext, 1982), 166, 76.

39. See the special numbers of the *Chicago Review,* "Stan Brakhage: Correspondences," 47:4 (Winter 2001) and 48:1 (Spring 2002) for Brakhage's relation to poets. Bernstein's essay "Frames of Reference" in *Content's Dream* makes clear his familiarity with Brakhage and other contemporaneous avant-garde filmmakers. In contrast with my own reading, Bernstein understands filmmakers like Brakhage and Ernie Gehr to be revisioning, rather than abandoning, the "transparency effect" (*Content's Dream,* 94–95). Interestingly, Bernstein specifically contrasts Brakhage's "transparent" celluloid with the "surface" of Pollock's canvases. Sitney, conversely, reads Brakhage precisely in terms of Pollock's abstract expressionism—in part as a filmmaker who "affirmed the physicality of the film material" (Brakhage, *Metaphors on Vision,* 139, 197–99), and in part as enacting a heroic, and romantic, "lyrical mode." Bernstein is no doubt reacting, to some extent, against that romantic lyricism. David James, in *Allegories of Cinema: American Film in the Sixties* (Princeton: Princeton University Press, 1989), his outstanding survey of the politics of American alternative films in the 1960s, contextualizes and attempts to recuperate part of that romantic idealism as an alternative and resistance to capitalist modes of production (29–36). James situates Brakhage's counterculture remove to a Colorado cabin in terms of Thoreau and Wordsworth, although a better analogue to Brakhage's "domestic avant-garde," with its exclusion of industrial modes of production, is surely Lambeth rather than Walden or Grasmere. James notes

that the one element of production Brakhage could not wrest from commercial industry was the manufacture of film stock (35); analogously, Blake and his wife were able to pursue all stages of illuminated book production except the manufacture of paper. This is obviously not the place for a nuanced comparison of Blake and Brakhage, but I would suggest that in spite of the latter's repeated objections to Blake's optics of apocalyptic transcendence, the two artists, particularly in terms of visionary and material praxis, are far more similar than contrary.

A misplaced idealism aside, there are several aspects of Brakhage's early work one might gladly overlook (as I intend to here): an uncritically romantic "mythopoesis," a naïve belief in some prelinguistic "innocent eye," and several of those enthusiasms of the 1960s and '70s which now seem so embarrassing (Wilhelm Reich's "orgone energy" not least among them). In the final analysis, however, Brakhage's practice—regardless of the metaphoric rhetoric which sometimes overwhelms his manifestos—speaks unmistakably, like Blake's, for the anti-transparent "visualization of sight."

40. Brakhage's often-quoted opening to *Metaphors on Vision* formulates his defamiliarizing position in these terms: "Imagine an eye unruled by man-made laws of perspective, an eye unprejudiced by compositional logic, an eye which does not respond to the name of everything but which must know each object encountered in life through an adventure of perception" (*Metaphors on Vision*, n.p.). One need not agree with Gombrich's entire refutation of Ruskin's "innocence of the eye" (*Elements of Drawing*) to know that "the innocent eye is myth" (*Art and Illusion*). Although Brakhage might not agree, his position is perhaps best understood as a reconfiguration of the codes of visuality rather than a utopic return to some prelapsarian (and prelinguistic) state.

41. In *Light Moving in Time,* his superb study of the visual aesthetic of avant-garde film, William C. Wees provides a much more detailed account of Brakhage's attempts to "give sight to the medium" of vision. For just one example, Wees perceptively interprets Brakhage's trademark handheld (8mm) camerawork, with its rapid jerky movements, as an equivalent of the eyes' saccadic movements (85 et seq.). In more general terms, Wees's overall arguments run parallel to my own on many points, and I am deeply indebted to his work—to which I strongly encourage anyone interested in visuality or film to turn—for engaging these issues far more thoroughly than I do here.

42. Oster, "Phosphenes," 83.

43. "Les poètes de sept ans" is in Arthur Rimbaud, *Complete Works, Selected Letters,* ed. Wallace Fowlie (Chicago: University of Chicago Press, 1966), 74–78. One might also recall Beckett's *Watt*: "The problem of vision, as far as Watt was concerned, admitted of only one solution: the eye open in the dark. The results given by the closed eye were, in Watt's opinion, most unsatisfactory" (Samuel Beckett, *Watt* [London: Picador, 1988], 231). More recently, in the American tradition, Lytle Shaw's "Ferns of the Carboniferous Period," part of the series *Cable*

Factory 20, includes among its collaged citations a lineated passage from Goethe's treatise on color:

> Where, in the slide show,
>> the eye receives a blow,
>>> and sparks seem to spread from it.
>> In some states of body, again,
>>> when the blood is heated,
>> and the system much excited,
>>> if the eye is pressed
>>>> first gently, and then more and more strongly,
>>> a dazzling and intolerable light may be excited.

44. Vito Acconci's *Eye Poke* asks its viewer to imagine the phosphenes that Acconci must be experiencing as he repeatedly stabs at his eyes, futilely fighting reflex in an attempt to keep them open as he pokes. Several of Brakhage's films might be thought of as the same work, but photographed from Acconci's point of view. In contrast with Acconci, however, Brakhage replaces the overt violence of *Eye Poke* with more subtle and positive connotations, although one should not forget the emulsion scraped from the image of the eyes of the blind man in *Reflections on Black.* These films take their place in the long tradition of ocular aggression in avant-garde cinema (which is always implicitly aimed at the open eyes of the viewer), most famously the razor scene in Louis Buñuel and Salvador Dali's *Un chien andalou,* but one might think of the equally disturbing operation in Paul Sharit's *T,O,U,C,H,I,N,G,* or the enucleation in the final moments of Pier Paolo Pasolini's *Salò: 120 Days of Sodom,* and any number of other moments. The significance of these abocular scenes within very different works is of course not identical, although the sharp metal used in each of them might suggest an allegory of cinematic splicing. Such scenes, however, date back to the inaugural moments of cinema: Edison's film of a man sneezing (a physiological event during which one cannot keep the eyes open) and the rocket which penetrates the eye of the moon in Meliès's *Voyage a la lune.*

45. Albert Rose, *Vision: Human and Electronic* (New York: Plenum, 1973), 46. Robert Desnos describes phosphenes in *La liberté ou l'amour!* (Paris: Gallimard), a book famously prefaced with a poem attributed (spuriously; the work is a pastiche by Desnos himself) to Rimbaud. In the ninth chapter, "Palace of Mirages," will-o'-the wisps are described as "garden flowers, half-seen in the darkness of your eyelids when you clench your eyes shut"; that this description occurs in a Proustian passage focused on memory is not incidental: phosphenes are the eyes' memory of themselves.

René Daumal's essay on "L'inérrable expérience" (*Le grand jeu* 4 [autumn 1932]: 2–5), one of the most lucid and least mystical accounts of extreme intoxication, describes the effects of inhaling carbon tetrachloride fumes one day, "pour voir ce qui arriverait [just to see what would happen]." What happened begins with the "fourmillement de points lumineus [swarming of luminous dots]" which are "bien connus de ceux qui ont subi une anethésie générale [well known to those who have gone under general anesthesia]," after which "les phosphènes prenaient soudain une intensité tel que, même les yeux ouvert, ils formaient devant moi un voile m'emêchant de rien voir d'autre [the phosphenes suddenly took on such an intensity that even with my eyes open they formed before me a veil which prevented me from seeing anything else at all]." As his experiments in the *raisonné dérèglement de tous les sens* might suggest, Rimbaud was an important and explicit influence on Daumal. Similarly, recall the conjunction of kerosene drinking and phosphenes in another surrealist work; the list of emotional discoveries in the third chapter of René Crevel's *Babylon* concludes: "And if she closed her eyes, she would see millions of stars" (trans. Kay Boyle [Los Angeles: Sun and Moon, 1996], 48).

46. Oster, "Phosphenes," 83.

47. From a lecture at Hampshire College, summer 1972 (audio tape no. 23, Media Study Inc., Buffalo, N.Y.); quoted in Wees, *Light Moving in Time*, 93. Brakhage makes similar comments elsewhere (*Scrapbook*, 48), and frequently repeats his Helmholzian rhetoric, speaking, for instance, of neural activity as a "short circuit" (*Scrapbook*, 134).

Brakhage insists that rather than an imaginative inventor of fantasies, he is "the most thorough documentary film maker in the world" because he documents "the act of seeing" (*Scrapbook*, 188). Despite his reservations about Brakhage's rejection of transparency, Bernstein echoes this assessment: "As for realism, from the point of view of reproducing the material conditions of seeing — including diffusion, distraction, fragmentation, blurring — works by Snow or Brakhage, and the like, are probably more deserving of the term" (*Content's Dream*, 103).

48. Cf. Brakhage, *Scrapbook*, 134.

49. Wees, *Light Moving in Time*, 3; R. L. Gregory, *Eye and Brain: The Psychology of Seeing*, 2nd ed. (New York: McGraw-Hill, 1973), 81.

50. Brakhage, *Scrapbook*, 51, 48; cf. 115, 120.

51. Lenny Lipton, "A Filmmaker's Column," *Take One* 4, no. 1 (1974): 46.

52. Ernie Gehr, "Interview with Jonas Mekas," *Film Culture* (March 1972): 32. Corroborating the interpretation that his film engages the mechanics of the mental and optical apparatuses, Gehr remarks: "If it had just been a film about grain, I might have released a 5 minute film" (35). As Roland Barthes would put it: "A little formalism turns one away from History, but . . . a lot brings one back to it."

I draw my description of the filming process from Gehr's interview with Jonas Mekas, as well as Scott McDonald's frequently reprinted essay, "Ernie Gehr: Camera Obscura/Lens/Filmstrip." In its original form, the film was apparently over twice as long and accompanied by a soundtrack (Brakhage, *Metaphors on Vision*, 437).

53. Morison, *Principles*, 5 (emphasis added).

54. Warde, *Crystal*, 93. The examples are ubiquitous, but see, for instance, Morison, *Principles*, 10–11; and Warde, *Crystal*, 84.

55. Eric Gill, *An Essay on Typography*, 2nd ed. (London: Sheed and Ward, 1936), 47.

56. These claims are even clearer in Morison's accounts of typographic history than in his manifestos, although even there he repeatedly appeals, like Warde, to social ordering as the strength of "good" design. Robin Kinross euphemistically refers to this position as the new traditionalists' philosophy of the "civilizing container" (*Modern Typography*, 66).

57. Warde, *Crystal*, 7, 171–73. Whatever the metaphorical richness, the association is not limited to Warde's paragraph. The Curwen Press, one of the primary venues of the new traditionalism's typographic "club," as Kinross puts it, "came to denote a world of gentle refinement: literate but not too serious, it was associated particularly with good food and wine" (*Modern Typography*, 59).

58. Richard Lanham, *The Electronic Word: Democracy, Technology, and the Arts* (Chicago: University of Chicago Press, 1993), 266; Morison, *Principles*, 7.

59. "Obstinate physicality" is Bernstein's phrase (Brito, *A Suite*); he also makes clear the process-oriented nature of the "veils" project in the catalogue essay "With Words"; the "veils," he says "came from a sense of the act of writing, that energy having as its *byproduct* the visual image" (*Content's Dream*, 291).

60. Martin Jay, *Downcast Eyes: The Denigration of Vision in Twentieth-Century French Thought* (Berkeley: University of California Press, 1993), 2.

61. Blake, *Complete Writings*, 426, 193.

62. Let me provide just a sampling of the relevant works, some of which are cited fully in the bibliography. Marjorie Perloff discusses poetry's relation to the modes of pubic discourse, including the rhetoric of transparence, in *Radical Artifice: Writing Poetry in the Age of Media* (Chicago: University of Chicago Press, 1991). Richard Lanham considers the wider-ranging implications of textual transparency in *The Electronic Word: Democracy, Technology, and the Arts* (Chicago: University of Chicago Press, 1993), as does Charles Bernstein himself in "Artifice of Absorption" (in Bernstein's *A Poetics*), where he picks up some of the arguments made by Ron Silliman in *The New Sentence*, which attempt to understand such ideologies in terms of political economy. Brian Rotman's delightfully supple, if historically imprecise, *Signifying Nothing: the semiotics of zero* (Houndmills: Macmillan, 1987), links the new scopic regime of one-point perspective to the emergence of mercantile capitalism in Renaissance Europe, where the vanishing point, the "zero" necessary for the development of bookkeeping, and the development of paper money all occupied the same conceptual position within their respective economies. Similarly, in *The Condition of Postmodernity* (London: Basil Blackwell, 1989), David Harvey situates changes in visual regimes in relation to more recent changes in political economy. Claude Gandelman engages those conditions of postmodernity less fully in his discussion of oculocentrism and logocentrism,

"Oculocentrism and Its Discontents," in *Reading Pictures/Viewing Texts* (Bloomington: Indiana University Press, 1991).

For more sweeping accounts, William Wees provides an overview of the changing historical "visualization of sight" in *Light Moving in Time* (see especially chapter 2), a history which Jonathan Crary also recounts in his argument for the modern reconfigurations of the spectator, *Techniques of the Observer.* Despite its substantial length and breadth, Martin Jay's survey of the role of vision in twentieth-century French philosophy, *Downcast Eyes,* does more to suggest further work, particularly in non-francophone philosophy, than to exhaust the inquiry. These accounts are (often implicitly and perhaps unknowingly) picking up on earlier work in the history of science, such as that done by Diksterhuis, de Santillana, and Linderberg.

The art historical literature on linear perspective is substantial, although one might begin with Erwin Panofsky, *Perspective as Symbolic Form,* trans. Christopher Wood (Cambridge: Zone Books, 1991): Hubert Damisch, *L'origine de la perspective* (Paris: Flammarion, 1987); William Ivins, *On the Rationalization of Sight* (New York: Metropolitan Museum of Art Papers no. 8, 1938); and Samuel Edgerton, *The Renaissance Rediscovery of Linear Perspective* (New York: Basic Books, 1975), to get a sense of the important differences between accounts of the same phenomenon. Joel Snyder's argument for the pictorialization of vision in "Picturing Vision" (*Critical Inquiry* 60, no. 3 [March 1990]) addresses many of the issues—such as "realism," convention, and the relationship between artistic and scientific theory—which lie behind most of the other critical accounts of visuality. With regard to the more explicit arguments for the implications of the development of perspectival systems, sympathetic projects have been undertaken in Michael Baxendall's archaeology of the "period eye" in *Painting and Experience in Fifteenth-Century Italy* (Oxford: Oxford University Press, 1972); Norman Bryson, *Vision and Painting: The Logic of the Gaze* (New Haven: Yale University Press, 1983); Svetlana Alpers, *The Art of Describing: Dutch Art in the Seventeenth Century* (Chicago: University of Chicago Press, 1983); Jacqueline Rose, *Sexuality in the Field of Vision* (London: Verso, 1986); and in Christine Buci-Glucksmann's *La folie du voir: De l'esthetique baroque* (Paris: Galilée, 1986), and to a lesser extent *La raison baroque: De Baudelaire à Benjamin* (Paris: Galilée, 1984).

63. Jay, "Scopic Regimes," 4.

64. Erwin Panofsky, *Renaissance and Renascences in Western Art* (Stockholm: Almqvist and Wiksell, 1960), 517. I take my etymology from the *Oxford English Dictionary,* but I should note that some accounts of the history of the word "perspective," in the sense of *construzione legittima,* are less certain, suggesting a possible modification of the medieval Italian *prospettiva,* a "scenic view," from the Latin *prospectus.* Regardless of its actual history, the English "perspective" betrays no trace of the prefix *pro* and maintains a graphic suggestion of looking *through.*

Joel Snyder claims that "by the end of the fourteenth century, the 'window pane feeling' had been well established" ("Picturing Vision," 518); although recall my earlier comments and qualifications on this figure of the window.

65. Jay, "Scopic Regimes," 16.

66. Hal Foster, introduction to *Vision and Visuality* (Seattle: Bay, 1988), ix.

67. Wittgenstein, *Investigations*, §66. For one consideration of Wittgenstein's visual tropes, see W. J. T. Mitchell's "Wittgenstein's Imagery and What It Tells Us," *New Literary History* 19, no. 2 (winter 1988): 361–70, as well as chapters 2 and 8 of his *Picture Theory* (Chicago: University of Chicago Press, 1994).

68. Wittgenstein, *Investigations*, 2:199. Throughout these notes, my references to Wittgenstein's text refer to proposition numbers, unless preceded by a "2," which indicates a page number in the second section of the *Investigations*.

69. Ibid., §144. Although German has a cognate for the anatomical *die pupille,* the homonym, of course, obtains only in the English translation (if this strikes you as somehow invalidating, please reconsider what follows from the "materiality of the signifier").

70. Ibid., 212.

71. Compare this relation of the visual field to a transcendent position with Wittgenstein's discussion of the "visual room" in the *Investigations,* which "has no master, outside or in" (§398).

In the following chapter I take up the idea of the textual sublime, but one might note here that the diagram in Wittgenstein's *Tractatus* at 5.6331—which appears in a book largely dedicated to the notion of "transcendence"—is the very figure Peter de Bolla maps onto the historical discourse of the sublime; Wittgenstein "places the eye where [Frances] Reynolds situates sublimity" (Peter de Bolla, *The Discourse of the Sublime: Readings in History, Aesthetics, and the Subject* [Oxford: Basil Blackwell, 1989], 49).

72. Wittgenstein, *Blue*, 31, 32. For a very interesting complement to Wittgenstein's text, one might consider Jean Louis Schefer's meditative essay "Quelles sont les choses rouges?" (*Art Studio International* 16: 18–31), in which he reasons: "*red things* don't exist." Noting that for Aristotle, red occurs "by way of vision: as the accident of vision . . . [as] a surface painted by the eyes," red, for Schefer, "doesn't actually constitute the body of red things: it makes them come as close as possible to . . . the surface that we ourselves become when we look at red."

73. Wittgenstein, *Blue*, 60.

Chapter 4

1. Wittgenstein, *Investigations*, §115.

2. Some of the final poems in *Camp Printing*, which move from mere overprinting to deploy their texts in geometric compositions of pieced blocks, explic-

itly recall the circular collages of Carlo Carrà, such as his *Interventionist Manifesto* (1914).

Contemporaneous with these poems, Waldrop was also producing overprints more like the textured screens of *Veil;* compare the thirteenth turning of her *Letters from Rosmarie and Keith Waldrop* (Providence: Burning Deck, 1970). For an example of a poem that stands, formally, between the layers of Bernstein's "veils" and the kinetic repetitions of *Camp Printing,* consider the overprinted sheets from Bob Cobbing's *Why Shiva Has Ten Arms* (London: Writers' Forum, Folder no. 7, 1969).

3. In an essay that starts from a very similar premise and proceeds to some very different conclusions, Jacinto Lageira writes: "à partir du futurisme . . . le 'poème visuel,' au sens large, va constituer un langage en soi à partir d'éléments linguisitques d'où est éliminé le sémantique, et qui tend à rejoindre la configuration du tableau [in the wake of futurism, . . . the 'visual poem,' in the broad sense of the term, comes to constitute a language in itself, developing out of linguistic elements from which the semantic has been eliminated, and which approaches the condition of pictorial composition]" ("Le poème du langage," in *Poesure et peintre: "D'un art, l'autre,"* ed. Bernard Blistène and Véronique Legrand [Avignon: Réunion des Musées Nationaux, Musées de Marseille, 1993], 319.

4. Silliman, *New Sentence,* 13.

5. Similar poems have appeared from Christian Morgenstern and the pseudonymous Joyce Holland, to name just one early and one late practicioner. See the former's *Gallowsongs* and the latter's "dash poem" contribution to *This* 3.

6. An even more perfect balance is struck in one of Bill Bissett's contemporaneous poems. Bissett frequently employs overprinting (or typing) techniques, which if not always so illegible do tend toward this degree of symmetry, suggesting an obsessive repetition absent from Waldrop's poems.

For a similar reading of an "unintelligible" poem, see Jean-Jacques LeCercle's reading of Edward Lear's "nonsense" letters (*The Violence of Language* [London: Routledge, 1990]); Richard Bradford's discussion of eighteenth-century experiments with typographic meaning ("The Visual Poem in the Eighteenth Century," *Visible Language* 23, no. 1 [1990]); and Michael Twyman's more recent account of "typography without words" (*Visible Language* 15, no. 1), which makes clear that such readings—as well as the aesthetics of a poem like Man Ray's—pass into the discourse of design theory.

Similar conventions adhere for painting as well; Mondrian—in one of his more embarrassing moments—insisted on the feminine horizontal and the male vertical; Walter Benjamin held out for the verticality of painting against the horizontality of drawing; and Jon Erickson, with a passing reference to the referentiality of de Kooning's paintings, claims that the "question of landscape will always appear in any painting that divides its planes horizontally, whether intended by the artist or not. Indeed, *horizontal* comes from the *horizon:* the defining feature of our visual world" (Jon Erickson, *The Fate of the Object: From Modern Object to Postmodern Sign in Performance, Art, and Potry* [Ann Arbor: University of Michigan Press, 1995], 218). The footnote to this sentence reveals the source of Erickson's insight: "In the commercial graphic art world, an illustration layout placed vertically is called a 'portrait' and horizontally a 'landscape.' This designation based on positioning, regardless of content, verifies the painting as picture even if only according to canvas shape, no matter how minimal the content." However intriguing these assertions, one clearly would not want to make any grand claims about the meaning of canvas shape, other than to note that viewers do sometimes take it to have *some* inherent significance.

7. Additionally, that mechanical information implies social and economic information as well: the number of people required to operate a press or machine binder, their requisite level of training, the complexity of their organization, as well as the capital required to access, or own, print technologies.

8. A note on terms: beyond denoting "rules for proceeding" and the obvious connotations of digital communication (those characters at the opening and close of a message that enable one machine to communicate with another), "protocol" should here evoke both palimpsests and collage, neither irrelevant to the works under discussion in this book. In Greek, the *protokollon* (*prot* + *kollan* = to "glue together") was the first sheet of a papyrus roll, which bore data of manufacture.

9. Citing Bob Cobbing, D. A. Levy, and Bernstein in passing, Steve McCaffery offers a similar analysis:

> Overprint (the laying of text over text to the point of obliterating all legibility) is Bissett's method of deterritorializing linguistic codes and placing language in a state of vertical excess. Overprint destroys the temporal conditions of logic and causality, obliterating articulation and destroying message by its own super-abundance. In this way semantic property reduces to a common, un-differentiated equivalent graphic substance, whilst spatial difference is rearranged to intercept the material surface of the code causing it to physically collide and jam" (Steve McCaffery, *North of Intention: Critical Writings 1973– 1986* [New York: Roof Books, 1986], 103).

I discuss the reduction of the semantic to the material, as well as the idea of textual excess, below.

10. De Saussure employs an inconsistent vocabulary, sometimes using the more familiar *anagramme,* deciding briefly in favor of *paragramme* since the distribution of vocalics through the poem was more spatially complex than simply initial placement, and then generally favoring *hypogramme,* in part to underscore his faith in a governing subtext for the distribution of linguistic material. From *hypogramme,* presumably, Jean Starobinski takes the title of his invaluable study of de Saussure's

notebooks, *Les mots sous les mots,* and the appropriateness of imagining "words written over words," in the context of works like *Veil* and *Camp Printing,* should be self-evident.

One of the earliest reactions to Starobinski's revelations of the notebook cache (first in *Mercure de France* in 1964 and then in a festschrift for Roman Jakobson in 1967) is Michel Deguy's review essay "La folie de Saussure" (*Critique* 260 [January 1969]: 20–26). Georges Mounin's essay on "Les anagrammes de Saussure" appeared in *Studi Saussuriani,* ed. Robert Godel (Bologna: Società Editrice il Mulino, 1974: 235–41), the same year that *Semiotext(e)* devoted two special issues to de Saussure: "The Two Saussures" (1, no. 2 [fall 1974]) and "Saussure's Anagrammes" (2, no. 1 [spring 1975]); among particular interest in these volumes are the facsimiles of two of Saussure's notebooks, as well as the contributions by Michael Riffaterre and Sylvère Lotringer, whose previous review essay "The Game of the Name" (*Diacritics* 3, no. 2 [summer 1973]: 2–9) is also essential. George Redard's reaction to the *Semiotext(e)* colloquium was published as "Deux Saussure?" in *Cahiers Ferdinand de Saussure* 32 (1978): 27–41. Within a couple of years, J.-.M. Adam and J.-P. Goldstein could devote an entire chapter to "Les anagrammes ou la déconstruction" in *Linguistique et discours litteraire* (Larousse, 1976), 42–59; and already by 1977 Michel Dupuis felt compelled to offer a sober and conservative counter to the more speculative uses of Saussure's notebooks ("À propos des anagrammes saussuriennes," *Cahiers d'analyse textuelle* 19 [1977]: 7–24), calling for a scholarly assessment of the archive material, a challenge which David Shepheard takes up, in part, in his discussion of "Saussure's Vedic Anagrams" (*Modern Language Review* 77 [July 1982]: 513–23). By all accounts, Peter Runderli's *Ferdinand de Saussure und die Anagramme* (Tübingen, 1972) is an important work; the German, unfortunately, puts his text beyond my knowledge.

Further writing on the *anagrammes* can be found in David L. Clark's "Monstrosity, Illegibility, Denegation: De Man, Nichol, and the Resistance to Postmodernism," in *Negation, Critical Theory, and Postmodern Textuality,* ed. Daniel Fischlin (Dordrecht: Kluwer Academic Publishers, 1994); Julia Kristeva's *Revolution in Poetic Language* and "Pour une semiologié des paragrammes" (*Tel Quel* [spring 1967]); and several of the exemplary essays in Steve McCaffery's *North of Intention,* "The *Martyrology* as Paragram" and "Writing as a General Economy" in particular. Finally, Michel Meylakh places de Saussure's studies in the context of Slavic traditions ("À propos des anagrammes," *L'homme* 16, no. 4 [October-December 1976]: 105–15), a topic that has been addressed more recently by Walter Comin-Richmond ("Krycenyx's *Maloxolija V Kapote:* The Anagrammitization of Literature," *Slavic and East European Journal* 38, no. 4 [1994]: 618–35).

Despite their similar interest in the generation of meaning from the slightest phonemic difference ("cat" and "hat," for example), no one, as far as I know, has mentioned the fact that "De Saussure" and "Dr. Seuss" are almost perfect anagrams.

11. Paul de Man, *The Resistance to Theory* (Minneapolis: University of Minnesota Press, 1986), 37.

12. Although de Saussure would continue to refuse to acknowledge that inhumanness, it would also be discernible in the roughly contemporaneous work which supplanted his paragrammatic investigations and for which he is famous. In the structural schema advanced in the *Cours de linguistique générale,* meaning is only generated differentially from out of the model of linguistic structure; once again, the *material* produces, displacing the power of positive human willing. Indeed, one might compare this discussion with the "linguistic crisis" that Linda Dowling posits as the source of decadence (*Language and Decadence in the Victorian Fin de Siècle* [Princeton: Princeton University Press, 1986]). The new Victorian science of linguistics, in Dowling's reading, "raised a specter of autonomous language—language as a system blindly obeying impersonal phonological rules in isolation from any world of human values and experience" (xii). My thanks to Brian Reed for bringing Dowling's work to my attention.

De Saussure, of course, would disclaim such a statement about "materiality," but he always does so with a stridency that protests rather too much, flatly denying the primacy of the material (not to mention writing) and making recourse to the voodoo of "l'image vocale." Jacques Derrida, the reader most attentive to such slights (cf. *Of Grammatology*), performs a not-dissimilar sleight of hand, emphasizing the materiality of the signifier while allowing it to avoid any "presence" by escaping through the trapdoor of a *mise en abîme.* Both strategies are more or less clever, but cheating never really wins the game.

13. De Man, *Resistance,* 96.

14. In this passage, de Man is clarifying an earlier remark, which is worth repeating for the dark turns revealed in its final, hesitating speculations:

The way in which I can try to mean is dependent upon linguistic properties that are not only [not] made by me, because I depend on the language as it exists for the devices which I will be using, it is as such not made by us as historical beings, it is perhaps not even made by humans at all . . . it is not at all certain that language is in any sense human (*Resistance,* 87).

De Man seems more fascinated by this conclusion than reluctant to reach it.

15. The quote is from de Man, *Resistance,* 96. My example, which shifts de Saussure's phonetics to a visual model, obviously benefits from the opposing registers of the two words, which in part explains its frequent appearance, from Jackson Mac Low's *Words nd Ends* to Susan Howe's *Articulation of Sound Forms in Time* ("Sarah's laughter"), as well as the fifth book of B. P. Nichol's *Martyrology* ("the word shift: 'laughter in slaughter'"), all of which echo James Joyce's "laughtears," which John Cage so loved and frequently quoted. In the vocabulary of Russian formalism-futurism, this is a perfect example of сдвиг (*sdvig*), the "shift" which someone like Zdanevich might describe acting on the "verbal mass" of "laughter"

so that its gravitational pull attracts the genitive "s" away from "Sarah." *Sdvig* is only one of many names, as we shall see, given to the operation of language's inhumanity. As this book should make clear, many avant-garde writings are in fact the application of alternative reading strategies which have left a written record in their wake. In addition to сдвиг, one might think of homophonic translations like Zukofsky's Catullus, or those early Clark Coolidge poems which seem to have been read down the edge of a justified page, for just two examples.

For a more thorough reading of de Man's late writing, see David Clark's essay "Monstrosity, Illegibility, Denegation: De Man, Nichol, and the Resistance to Postmodernism," which starts from an understanding of the inhuman that is very close to mine, but then goes on to speculate about death, monstrosity, and denegation. Combining his arguments with an attentive reading of B. P. Nichol's *Martyrology*, Clark also begins to suggest the rewards of an "applied paragrammatology."

16. De Man, *Resistance*, 101.

17. Ibid., 89.

18. Jean-François Lyotard, *The Inhuman: Reflections on Time*, trans. Geoffrey Bennington and Rachel Bowlby (Stanford: Stanford University Press, 1991), 11.

19. George Oppen, *Collected Poems* (New York: New Directions, 1975), 186.

20. De Man, *Resistance*, 84.

21. Jacques Derrida, "De l'économie restreinte a l'économie générale: Un Hegelianisme sans réserve," in *L'écriture et la différance* (Paris: Éditions du Seuil, 1967), 376; translated as "From Restricted to General Economy: A Hegelianism without Reserves," *Semiotext(e)* 2, no. 2 (1976): 29.

22. In addition to the "inhuman" of Lyotard and de Man, recall, for example, Michel Serres's "Demon" or Jean-Jacques LeCercle's "violence of the supplement"; Guy Debord, in fact, pins his hope of a truly revolutionary poetics on the "fundamentally strange and foreign" nature of words (Debord, "All the King's Men," 29). In Wittgensteinian terms, such language refuses to "say": "There is indeed the inexpressible. This *shews* itself; it is the mystical." In Lacanian terms, the "inhuman" is familiar as *lalangue,* and it is clearly related to the "Other"; "language, world, the fact of a movement of signification beyond human meaning" (Stephen Melville, "In Light of the Other," *Whitewalls* 23 [fall 1989]). If that sort of thing interests you, see Jean-Claude Milner, *L'amour de la langue* (Paris, 1978), for more on a post-Saussurean Lacanian linguistics.

23. Jean Baudrillard, *L'autre par lui-même* (Paris: Éditions Galilée, 1987), 28, 29.

24. Ibid., 82.

25. Ibid., 72.

26. Ibid., 76, 80.

27. Ibid., 55.

28. Steve McCaffery's invaluable writing brings together several of the topics I have addressed in this chapter, including a paragrammatic understanding of writ-

ing as a general economy. McCaffery focuses on how subjectivity is put into question by libidinal economies, but his arguments are in full congress with a more de Manian inflection. Noting that "those varieties of wordplay (pun, homophony, palindrome, anagram, paragram, charade) which relate writing to the limits of intentionality and the Subject's own relation to meaning" are instances "where language emerges as a general force whose operation is no longer authenticated, nor controlled by conscious instrumental reason and the intentional subject" (*North of Intention*, 58, 66), McCaffery explains:

> we must further admit to the infinite resourcefulness of language itself to produce aimlessly and fulfill in effect all the features Bataille assigns to a general economy: unmasterable excess, inevitable expenditure and a thoroughly nonproductive outlay (209).

For other arguments on the general economy of writing, though none so attentive to the microlevel of the text, see Arkady Plotnitsky's more sustained and philosophically grounded *Reconfigurations: Critical Theory and General Economy* (Gainesville: University Press of Florida, 1993); Jacques Derrida's challenging and uncompromising reading of Bataille's own writing as a general economy, "From Restricted to General Economy: A Hegelianism without Reserves"; and Jean Baudrillard's deliriously ungrounded essays on communication, which crib much of their diction and ideas directly from Bataille. It would be difficult to overestimate the importance of Bataille's thought on contemporary "theory," as the models of excess in such familiar terms as "le hyperréal" and "le supplément dangereux" only begin to evince.

29. For Bataille's expansion on the idea of a general economy, see *La part maudite* (Paris: Les Éditions Minuit, 1967) and *L'histoire de l'érotisme* and *La souveraineté* (published as vol. 8 of the *Oeuvres complètes* [Paris: Éditions Gallimard, 1976]). An English translation by Brian Hurley of all three works is available in two volumes as *The Accursed Share: An Essay on General Economy* (New York: Zone, 1988, 1991)

30. Georges Bataille, *L'expérience intérieure* (Paris: Gallimard, 1954), 233.

31. Ibid.

32. In the notes which constitute *L'expérience intérieure*, Bataille defines poetry as utile language deployed in inutile ways ("do not forget that a poem, although it is composed in the language of giving information, is not used in the language-game of giving information"), and he confesses:

> De la poésie, je dirai maintenant qu'elle est, je crois, le sacrifice où les mots sont victimes. Les mots, nous les utilisons, nous faisons d'eux les instruments d'actes utiles. Nous n'aurions rien d'humain si le langage en nous devait être en entier servile. Nous ne pouvons non plus nous passer des rapport efficaces

qu'introduisent les mots entre les hommes et les choses. Mais nous les arrachons à ces rapports dans un délire (173).

Of poetry, I will now say that it is, I believe, the sacrifice where words are victims. Words—we use them, we make of them the instruments of utile acts. We would scarcely be human at all if language had to be entirely servile in us. We could never get by without the efficacious rapport that words establish between people and things. But we tear words from these links in a delirium.

Bataille makes a similar distinction between a meaningless poetic language and a significant language in "Hegel: La mort et le sacrifice," *Deucalion* 5 (1955): 40. In contrast with the semantic meaning of a utile language, "That which is not servile is unspeakable" (214), and "by definition, the *excess* is outside reason" (*L'histoire de l'érotisme*).

33. Even to recognize a general economy *as such* may be enough to redirect the profitlessness of its expenditures and remake it as a restricted economy; one may have to be content with understanding that a system can, or even must, be conceivable as a general economy without knowing exactly how its losses are dissipated.

34. Derrida, "From Restricted to General Economy," 397/43.

35. Following from the explications of de Man's later writings made by Cynthia Chase (*Decomposing Figures: Rhetorical Readings in the Romantic Tradition* [Baltimore: Johns Hopkins University Press, 1986]) and Marc Redfield ("Humanizing de Man," *Diacritics* 19, no. 2 [1989]: 35–54), David Clark offers a similar analysis in terms of "denegation" and "readability" ("Monstrosity," 276 et seq.). For readers interested in arguments roughly parallel to mine, but made in more "theoretical" terms, I recommend all three accounts, and Redfield's review essay in particular.

36. Baudrillard, *L'autre*, 80.

37. Wittgenstein, *Investigations*, §210. In addition to the "arbitrary cipher" he actually draws out there and at §166, Wittgenstein proposes a dingbat language of signs, with "arbitrary flourishes" replacing familiar letters in a string of inscriptions radically disconnected from any referential meaning (§169): "&∞§≠ §≠?ß +% ∞!'§*." Such scripts are taken up throughout the *Philosophical Investigations*, where Wittgenstein is interested in precisely that moment on the jagged torus where one might equivocate between saying "Here is a Chinese sentence" and "No, that only looks like writing; it is actually just an ornament" (§108). In this context, mentions of "orthography," such as the one in proposition 121, do not seem merely random examples.

38. De Man, *Resistance*, 89; Lotringer, "The Game of the Name," 4.

39. McCaffery also has a sense that such poems are limnal; with echoes of T. S. Eliot's "The Hollow Men" ("shape without form, shade without colour, / Paralysed force, gesture without motion"), he writes: "Overprint achieves a state of being without being-in, a living without life, motion without definition, writing without the written" (*North of Intention*, 104).

40. Bernstein, *Poetics,* 65; Ludwig Wittgenstein, *Tractatus Logico-Philosophicus,* trans. C. K. Ogden (London: Routledge, 1990), 5.62.

41. Blake, *Complete Writings,* 490.

42. Recent discussions have described the provocation of the sublime experience in precisely these terms of "an excess of the plane of the signifier" or the "infinity of materiality" (Thomas Weiskel, *The Romantic Sublime* [Baltimore: Johns Hopkins University Press, 1976], 103; Frances Ferguson, *Solitude and the Sublime: Romanticism and the Aesthetics of Individuation* [New York: Routledge, 1992], 14). "Mathematical" is of course Kant's term, which he elaborates in the second book of the *Critique of Judgment,* while "in a manner analogous to terror" comes from Burke's famous description in section 7 of his *Philosophical Inquiry.*

43. Samuel Holt Monk, *The Sublime* (Ann Arbor: University of Michigan Press, 1960), 93; Ferguson, *Solitude,* 8. To be precise, there are no sublime objects, only those that might elicit the experience of the sublime. Given the opacities of vision that I have argued are such an integral part of experiencing a work like *Veil,* readers should not forget that one of the prototypically sublime moments is "gazing on a *cataract*" (as Coleridge puts it in "On the Principles of Genial Criticism").

The specifics of a particular sublime (Burkean, Kantian, Schillerian, Coleridgean, and so on) aside, Vincent A. De Luca's general summarization of these sublimes should appear more or less familiar to readers of works like *Veil* (allowing for varying personal degrees of "stimulation" and "exaltation"): "In the theory of the period the sublime experience is typically presented as a three-fold moment: an encounter with the stimulating object, an episode of discontinuity (usually described as vertigo or blockage or bafflement), and a sudden and ecstatic exaltation" (Vincent A. De Luca, "A Wall of Words: The Sublime as Text," in *Unnam'd Forms: Blake and Textuality,* ed. Nelson Hilton and Thomas Vogler [Berkeley: University of California Press, 1986], 218–19). Nor have I forgotten Knapp's caveat about the caveats about summarizing the sublime.

Mallarmé, not surprisingly, evokes the paragrammatic sublime in his essay "The Book: A Spiritual Instrument," where he speaks of the "miracle of the word: words led back to their origin, which is the twenty-four letters of the alphabet, so gifted with infinity that they will finally consecrate language. Everything is caught up in their endless cariations and then rises out of them in the form of the principle. Thus typography becomes a rite." That rite, as we saw, is one of sacrifice.

44. The bibliography on the sublime has now almost attained the "infinite magnitude" of Kant's mathematical sublime. To understand all of these discussions as engaging the same subject simply because they employ the same term would be a gross error, but an inquiry into "the sublime" would obviously begin with the treatise attributed to Longinus, Kant's *Critique of Judgment,* Burke's *Philosophical Inquiry into the Origin of Our Ideas of the Sublime and Beautiful,* and Schiller's *Letters on the Aesthetic Education of Man,* before proceeding to Addison, Blake, and Coleridge—and perhaps even Schopenhauer if you're really feeling up to it. The

best general overviews can still be found in Walter John Hipple, *The Beautiful, Sublime, and Picturesque in Eighteenth-Century British Aesthetic Theory* (Carbondale: Southern Illinois University Press, 1957); Samuel Holt Monk's *The Sublime;* Thomas Weiskel's *The Romantic Sublime;* and Peter de Bolla's *The Discourse of the Sublime.* Among the many more specific studies, of particular interest for the issues raised in this chapter are Paul de Man's reading of Kant in *Aesthetic Ideology* (Minneapolis: University of Minnesota Press, 1996); Frances Ferguson's theorization of the sublime contra de Man in *Solitude and the Sublime;* and Lyotard's several claims for recuperating a "postmodern" sublime. These works should be surpassed by the long-anticipated book on the sublime forthcoming from Gregg Biglieri.

Putting aside the dangers of collapsing Kant and Burke so blithely as I have just done, limitations for the idea of a "textual sublime," in any precise or technical sense of the word drawn from classical or eighteenth-century philosophy should be immediately obvious. To begin with, the text is not a natural object (requisite for the Kantian sublime), the "inhumanness" of language does not clearly return one to a feeling of humanist superiority and a knowledge of the immortality of the soul, and so on. Perhaps most important, however, the Longinian sublime has been read in ways that would set it in diametric opposition, rather than collusion, with my argument. In a work starkly antithetical to mine, Charles J. Rzepka defines the sublime as transcending the materiality of the signifier and achieving a transparent text of perfect communication. Rzepka also argues, without mention of Bataille, for a "general economy" of writing that is also very different from the one I have presented.

45. De Luca, "A Wall of Words," 232, 218.

46. Ibid., 232.

47. In what he calls *le ritual de la transparence* (the ritual of transparence), Baudrillard's contemporaneous description is worth comparison:

Pour qu'il y ait regard, il faut qu'un objet se voile et se dévoile, qu'il disparaisse à chaque instant; c'est pourquoi il y a dans le regard une sorte d'oscillation . . . . Dans une image, certaines parties sont visibles, et d'autres non, les parties visible rendent les autres invisible

In order to really look at an object, it must veil and unveil itself, it must disappear each instant, because looking is a kind of oscillation . . . . In an image, certain aspects are visible, others not, and the visible parts render those others invisible (*L'autre,* 30).

48. De Luca, "Wall of Words," 219.

49. Ibid., 232.

50. The phrase "wall of words" repeats through *Veil,* where it refers to Jim Brody's collective nickname for Bernstein, Nick Piombino, and Bruce Andrews—

all of whom lived on New York City's upper West Side at the time—as "the west side wall of words" (private correspondence). In "Blow-Me-Down Etude" the phrase returns, appropriately altered, as "The Westside wail of words" (Charles Bernstein, *Rough Trades* [Los Angeles: Sun and Moon, 1991], 94).

51. Bill Bissett makes recourse to the same convention in the left-hand column of his poem "train" (*inkorrect thots* [Vancouver: Talon Books, 1992]).

52. De Luca, "Wall of Words," 218, emphasis added; McCaffery, *North of Intention,* 208; Starobinski, *Les mots,* 122; de Man, *Resistance,* 51; and Baudrillard, *L'autre,* 60–63; see also Baudrillard's *Symbolic Exchange and Death* (London, Thousand Oaks: Sage Publications, 1993). As the ubiquitous references suggest, one would not want to underestimate the significance, or the mythic stature, of de Saussure's *paragrammes* for recent "theory."

53. De Man, *L'autre,* 23. To indicate yet another discourse operating on precisely these terms and also return to the resistance of totalizing scopic regimes and the ordering of vision by manmade laws, the effect of reading a work like *Veil* becomes something like *la folie du voir,* the baroque "madness of vision" that Christine Buci-Glucksmann has recovered for postmodern memory. With its "fascination for opacity, unreadability, and . . . indecipherability" and its "dependence on the materiality of the medium," the "palimpsests of the unseeable" in that madness of vision effect a general economy of "dazzling, disorienting, ecstatic surplus" (Jay, *Downcast Eyes,* 16–17).

54. For one example of a very sophisticated *mettre en jeu* of different theoretical and philosophical concerns, via overprinting, consider the mirrored page from Lyn Hejinian and Travis Ortiz's *The Staking Effect.* At issue, in the context of the larger poem, are specific concepts put forth by Jean-François Lyotard, Jalal Toufic, and Mikhail Bakhtin—as well as more general issues relating to repetition, silence, and—of course—collaboration.

Chapter 5

1. In Leon Roudiez's definition, any reading that challenges the normative referential grammar of a text by forming "networks of signification not accessible through conventional reading habits" would be paragrammatic (quoted in Kristeva, *Revolution,* 256). In "Silent Performances: On Reading John Cage," Arthur J. Sabatini mentions de Saussure's anagrams in relation to Cage's mesostics, though he does not develop the conjunction (Sabatini, *John Cage at Seventy-Five,* 74–96). Velimir Xlebnikov actually composed certain poems by encrypting proper names into the lines (cf. Ronald Vroon, *Vladimir Xlebnikov's Shorter Poems,* 178 et seq.).

2. To be precise: as with his fourth writing-through of *Finnegans Wake,* Cage

added a further constraint by not permitting the repetition of the same syllable used to present a given letter of the name. In a less strict mesostic, the first letter may be repeated.

In her review of *American Poetry: The Twentieth Century* (*The New Republic*, 19 June 2001), Helen Vendler does not seem to understand the mesostic form which she dismisses as "too easy." As proof that John Cage's *Composition in Retrospect* is an "uninteresting experiment," Vendler tries her own hand at the mesostic, however, had she actually followed Cage's rule almost a third of her lines would not be permitted.

After hearing Joe Gargery's account — " 'Why, here's a J . . . and a O equal to anythink! Here's a J and a O, Pip, and a J-O, Joe . . . . One, two, three. Why here's three J's and three O's, and three J-O. . . .' " — it's difficult not to imagine him completing the string with "Y-C-E," like Cage: "I just went straight on, A after J, E after M, J after S, Y after O, E after C. I read each passage at least three times over" (John Cage, *Writing Through Finnegans Wake*, n.p.).

3. James Joyce, *Finnegans Wake* (New York: Penguin, 1976), 120.

4. I want to draw attention to Albert Gelpi's discussion of *Words nd Ends from Ez* in "The Genealogy of Postmodernism: Contemporary American Poetry" (*The Southern Review* [summer 1990]), in part because it is one of the few mentions of the poem in the critical literature and in part because the urgency of this chapter derives from a desire to answer those who — like Al — have taught me to love poetry with a passionate intelligence, but who do not see the pleasures and interest offered by writers like Cage and Mac Low (and Christopher Dewdney, whom I discuss later in this chapter).

Gelpi suggests that Mac Low's poem is "senseless" (532), unreadable "jibberish" that does "not warrant attention" beyond its "absurdity" (529), and before accusing Mac Low of not being a "serious . . . poet" but rather one of "the tricksters," Gelpi asks: "how many of the very few who pick up MacLow's book will get any farther into its seventy-seven pages than it takes to unriddle the gimmick?" (529). Patterns of reading and the demands of radical writing are important issues, but I, for one, would never want to mistake the *quantity* of a readership for the *quality* of those who can rise to the challenge.

5. Jackson Mac Low, *Words nd Ends from Ez* (Bolinas: Avenue B, 1989), 25.

6. Ibid., 54; John Cage, *X: Writings '79–'82* (Middletown, Conn.: Wesleyan University Press, 1983), 110. See Linda Voris, "Along the Spreading Surface: The Sequence of Gertrude Stein's Compositional Tasks in the 1920s" (dissertation), University of California at Berkeley, 1998.

7. For more on Cage's Norton lectures, see Marjorie Perloff, *Radical Artifice*, 200–16. It is possible, though unlikely, that Wittgenstein served as the source for Mac Low's second acrostic poem, with pride of place going to Mark Twain's *Life on the Mississippi* (Mac Low, *Stanzas for Iris Lezak*, 401). For more on Mac Low's

DIASTEX method, see his "afterword" to *Barnesbook: Four Poems Derived from Sentences by Djuna Barnes* (Los Angeles: Sun and Moon, 1996), 47–53). I discuss another of the DIASTEX poems, "Barnes 4," later in this chapter.

In a 1984 interview with Andrew Payne, Steve McCaffery muses in passing: "It would be interesting to approach Cage's and Mac Low's writing through Wittgenstein's notion of the language game" (*North of Intention,* 119–20); I hope this essay achieves some small measure of the interest he predicted.

8. For a discussion of the influence of Wittgenstein on Johns and Joseph Kosuth, which might have gone much further in making its case, see Jessica Prinz's *Art Discourse/Discourse on Art* (New Brunswick, N.J.: Rutgers University Press, 1991); Marjorie Perloff's "coda" to *Wittgenstein's Ladder: Poetic Language and the Strangeness of the Ordinary* (Chicago: University of Chicago Press, 1996), which might also have been expanded, and in which she presents Kosuth's witty treatment of Wittgenstein; and Kosuth's *Letters from Wittgenstein, Abridged at Ghent* (Ghent: Imschoot-Uitgevers, 1992)—a book that might itself be thought of as a sort of "writing-through."

9. Cf. Steve McCaffery's note in *Vort: Twenty-First Century Pre-Views* 3, no. 2 (1975): 63. The quotation from Cage appears on the back cover of Mac Low's *Words nd Ends.*

10. William Shakespeare, *Hamlet,* act 2, scene 2, lines 190–91.

11. Wittgenstein, *Investigations,* §156; cf. §§156–62 et passim. The second part of this chapter will propose an answer to Wittgenstein's version of Hamlet's joke: "What would you be missing if you did not *experience* the meaning of a word?" (*Investigations,* 2:214).

12. Ibid., §344, 2:212.

13. The most sustained *gedankenexperiment* about "reading machines" in the *Investigations* occurs at §157, anticipating the machinic metaphors of §193 et passim; the figure of the idling engine as a correlative for the confusions of philosophy when language has "gone on holiday" recurs most forcefully at §§88 and 132.

14. Wittgenstein, *Investigations,* §108. Although the sense of §36 suggests a more general reference, this choice of "phantasm" in §108 resonates with the earlier use of "spirit" and, when combined with the evocative term "medium," offers a more literal reading of "language": "Where our language suggests a body and there is none: there, we should like to say, is a *spirit.*"

15. Ibid., §120.

16. Ibid., §165.

17. Ibid., §108, §203.

18. Ibid., §242.

19. Ibid., §160, §198.

20. Agnes Martin's paintings can be read as the perfect emblem for Wittgenstein's schematic of disciplined writing. This is obviously not the place for a full

treatment of her work, which I find terrifyingly fascist in its mystical pretensions to presence, rhetoric of "purity" and "hygiene," aggressive insistence on order, uniformity, regularity and regulation, repetition, and linearity (everything involved with being "in-line"), and so on. One might, however, note the hand-drawn graphite lines that run—like written texts (the use of pencil is not coincidental)—from left to right across the canvas, bordering the painted stripes. Discernible beneath the tremor and waver of this "text," however, a careful viewer can make out the impression of a straight-edge blade which has cut into the primed canvas and underlies—both literally and metaphorically—those graphite lines. On the one hand, it is a retelling of the old story of Malevich's lyric suprematism and the geometry of constructivism. But Martin's lyric line offers no resistance to the totalitarianism of her project; the pencil lines serve as regulating "guide lines," so that their "writing" is the text of complicity; they are the trace of the performance of a disciplined subject under the pressures of authority: obsession, single-mindedness, fanaticism, controlled response. These paintings are the visual equivalent of being ordered to write on the board a hundred times "I will not . . ." and so they stand as the serious punchline to John Baldessari's "I will not make any more boring art" (1971).

21. Wittgenstein, *Investigations,* §131.

22. Ibid., §140.

23. Ibid., §146.

24. Ibid., §193. What if, like T. E. Hulme, we recognized that which is usually thought of as "the grit in the machine" as instead "the fundamental element of the machine"?

25. Wittgenstein, *Investigations,* §133.

26. Ibid., §176. Compare the sections of Wittgenstein's *Remarks on the Foundations of Mathematics,* §§29–31.

27. For the argument that proper names are rigid designators, see Saul A. Kripke, *Naming and Necessity* (Cambridge: Harvard University Press, 1980): 49–63 et passim.

28. Wittgenstein, *Investigations,* §401.

29. Jackson Mac Low, "Museletter," in *The L=A=N=G=U=A=G=E Book,* ed. Bruce Andrews and Charles Bernstein (Carbondale: Southern Illinois University Press, 1984), 26.

30. I take the phrase "lyrical interference" from Olson, of course. The logic by which Slavic futurism often turned to the other extreme—"ego-futurism," Mayakovskii's top-of-the-voice *Я!*—might be worth thinking through.

The precedent—once again—for resorting to rules in order to rid the artistic act of the ego is of course Marcel Duchamp. One of the (several and contradictory) claims Duchamp made for the ready-made was that its selection was an act of aesthetic indifference embodying the total absence of "taste" (Cabanne, *Dialogues with Marcel Duchamp,* 48), and the guarantor of that indifference was an arbitrary rule: "on such and such a time." That one ought not simply take Duchamp at his word, or that this may not be the best way to understand the ready-mades, should go without saying.

31. Emblematic of this problem is the *musicircus,* one of Cage's most blatant attempts to diminish the ego and "act as if there is no use in a center." Explicitly established as an anti-hierarchical and anarchic event, the *musicircus* is bounded by broad constraints: a particular time and place, neither admission fees nor payments to the sufficiently large number of musicians performing in diverse genres and distributed through the space in random and indiscreet ways so that they provide a promiscuity of noise. For the enactment I saw at Stanford University in early 1992, this meant that one entering the spread-out complex of music school buildings might find a jazz ensemble in the hallway a few steps from the punk band on the stairwell, and outside the office in which the sitar player had set up . . . all of the sound mixing as the mobile auditor moved past the man with the musical pinball machines and towards the Gregorian chanters, mixing with other visitors and performers already finished or yet to play. Also performing—as conspicuously advertised—was John Cage himself, reading from his composition *Muoyce.* One did not just stumble across him, however, standing in the hallway next to the marching band, or in one of the glass-cubicle practice rooms with a lounge singer on one side and a concert pianist on the other; he was sequestered at the *very center* of the complex, behind closed doors in a large dark room (the only light a desk lamp aimed directly over his head), and despite the presence of a microphone reading in a barely audible whisper: the very model of passive aggression. Not surprisingly, this arrangement had the effect of creating both an initial mystery that focused attention on Cage (where was he?), and also—for those who finally found him—an atmosphere of having entered the sacred cave of the sibyl. Around the illuminated desk where Cage uttered his hushed whispers, the audience stood in the dark: necessarily drawn close, reverently silent, and straining with attention in an attempt to even make out what he was saying. Norman O. Brown, a contrary presence throughout the events held at Stanford that week, voiced similar reservations about the *musicircus.* Charles Junkerman notes the potentially paradoxical centering of the event but graciously offers a generous if not entirely convincing apologia ("nEw/foRms of living together," in *John Cage: Composed in America,* ed. Marjorie Perloff and Charles Junkerman [Chicago: University of Chicago Press, 1994], 49–50).

One might further note that even the most successful attempt to eliminate the ego by chance operations would have a certain historical twist as well, given the degree to which we have increasingly become "statistical subjects" over the last 150 years.

32. The line appears in the appendix to Bob Brown's *Readies* anthology (162).

In addition to playing off Pound's nickname, Brown relies on the names for the graphemes "e" and "z" to equate Pound's poetry with what is "easy"; mimicking a colloquial adverbial form of "easily" appropriate to the informally abbreviated "Ez," Brown's sentence translates to "what guy can't easily write a canto?" Similarly, playing off the rhyme (in the eye as well as the ear) of "cant" and "canto," Brown exploits the apostrophe's purely graphic differentiation between "can't" and "cant" to productively confuse the difference between "can not" and "the conventional, trite, or insincere use of language" which he jocularly implies Ezra's universally producible poems might be. Brown is replying to Pound's assertion that "ANY BLOKE CAN EXPERIMENT," which stood alone as a section to his essay "Our Contemporaries and Others," in *The New Review* 2 (May, June, July, 1931): 151. In the contemporaneous *Demonics*, Brown makes similar play with what "Ezra says"; one poem is entitled "Ez, I sez, sez I, Ez" (83).

The Cantos itself records "Ez" as Pound's nickname (cf. 502), and for notice of Pound's own onomastic paronomasia and the inescapable play between Pound and £, see Richard Sieburth, "In Pound We Trust: The Economy of Poetry/The Poetry of Economics," *Critical Inquiry* 14 (autumn 1987): 162 et passim, and the pages he references from J.-M. Rabaté's *Language, Sexuality, and Ideology* (173–82; 234–41).

33. Mac Low, *Words*, 64.

34. Ibid., 59.

35. In a musical analogy, this relationship between constraint and expression in the mesostic might correspond to the composition of counterpoint around a cantus firmus, or more aptly still, the free expression around the rules of the dodecaphonic tone row (Cage's study of counterpoint with Schoenberg is not incidental biography). Mac Low, moreover, has experimented with compositions that explicitly code letters of the alphabet to the twelve tones of the scale so that words can become something like tone rows (Cage, *John Cage: Writer* 147–48), and Elizabeth Cross has composed similarly analogic pieces ("Schoenberg Dance 12," in *Chain* 3, no. 1 [spring 1996]: 48–50).

36. Wittgenstein, *Investigations*, §84.

37. Ibid., §81.

38. Mac Low is well aware of the paradoxes involved and freely and frequently admits to the contradictions (cf. "The Poetics of Chance," 175; or "Museletter" 27).

39. Wittgenstein, *Investigations*, §201.

40. Jackson Mac Low, "The Poetics of Chance & the Politics of Simultaneous Spontaneity, or the Sacred Heart of Jesus (Revised and Abridged)," in *Talking Poetics from Naropa Institute: Annals of the Jack Kerouac School of Disembodied Poetics*, vol. 1, ed. Anne Waldman and Marilyn Webb (Boulder, Colo., and London: Shambhala, 1978), 174. One might find it useful to think of the tensions in diastic practice as the fundamental and long-lived conflict between *tariki* and *jiriki* em-

phases in Zen: whether enlightenment is achieved through one's own power or from an external authority. I do not intend to pursue anything like a theological debate over the conformance of the diastic poems to various Buddhist doctrines, but those interested in such questions might begin by considering what a poetics of true nonattachment might involve.

41. Wittgenstein, *Investigations,* §125.

42. Jackson Mac Low, "Seventh Light Poem," in *Representative Works: 1938–1985* (New York: Roof, 1986), 142.

43. Wittgenstein, *Investigations,* §131.

44. Note, for example, how the speed with which critics rush to dismiss rule-generated poetry ("that's not poetry!"; "a computer could do that!"), or the glee with which they catch the poet out ("aha, it's not *really* nonintentional after all!"), and the equally charged dash to defend such procedures in turn, are triggered with the same ease. One need not overpsychologize these reactions to find them surprising when the facts of the matter, after all, bear little debate: Cage's mesostic technique openly announces its equal measure of determined procedures and volitional choice, and Mac Low readily admits the limits of (non)intentionality in his diastic compositions. Similarly, in Christine Froula's account, which I will address in the second section of this chapter, errors in *The Cantos* become less a measure of Pound's activity than a measure of the totalitarian desires of his readers and editors: their judgment of literal accuracy, their intolerance of the slightest deviance, and their belief in the absolute, transhistorically correct, objective "fact."

In the end, the diastic poems may be cautionary tales not so much about the totalitarianism of Pound's poetry, or the nature of rule-following, or the climate of Cold War politics in which they were composed, but rather of our desires about polarities and absolutes, and about the very structures and workings, therefore, of totalitarianism itself—the fascist in each of us, as Guattari would say.

45. Mac Low, *Words,* 13; Cage, *X: Writings,* 110.

46. Mac Low, *Words,* 82; Ezra Pound, *The Cantos of Ezra Pound* (New York: New Directions, 1991), C107:770. Given the differences between commonly available editions of Pound's *Cantos,* the canto number will precede the page number in citations to the poem.

47. Cage, *X: Writings,* 109.

48. Mac Low, *Words,* 13.

49. Ibid., 75.

50. Ibid., 14.

51. Ibid., 43, 57; Pound, *Cantos,* C76:476.

52. Mac Low, *Words,* 68, 62, 44.

53. Ibid., 69.

54. In the coda to this book I will consider the inverse of this generic crossing: the ways in which scholarly apparatuses have come to be read qua poetry. Cage

was certainly aware of the frisson between source text and diastic; he credits the inspiration for the mesostics to Marshall McLuhan's notion of "brushing information" (John Cage, "An Autobiographical Statement," *Southwest Review* 76 [winter 1990]: 66).

The relation of the writing-through to the sacrifice of general economy could be developed further. Steve McCaffery writes: "Peritionyng lets an exchabge thin a parasitic approptiarion the poews sityate closre to a specifiic type of clinsmen: the porlotch, a ritual destroying, fragmintign anf scarterimg of ap existamt waealht" (McCaffery, "Zarathrustran 'Pataphysics," *Open Letter: A Canadian Journal of Writing and Theory*, 9th series, no. 7 [winter 1997]: 20).

55. For more on the Situationist concept of *détournement*, see the opening chapter.

56. Pound, *Cantos*, C54:284, 285, 280, 306, 281.

57. A haiku-like section from Jonathan Williams's "Some Slowowls of Theodore Chamberlain" is apropos: A proud Zen, / azure pound: / daze, or pun?" (n.p.).

58. Pound, *Cantos*, C78:493.

59. Mac Low, *Words*, 59; Pound, *Cantos*, C81:535, C80:524.

60. Pound, *Cantos*, C86:577, C105:764.

61. Ibid., C96:676.

62. For an account of the way in which the significant look of *The Cantos* has changed through its editions, see the relevant chapters in Jerome J. McGann's contribution to the collection *A Poem Containing History: Textual Studies in "The Cantos,"* ed. Lawrence Rainey (Ann Arbor: University of Michigan Press, 1997), which recasts material from the relevant chapters in McGann's *The Textual Condition* (Princeton: Princeton University Press, 1991) and *Black Riders*.

63. Ezra Pound, *ABC of Reading* (New Haven: Yale University Press, 1934), 21.

64. Pound, *Cantos*, C85:568–69, C86:576–77.

65. McGann, *Textual Condition*, 108.

66. Bob Perelman, *The Trouble with Genius: Reading Pound, Joyce, Stein, and Zukofsky* (Berkeley: University of California Press, 1994), 43 et seq. " 'History is a school book for princes,' " Pound quotes in "Canto LIV" (280), and *The Cantos* themselves, of course, were conceived of as a "poem including history" (Pound, *ABC*, 46).

67. Pound, *Cantos*, C53:269.

68. Ezra Pound, *Collected Early Poems*, ed. Michael John King (New York: New Directions, 1976), 271.

69. Andrews, *Paradise*, 53.

70. Sieburth, "In Pound We Trust," 167. Sieburth also introduces Bataille into his own discussion of *The Cantos* (149), though with an emphasis on libidinal economies. More important, he proposes a critical challenge which I hope to have successfully met:

Against a number of recent readings that have too hastily sought to reduce Pound's work to a closed, phallo- or logocentric Fascist discourse, it is worth emphasizing the profound reversibility (or to use Bataille's terms, 'scissiparity') of many of the oppositions within which his thinking seems to move (165).

71. Pound, *Cantos*, C2:6, C7:25.

72. Mac Low, *Words*, 14.

73. Pound, *Cantos*, C116:810.

74. Charles Bernstein, "Pound and the Poetry of Today," *Yale Review* [new series] 75 (summer 1986): 640.

75. Ibid.

76. The lesson is an important one whether it is learned from Pound or Stein, Bunting or Zukofsky, Mac Low or Cage. Indeed, let me be clear that this is a claim that cuts both ways. This is obviously not the place to stage a full argument, but let me suggest, for instance, that however often Gertrude Stein has been taken as the hero of feminist and lesbian resistance to "patriarchal poetry," as a "good modernist" championing indeterminacy and play, there is perhaps no more *fascist* text in the modernist canon than *The Making of Americans*. With apodictic, demonstrative sentences setting out to classify and categorize every type of person, it is the novelization of the police-state archive. This reading, I want to underscore, stands independently of Stein's role as either the patriarch of her household with Alice or as apologist for Pétain's Vichy regime.

A final, brief word against necrophilia: whatever the ultimate judgments on these texts, the academic reception of Pound and Stein points to the intellectually impoverished biographic moralism that still underwrites much of what passes for literary scholarship. The assumption that one comes to literature in a hagiolatrous search for authors who can serve as personal heroes has overlooked what is surely one of the primary moral lessons of *The Cantos* itself: the danger of fueling charismatic hero worship. We endanger ourselves when we approach Pound with the same uncritical (if condemnatory) regard with which he in turn had exhumed Confucius, Malatesta, and Mussolini.

77. How carefully have you been reading? How carefully have I been writing? Has the disjunction between my claims for radical form and the thoroughly conventional mode of this essay yet struck you as disquieting? I have asked these questions before. One might of course make excuses for the apostasy of this disquisition — the essay as bodhisattva — but after such compromise, what forgiveness?

78. For a reading of the *I Ching* hexagrams qua poetry, see Jonathan Price, "The I Ching as Visual Poem," in *Visual Literature Criticism: A New Collection*, ed. Richard Kostelanetz (Carbondale: Southern Illinois University Press, 1979).

79. Wittgenstein, *Investigations*, §372.

80. Ludwig Wittgenstein, *Remarks on the Foundations of Mathematics*, ed. G. H.

Wright, R. Rhees, and G. E. M. Anscombe, trans. G. E. M. Anscombe (New York: Macmillan, 1956), 160e. Wittgenstein suggests that reading might be like rule-following at an even deeper level: the feeling of being "guided" (*Investigations*, §170). Wittgenstein's rule-following student, looking up answers in a table and figuring out how to go on from one term to the next, it might be added, evokes nothing so much as Cage checking with the simulated *I Ching* tables and figuring out the rules for how to go on from one term to another.

81. Pound, *Cantos*, C61:340.

82. See Tim Redman, *Ezra Pound and Italian Fascism* (Cambridge: Cambridge University Press, 1991). That in the final, delusional days of the exiled regime Pound struggled to publish Italian translations of Confucian classics, and that he could urge the remaining, isolated *fascisti*—in a last-ditch defense of their hopelessly besieged positions—to simply "reread the . . . Classics," manifests the depth and pathos of the desperation with which he discharged his office as court troubadour. Those wary of Pound's conception of "the Classics" can certainly empathize with his much earlier confession: "The thought of what America would be like / If the Classics had a wide circulation / Troubles my sleep" (Ezra Pound, *Personae: Collected Shorter Poems* [London: Faber and Faber, 1952], 183).

83. Pound, *Cantos*, C114:805; Mac Low, *Words*, 45.

84. Jann Pasler establishes Cage's tendency to appeal to authority, even when "the master" invoked would not have corroborated the claim Cage attributes to him.

85. Pound, *ABC*, 92.

86. Ezra Pound, *Selected Poems* (New York: New Directions, 1957), 21.

87. Pound, *Cantos*, C98:699–700, C102:742.

88. Ibid., C24:110.

89. The methodology of the "Barnes" poems is complex, and those with a serious interest should consult Mac Low's notes to *Barnesbook* directly. In short: chance procedures selected and ordered eight sentences from Djuna Barnes's oeuvre; those sentences were then taken as a source text and run through a computerized automation of one of Mac Low's diastic writing-through methods; finally, Mac Low edited the output by elimination, rearrangement, and repunctuation.

One of the most interesting aspects of Mac Low's computerized diastics, and one that deserves further contemplation, is that the entire source text can be used—*mise en abime*—as the index with which to write-through itself. As if a seeded cloud rained hydrogen in showers which fell only within the cloud's interior, silvering its sides.

90. My focus here is not to suggest that more referential plays of signification in "Barnes 4" should be discounted. For just one instance of the light, deftly managed, but precise networks which bind ostensibly unrelated lines from the poem, consider the line "And to the Greek, ground"; to follow the etymology of "ground"

back to the Greek would find *chrainein*, "to touch slightly," or in other words, to "whisper against." As Cage says of Mac Low: "he gives exact attention."

91. Christopher Dewdney, "Fractal Diffusion," in *The L=A=N=G=U=A=G=E Book*, ed. Bruce Andrews and Charles Bernstein (Carbondale: Southern Illinois University Press, 1984), 180; Mac Low, *Words*, 44.

92. Wittgenstein, *Investigations*, §193.

93. McCaffery, "Zarathrustran 'Pataphysics," 14, 17.

94. Mac Low, *Words*, 58.

95. Ibid., 51.

96. Ibid., 60, 41.

97. Ibid., 34.

98. Ibid., 41–42.

99. Ibid., 41.

100. Ibid., 40, 29.

101. Ibid., 34, 58. Kathleen Fraser, long a diligent poet of the error, has asked: "Isn't the typo, after all, a word trying to escape its single-version identity?" (*il cuoure: the heart* [Middletown, Conn.: Wesleyan University Press, 1997], 197).

102. Alwyn Lee, "The Second Chance," ed. Jesse Birnbaum, researched by Martha McDowell, *Time* (June 2, 1967): 67.

103. Pound, *ABC*, 46. As Friedrich Kittler has argued, such fidelity of transcription—the high accuracy and low filtering of medial technologies such as the phonograph, the cinema, and (so important for Pound) the typewriter—defines the modern "discourse network" (*Aufschriebesysteme*). Such devices reproduce "noise" with such indiscriminate vulgarity that they lay everything bare; in Pound's own Baudrillardian portmanteau, they let us hear the "wail of the pornograph" (*Cantos*, C29:143). Gertrude Stein alludes to precisely this condition of early twentieth-century medial technologies in the opening of *Paris, France:* "When we were having a book printed in France we complained about the bad alignment. Ah they explained that is because they use machines now, machines are bound to be inaccurate" (*Paris, France* [New York: Liveright, 1996], 8). As Kittler and Pound understood, the problem, of course, is that the machines are far *too* accurate and inflexible.

104. Ezra Pound, *Guide to Kulture* (New York: New Directions, 1970), 98. In this sense, Susan Howe has best carried on the Pound tradition of arguing, poetically, for the importance of both bibliographic detail in the records we have—the paper stock, bookplates, colophons, seal marks, marginalia, handwriting, binding (these are all from *The Cantos*), and so on—as well as an attentive reading of the silences in the historical record. Pound, it scarcely needs mention, did not share the decidedly feminist focus of Howe's project.

105. Pound, *Cantos*, C13:60.

106. Ibid., C7:25.

107. Ibid., C8:28.

108. Ibid., C77:481–82, C8:28.

109. For a reproduction of the fragment and the story of its transmission, see Hugh Kenner, *The Pound Era* (Berkeley: University of California Press, 1971), 5–6, 50–56). When published in *Lustra* ([New York: Knopf, 1917], 55), each line is followed by a three-point ellipses; the version I reproduce is taken from Pound's revised and definitive version in *Personae* (115).

110. Mac Low, *Words*, 32.

111. Christine Froula, *To Write Paradise: Style and Error in Pound's "Cantos"* (New Haven: Yale University Press, 1984), 153.

112. Ibid., 140.

113. Ibid., 139.

114. Pound's unpublished letter (dated September 2, 1957) is now in the Yale Collection of American Literature, Beinecke Library; the line is quoted in Froula, *To Write Paradise*, 145–46.

115. See their respective contributions to the publication of the proceedings, edited by Lawrence Rainey, of a special panel on textual scholarship and *The Cantos* (*A Poem Containing History: Textual Studies in "The Cantos"*). I obviously disagree with Kenner's conclusion that we can safely correct printers' misdeeds with a clear conscience ("what's amiss that's uncontrovertibly a printer's misdeed can be safely corrected" [Kenner, "Notes on Amateur Emendations," in *A Poem Containing History*, 28, *cf.* 27]).

116. Peter Glassgold, "A Statement From New Directions," in *A Poem Containing History*, 275. One should note that Laughlin, as (then) editor of New Directions, had a vested interest in the current version of *The Cantos,* which was under his imprint and under discussion in comparison with a proposed scholarly edition. One should further note that this imputation of Pound's wishes comes at least fourth-hand: Laughlin's message was transmitted by Griselda Ohannessian, who conveyed it to Peter Glassgold, who delivered it at the conference whence its transcript was published in the collection edited by Lawrence Rainey.

117. Pound, *Cantos,* C1:5, C30:148.

118. Ibid., C10:47. See Lawrence Rainey, "'All I Want You to Do Is to Follow the Orders': History, Faith, and Fascism in the Early Cantos," in *A Poem Containing History*, 76 et seq., for an account of this passage and a reproduction of both the original source and Pound's notes. Rainey is as thorough as one could wish, though he overstates the mystery of the passage.

119. Pound, *Cantos,* C62:341.

120. Ibid., C78:481.

121. The form is, however, familiar from his correspondence.

122. Pound, *Cantos,* C87:585.

123. Ibid., C56:302.

124. Mac Low, *Words*, 82.

125. James Joyce, *Ulysses: The Corrected Text,* ed. Hans Walter Gabler, Wolf-

hard Steppe, and Claus Melchior (New York: Random House, 1986), 151–52 (in chapter 2), 228–29 (in chapter 9).

126. Joyce, *Finnegans Wake*, 425.

127. For my thinking on Joyce and error, I am indebted to a series of conversations with John Bishop in the spring of 1995; I continue those discussions here with gratitude and fondness.

128. Joyce, *Finnegans Wake*, 120; Fritz Senn, "Joyce's Misconducting Universe," in *International Perspectives on James Joyce*, ed. Gottlieb Gaiser (Troy: Whitson, 1986), 164.

129. Joyce, *Finnegans Wake*, 109, 126. Vroon notes a similar difficulty with regard to the textual status of Velimir Xlebnikov's oeuvre (*Xlebnikov's Shorter Poems*, 26).

130. Joyce, *Finnegans Wake*, 276.

131. Froula, *To Write Paradise*, 142.

132. Vicki Mahaffey, "Intentional Error: The Paradox of Editing Joyce's *Ulysses*," in *Representing Modernist Texts: Editing as Interpretation*, ed. Charles Bornstein (Ann Arbor: University of Michigan Press, 1991), 182.

133. Richard Ellmann, *James Joyce* (New York: Oxford University Press, 1959), 662.

134. Eugène Jolas, "My Friend James Joyce," in *James Joyce: Two Decades of Criticism*, ed. Seon Givens (New York: Vanguard, 1948), 13. These passages from *Finnegans Wake* occur throughout, but see especially the chapter following p. 104.

135. Ellmann, *Joyce*, 600.

136. I recognize that the force of this claim requires the elaboration of an argument which would be out of place in the present context. Suffice it to say that I regard the myriad attempts to read *Finnegans Wake* as a conventional novel—with an overall story and populated by personae like HCE and ALP—as unfounded, if not so absurdly inappropriate as to risk the grotesque. These received readings exhibit, more or less movingly, the extremes with which we resist the inhumanness of language. Taken as novellae in their own right, for instance, the books by Tindall and Burgess would be fairly amusing; as literary criticism they are merely perverse. As I hope this chapter demonstrates, I am all for hallucinated readings, but when they proceed without textual justification they merely pass into pathology. For examples of more sober accounts of the (non)narrative structure of *Finnegans Wake*, see Derek Attridge, "Deconstructing Digression: The Backbone of *Finnegans Wake* and the Margins of Culture," in *Peculiar Language: Literature as Difference from the Renaissance to James Joyce* (Ithaca: Cornell University Press, 1988), 188–238; Jean-Michel Rabaté, "Narratology and *Finnegans Wake*," in *James Joyce: The Centennial Symposium*, ed. Morris Beja et al. (Champaign: University of Illinois Press, 1986), 137–46; and Charles Altieri, "*Finnegans Wake* as Modernist Historiography," *Novel* (winter/spring 1988): 238–50.

137. Joyce, *Finnegans Wake*, 121.

138. Cage, *Silence*, 59.

139. One should note that grammatical patterns are perhaps the most recognizable and familiar aspect of *Finnegans Wake* (see Quartermain, *Disjunctive Poetics*, 114–16, for a particularly nuanced reading of this tension. The ghost of English syntax, however, plays an important role in rendering legible the much more unstable level of individual words, many of which would otherwise appear as mere disarticulated babble.

140. Joyce, *Finnegans Wake*, 114.

141. Ibid., 341, 118.

142. Ibid., 423.

143. Mahaffey, "Intentional Error," 185; Joyce, *Finnegans Wake*, 20.

144. Quoted in Vahan D. Barooshian, *Russian Cubo-Futurism, 1910–1930: A Study in Avant-Gardism* (The Hague: Mouton, 1974), 109.

145. Mac Low, *Representative Works: 1938–1985* (New York: Roof Books, 1986), 182.

146. Cage, *X: Writings*, 1, 173.

147. Paul de Man, "Phenomenology and Materiality in Kant," in *The Textual Sublime: Deconstruction and Its Differences*, ed. Hugh Silverman and Gary Aylesworth (Albany: SUNY Press, 1990), 107.

148. I am grateful to Peter Nicholls, who references Bourget and provides the translation (Nicholls, *Modernisms: A Literary Guide* [Berkeley: University of California Press, 1995], 59).

149. *Vort* number 8, 70.

150. Cage, *X: Writings*, 110.

151. Joyce, *Finnegans Wake*, 120.

152. Pound, *Cantos*, C12:57, C10:47.

153. Mac Low, *Words*, 16; Pound, *Cantos*, C9:37. Conversely, *Words nd Ends* transforms Pound's innocuous "And the worst of 'em all" (*C* 41:202) into the characteristically acrid but rather more vulgar "f 'em All" (30), recalling the earlier lines: "ieU ckiN al / . . . a cUss" (17).

154. Blake, *Complete Writings*, 154; Pound, *Cantos*, C14–16:61, 62–64.

155. Pound, *Cantos*, "Addendum for [Canto] C," 812.

156. Ibid., C14:62, C45:230.

157. Ibid., C14–15:65.

158. Ibid., C15:65.

159. Ibid., C14:63, C15:64; cf. C14:62.

160. Ibid., C14:61.

161. Ibid., C116:811; Joyce, *Finnegans Wake*, 67, 66; Pound, *Cantos*, 199.

162. Pound, *Cantos*, C14:62, C15:65, C14:61.

163. Ibid., C15:65.

164. Mac Low, *Words*, 17.

Chapter 6

1. Ezra Pound, "Retrospect: Interlude," in *Polite Essays* (London: Faber and Faber, 1937), 131, 130.

2. Robert Hobbs, *Robert Smithson: Sculpture* (Ithaca, N.Y., and London: Cornell University Press, 1981), 104. Smithson toured prehistoric English monuments in 1969 (Hobbs, *Smithson*, 171). Robert Morris, one of those who had also made the pilgrimage, was discussing the "interpretation of Stonehenge as an astronomical computer" by at least 1968 (Robert Morris, "The Art of Existence," *Artforum* 9, no. 5 [January 1971]: 30).

3. Smithson, *Collected Writings*, 95.

4. Pound, "Retrospect," 130.

5. In Smithson's own words, "the duplicity within the site involves the dialogue between inner and outer . . . . There's a disjunction in terms of the two sites" (Smithson, *Collected Writings*, 218).

6. See Jacques Derrida, *Of Grammatology*, trans. Gayatri Spivak (Baltimore: Johns Hopkins University Press, 1974), 141 et seq.

7. Smithson, *Collected Writings*, 153. Smithson evinces his understanding of the nonsite's ability to put terms under erasure in this way: "To be located between those two points [i.e., site and nonsite] puts you in a position of elsewhere, so there's no focus. This outer edge and this center constantly subvert each other, cancel each other out" (194).

8. Lawrence Alloway, "Robert Smithson's Development," in *Art in the Land: A Critical Anthology of Environmental Art*, ed. Alan Sonfist (New York: E. P. Dutton, 1983), 130. Cf. Alloway's similar statement in Hobbs, *Smithson*, 42.

9. Smithson, *Collected Writings*, 244.

10. I would provisionally suggest that the figure of the crystal, like Burroughs's "virus" or Spicer's "Martian," indexes the inhumanness of language: a radically alien structure that is nonetheless recombinantly active and "alive" (crystals "grow"). Whatever its resonance, Smithson's mineral language takes its place in a substantial and very interesting literary tradition of geolinguistics, which encompasses writers as diverse as J. G. Ballard (who directly influenced Smithson) and Clark Coolidge (who was directly influenced by Smithson in turn), to name just two. A distinctly Canadian tradition is also discernible, including Christian Bök, Christopher Dewdney, and Steve McCaffery.

11. Smithson, *Collected Writings*, 107.

12. Ibid., 108.

13. Basil Bunting, *Complete Poems*, ed. Richard Caddel (Oxford: Oxford University Press, 1994), 45.

14. Smithson, *Collected Writings*, 155.

15. Ibid., 61. The original essay was signed, pseudonymously, "Eton Corrasable,"

which anagrams neatly to "Robert as a clone" (among other intriguing and poetic possibilities). Smithson reiterates that he "was interested in language as a material entity, as something that wasn't involved in ideational values," as "printed matter—information which has a kind of physical presence for me" (294).

16. Thomas Clark and Colin Stern, *The Geological Evolution of North America: A Regional Approach to Historical Geology* (New York: Ronald, 1960); 2nd rev. ed. (nonuniform subtitle), 1968; 3rd rev. ed., coauthored with Robert Carroll (New York: Wiley, 1979). Smithson quotes from the second (revised) edition, page 151. The metaphor of the book was translated from the first (1960) edition of the textbook, where it had been applied to a jigsaw puzzle; in the passage that Smithson cites, two more general sentences from the first edition have been merged: "Just as the latter [i.e., an archaeologist] deciphers fragmentary inscriptions of dead languages, so the geologist reads his [*sic*] record in the rocks, interpreting and piecing together the scattered information," and "In the seas of the past, layer after layer of sediment accumulated like leaves of a book that a geologist may read page by page" (3, 5). By the third edition, published in 1979, the "tone of the time" had already changed. In the new, rather less dramatic text the metaphor had shifted to the archive: books in a library, from which a researcher extracts and compiles various arguments, and stacks of undated newspapers from different cities (58). Additionally, the passage in question was moved from its prominent place in the introduction (which carried the wonderfully Smithsonian title "Stratigraphy") to the fourth chapter.

17. Smithson, *Collected Writings*, 95.

18. Some bibliographic specifics, since they determine the shape of the resulting treatments: Ellis's study was first published in 1901, and although Williams cites the edition he used as 1926 this seems to be a misprint for 1936, the year of a new edition of the studies and one that fits the page layout of his excavations. Phillips used the 1892 British edition of Mallock's novel, which had originally appeared as a triple-decker serial (and lest a hasty reader miss the joke, the preface to Phillips's *Works and Texts* is signed "Bill Hurrell"). Coincidentally, the edition of *Paradise Lost* used by Johnson (whose reproduction, I should note, makes a slight enlargement) was also published in 1892 (by Thomas Y. Crowell and Company, New York, with an introduction by David Masson and biographical sketch by Nathan Haskell Dole). "Thus poetic language is the excavation of language by language" (Joseph N. Riddel, "From Heidegger to Derrida to Chance: Doubling and (Poetic) Language," in *Early Postmodernism: Foundational Essays*, ed. Paul A. Bové [Durham: Duke University Press, 1995], 220).

19. Tom Phillips, "Notes on *A Humument*," in *Tom Phillips: Works and Texts* (London: Thames and Hudson, 1992), 256. Davenport himself, significantly, had been publishing his translations of Greek fragments during precisely this time; his versions of Archilochus, Sappho, and Alkman appeared in 1964, 1965, and 1969, respectively. Lukas Foss, who is perhaps best known for his site-specific writing-

through of musical scores, set some of Davenport's translations to music and also influenced Johnson's writing-through. By the end of the 1970s, the attraction was still palpable; as Lyn Hejinian writes: "The old fragmentary texts, early Egyptian and Persian writings, say, or the works of Sappho, were intriguing and lovely, a mystery adhering to the lost lines" (Lyn Hejinian, *My Life,* 47).

20. Smithson, *Collected Writings,* 218. Smithson implicitly makes the same point when he links the development of the nonsite to "confronting the raw materials of the particular sectors," or when he declares "I'm more interested in the terrain dictating the condition of the art" (192).

21. Many pages from Phillips's *A Humument* (1st rev. ed. [London: Thames and Hudson, 1987]) appear to comment on its method of production. Among repeated references to "fragments," Phillips declares "that / which / he / hid / reveal I" (1), and he boasts of his "attempt to / cripple sentences" (5), announcing: "this was broken by / poetry" (4). A "Journal / of secret / scribing and hiding" (6), in which the original text is "suppressed or altered" (13), *A Humument* is a book that Phillips "wrote with blots" "so the changes made / the / book" (153, 7). The fracturing of the source text's grammar into divergent structures is self-reflexively emblematized by the indeterminate final word of Williams's "History XX," set apart on its own line: "the smell of the female / parts."

22. Smithson, *Collected Writings,* 178; cf. 192.

23. Ibid., 218.

24. Phillips, "Notes," 256.

25. Smithson, *Collected Writings,* 193.

26. Johanna Drucker, *The Century of Artists' Books* (New York: Grannary Books, 1995), 110.

27. Such effects, although integral to the work of art, are obviously dependent upon what seems to be the incidental character of their support. In Smithson's 1968 *Mono Lake Nonsite,* for instance, much of the force of the evacuated center of the map depends on the specifics of its production and the degree to which the oily sheen of the chemically treated photostat mirrors the glare of contaminated water under a northern California sun. Smithson's precedent was another "oceanic" map (Smithson, *Collected Writings,* 103): the "Ocean Chart" from Lewis Carroll's "The Hunting of the Snark," a work Smithson reproduces in his 1968 essay "A Museum of Language in the Vicinity of Art" (*Collected Writings,* 92–93), along with a reference to the similar chart—"A perfect and absolute blank!"— mentioned in Carroll's *Sylvie and Bruno Concluded.* That same year, in the journal *0–9,* Vito Acconci reproduced the photostat from Smithson's *Mono Lake Nonsite* and replicated its structure in his own visual poem "Drop." Acting, as Stein suggested, "so that there is no use in a center," "Drop" replaces Mono Lake with a page from the dictionary, a strategy adopted to very different effect by Alastair Johnston in his 1975 artist's book *Heath's German Dictionary.*

For another, more traditional valence of the trees in *Radi Os,* see Eric Selinger,

"'I composed the holes': Reading Ronald Johnson's *Radi Os*," *Contemporary Literature* 33, no. 1 [spring 1992]: 56).

28. In Phillips's book—and this is its distinction *as a book* and not in the limited-edition museum version of boxed but unbound prints—this level of thematic allusion is registered by the references to the cleft of the buttocks (cf. 19, 216, 256, 337, etc.). Soft pornography is one of the recurring motifs in *A Humument*, including passages that are sometimes quite funny, frequently ludicrous, occasionally rather touching—and repeatedly focused on the anus. Additionally, among the ostensibly nonce words that Phillips mines from Mallock's vocabulary are "nage," a term for the buttocks, and "truggling," which suggests the action an older man might perform with a younger (cf. the *OED*). I have argued elsewhere that the crack of the pages at the binding is the most erotically charged site of the book (*Signature Effects*, 1997).

When *Radi Os* was composed, Johnson's projected long poem bore the working title *Wor(l)ds;* subsequently retitling the poem *Ark* (and containing a center-set version of the first page of *Radi Os* as the opening to "Beam 21") adds a retroactive resonance to the repeated retention of the words "[d]ark" and "arch" in *Radi Os*—the arkeology of knowledge.

29. Selinger, similarly, reads "radi os" as a suggestion of X-rays (Selinger, "'I composed the holes,'" 55).

30. Smithson, *Collected Writings*, 364.

31. Ibid., 110.

32. Ibid., 96. Smithson's architectural metaphor might suggest Wittgenstein's similar use of such figures, and given their shared interest in limits, an extended comparison would surely prove productive. Indeed, Smithson's provisional theory of nonsites is decidedly Tractarian in its emphasis on "logical pictures" (364).

33. Ibid., 96.

34. Guy-Ernest Debord, introduction to *Documents relatif à la fondation de l'Internationale Situationniste,* ed. Gerard Barreby (Paris: Allia, 1985), 291; translated by Ken Knabb as "Introduction to a Critique of Urban Geography," in *Situationist International Anthology* (Berkeley: Bureau of Public Secrets, 1981), 7.

35. Smithson, *Collected Writings,* 108.

36. Gary Shapiro, *Earthwards: Robert Smithson and Art after Babel* (Berkeley: University of California Press, 1995), 49.

37. Smithson, *Collected Writings,* 111. The lexicon of Johnson's treatment is replete with terms of containment: "enclosed," "encompassed," "confined," "compass," "to / frame," "border,"—all suggesting the "bright confines" of the whitened page and the way in which Johnson's erasure leads "to smallest forms / their shapes immense, and / far within, / in their own dimensions / silences."

38. Smithson, *Collected Writings,* 78.

39. Smithson, *Collected Writings,* 95; he speaks elsewhere (228) of "a negative hole"; Steve McCaffery, *Theory of Sediment* (Vancouver: Talonbooks, 1991), 107.

40. McCaffery, *Theory*, 104–5.

41. Ibid., 111.

42. Bertrand Russell, "On Denoting," *Mind* 14 (1905): 479–93; reprinted in *The Philosophy of Language*, 3rd ed., ed. A. P. Martinich (New York: Oxford University Press, 1996), 199–207. The literature on this topic in linguistics is surprisingly substantial. For examples of the range of recent work on the definite article, see Betty Birner and Gregory Ward, "Uniqueness, familiarity, and the definite article in English," *BLS* 20 (1994): 93–102; John A. Hawkins, "On (in)definite Articles: Implicatures and (un)grammaticality Prediction," *Journal of Linguistics* 27 (1991): 405–42; and Richard Epstein, "Viewpoint and the Definite Article," in *Conceptual Structure, Discourse and Language,* ed. Adele E. Goldberg (Stanford: CSLI Publications, 1996), 99–112.

43. Smithson, *Collected Writings,* 218.

44. Phillips, "Notes," 256.

45. In the context of Phillips's postwar, atomic age poetry (one of the painted pages depicts an ominously blossoming mushroom cloud [*Humument,* 191]), the name has another resonance as well. "Toge" is a transliteration of the name of the Japanese poet Toge Sankichi, a "figure of epic proportions" who was introduced to the English-speaking world through Robert Lifton's popular *Death in Life* at precisely the moment Phillips began working on *A Humument* (Richard Minear, ed., *Hiroshima: Three Witnesses* [Princeton: Princeton University Press,1990], 277). Lifton describes Toge as "the most celebrated A-bomb poet—and in fact the only Hiroshima writer to become a popular hero . . . the epitome of the poet of protest" (Robert Lifton, *Death in Life: Survivors of Hiroshima* [New York: Random House, 1967], 441). As Phillips's later artwork "13-11-84: Souvenir of Hiroshima" attests, the subject touched him deeply, and he takes uncharacteristic care to spell out "H-i-r-o-s-h-i-m-a" letter by letter across one page of *A Humument* (141), a length to which he goes on only three other occasions. The Hiroshima page, moreover, also declares "The air seemed full of dead generations," and as if to corroborate his memorial, Phillips follows this scene two pages later with a *Japoneriste* garden and haiku-like poem.

46. The quote is Smithson's (*Collected Writings,* 212); the exception from Phillips can be found on page 231.

47. W. H. Mallock, *A Human Document: A Novel* (London: Chapman and Hall, [1892]), 1.

48. Ibid., 6.

49. Ibid.

50. Ibid., 6, 4.

51. Ibid., 4, 3. In the course of the novel, Mallock also makes numerous specific allusions, and Phillips includes his references to Veronese, Byron, Homer, Wordsworth, and Keats. In addition to the visual styles Phillips parodies—including, among many others, Delaunay (180), Muybridge and Victorian photography (187,

27), Cage (178), Lichtenstein (120), Wesselman (301), Cézanne (70), Seurat and the pointillists (230), cubism (105, 81), *les lettristes* (159), and even his own work (71)—literary in-jokes abound: Apollinaire (336), Baudelaire (353), Bob Brown (87), Charles Dodgson (212), E. M. Forster (185, 251), Pound (158), Rimbaud (70), Shakespeare (352), Virgil (218, 141), and Yeats (356).

52. Mallock, *Human,* 8.

53. Ibid., 6, 4.

54. Ibid., 3, 4.

55. McCaffery, *Theory,* 106.

56. Those skeptical about the significance of such effects are referred to the theoretical section of chapter 3. Those still anxious about intention may be assuaged by curator Huston Paschal: "Traversing the hemispheres, Phillips pursues his study of linguistics. (Language has always been integral to this painter's art.) He absorbs the seen and heard" (Phillips, *Works and Texts,* 20).

57. Smithson, *Collected Writings,* 190, 130, 216, 219, 194.

58. The obvious precedent for *RADI OS* is *MILT ON* (as Blake's title page has it), and Johnson's poem is decidedly Blakean. Johnson's neoplatonism and gnosticism give the poem a visionary ("shine inward, and / there plant eyes / that I may see and tell / Of things invisible") and apocalyptic (*apo kalyptein:* "and / parted / beneath / as a veil") tone, and the technique of treatment in *Radi Os* is not unrelated to Blake's own mode of book production. As Johnson himself notes, "*to etch* is 'to cut away,' and each page, as in Blake's concept of a book, is a single picture." The repeated references to "moulds" and "forms" in *Radi Os* emphasizes Blake's framing technique, and descriptions of acidic liquid ("the burning / dark designs" which form "image / Under / watery image") rhyme with Blake's similar metatextual references to the processes by which he created his extraordinary illuminated books: "printing in the infernal method, by corrosives . . . melting apparent surfaces away, and displaying the infinite which was hid" (Blake, *Complete Writings,* 101).

59. In what Phillips calls "the night / of / long white / words" (*Humument,* 83), the treated text reverses the conventional registers to produce a concealing light; the white of its page is "Dark with excessive bright" and as a "luminous / inroad of Darkness" that page conceals "With blackest / light" "the invisible" source text "on the bare / Between the / light" (Johnson, *Radi Os*).

60. Francis Ponge also saw (as it were) the sun as "la condition même du regard [the very condition of the glance itself]"; in its unobservable precondition of sight, the sun, for Ponge, "repousse le regard, vous le renfonce à l'intérieur du corps [repels the glance, driving it to the interior of your body]" ("Le soleil placé en abîme," in *Le grand recueil* [Paris: Gallimard, 1961], 3:162).

The combination of doubly present and absent images implicit in the afterimage is taken up less philosophically by Joan Retallack in "Afterrimages" [*sic*], each page of which is split to accommodate a free-form poem at the top and its "treatment" at the bottom. After completing the upper portion, Retallack claims to have allowed paper clips to fall by chance over the text and then recorded any letters that were visible within the bows of the clips. John McNally used a similar method of "self-treatment," although without the element of chance procedures, in his suite of poems "Custom" (unpublished manuscript "Out of Print").

61. Morris, "Art of Existence," 30.

62. Cobbing, who was using cut-ups as early as March 1956 (Robinson, "Bob Cobbing's Blade," 75), seems to have pride of place, although Burroughs gained widespread recognition through his 1965 *Paris Review* interview. That publication, in fact, brought him to the attention of Tom Phillips, who produced a series of poems by recording the margin words in newspaper columns before developing the procedure into the treatment used to make *A Humument*. Several pages of Phillips's book themselves display the trademark Burroughs/Gysin fold-in technique.

The influence of Cage on *A Humument* is also tangible; in addition to explicit references to "chance" (314, 328, 329), the repeated occurrence of "change" and "thrown" allude to the "chancy art" (29) of *I Ching* procedures (81), which were in fact used to determine the treatment of at least one page (99). "Words / hazard all," as Johnson writes in *Radi Os*. Or as Phillips has it (298): "chance words" (where "to word" is a verb).

63. As the epigraph to Jessie Weston's *From Ritual to Romance* (Garden City: Anchor, 1957) cautioned: "Many literary critics seem to think that an hypothesis about obscure and remote questions of history can be refuted by a simple demand for the production of more evidence than in fact exists" (cf. Francis Cornford, *Origins of Attic Comedy* [Garden City: Anchor, 1961]).

64. Phillips, *Humument*, 8.

Chapter 7

1. Campbell's book serves as a visual intertext to Duda Machado's poem "Imagem de Um Jardim" in *Zil* (Rio de Janeiro: Grupo de Planejameto Gráfico, 1977):

baque de pétalas
emudece o ar

jardim perfeito
onde se anula a tarde
jardim sem erro

jardim alheio
a qualquer idílio
ou atrocidade

2. Stéphane Mallarmé, *Oeuvres complètes* (Paris: Pléiade, 1945), 367.

3. Plato, *Republic*, 386c.

4. *BLAST*, reprint edition with a foreword by Bradford Morrow (Santa Barbara, Calif.: Black Sparrow, 1981), 18.

5. Ibid., 42.

6. Michael Camille, "Obscenity under Erasure: Censorship in Medieval Illuminated Manuscripts," in *Obscenity: Social Control and Artistic Creation in the European Middle Ages,* ed. Jan M. Ziolkowski (Leiden: Brill, 1998), 145–46.

7. Dirk Hohnsträter, "The Other Side of Memory: Reflections on Censorship," in *The Poetics of Memory,* ed. Thomas Wägenbaur (Tübingen: Stauffenberg, 1998), 299.

8. Jacques Derrida, *Dissemination,* trans. Barbara Johnson (Chicago: University of Chicago Press, 1981), 9.

9. Vitaly Kolmar and Alex Melamid's 1972 painting *Quotation* turns the tables by censoring an official government propaganda slogan; replacing each word with a square they turn the message into a grid of modernist abstraction: precisely what the official dictates of Socialist Realism would prohibit.

10. Jonathan Swift, *Gulliver's Travels,* pt. 3, ch. 5.

11. Derrida, *Dissemination,* 9.

12. *Granta* (summer 1989): 17–20; Anthony Cavendish, *Inside Intelligence* (London: Collins, 1990), xii et seq.

13. Brown, a member of the expatriate avant-garde artistic community in France in the 1920s, wrote his anthology at a moment when books "published in Paris" were being routinely scrutinized and banned by postal inspectors in the United States and England. The comic and derisory response to censorship in Brown's book, however, has a precedent from a decade earlier. When Brown compares the trade in banned literature to the contemporaneous smuggling of alcohol under Prohibition with the term "book-legging," his preface to *Gems* echoes G. P. Putnam's preface to the cleverly entitled *Nonsensorship,* a 1922 anthology of "Sundry observations concerning prohibitions inhibitions and illegalities," where the same portmanteau (as well as an opening reference to literary "gems") appears (Putnam, "We Have with Us Today," iii).

14. Bob Brown, appendix to *Readies for Bob Brown's Machine* (Cagnes-sur-Mer, Fr.: Roving Eye, 1931), 177, 185, 181 et passim.

15. Derrida, *Dissemination,* 253.

16. Ernest Fraenkel, *Les dessins trans-conscients de Stéphane Mallarmé: À propos de la typographie de "Un coup de dés"* (Paris: Nizet, 1960), 9.

17. Stéphane Mallarmé, *Selected Poetry and Prose,* ed. Mary Ann Caws (New York: New Directions, 1982), 82.

18. Stéphane Mallarmé, *Le "Livre" de Mallarmé: Premières recherches sur des documents inédits,* ed. Jacques Scherer (Paris: Gallimard, 1957), 55B.

19. Howe, *Singularities,* 63.

Bibliography

Alloway, Lawrence. "Robert Smithson's Development." In *Art in the Land: A Critical Anthology of Environmental Art,* edited by Alan Sonfist, 125–41. New York: E. P. Dutton, 1983.

Alpert, Barry. "Interview with Jackson Mac Low." *Vort: Twenty-First Century Pre-Views* 3, no. 2 (1975).

Andrews, Bruce. *Paradise and Method: Poetics and Praxis.* Evanston: Northwestern University Press, 1996.

Apollinaire, Guillaume. *Calligrammes.* Berkeley: University of California Press, 1980.

Apostolidès, Jean-Marie. "Du Surréalisme à l'Internationale Situationniste: La question de l'image." *Modern Language Notes* 105 (1990): 727–49.

Arvatov, Boris. " бут и кулътура вещи." In алъманах пролеткулъта, 75–82. Moscow, 1925. Translated by Christina Kiaer as "Everyday Life and the Culture of the Thing (Toward the Formulation of the Question)." *October* 81 (summer 1997): 119–28.

———. "Language Creation (On 'Transrational Poetry')." Translated by Anna Lawton and Herbert Eagle from *Lef* 2 (1923). In *Russian Futurism Through Its Manifestoes: 1912–1928,* edited by Anna Lawton, 217–31.

Atkins, Guy, and Troels Andersen. *Asger Jorn: The Final Years (1965–1973).* London: Lund Humphries, 1980.

Attali, Jacques. *Bruits: Essai sur l'économie politique de la musique.* Paris: Vendôme, 1977. Translated by Brian Massumi as *Noise: The Political Economy of Music.* Minneapolis: University of Minnesota Press, 1987.

Barooshian, Vahan D. *Russian Cubo-Futurism, 1910–1930: a study in avant-gardism.* De proprietatibus litterarum series maior 24. The Hague: Mouton, 1974.

Barreby, Gerard, ed. *Documents relatif à la fondation de l'Internationale Situationniste.* Paris: Allia, 1985.

Barthes, Roland. *Image, Music, Text.* New York: Hill and Wang, 1977.

Bataille, Georges. *L'expérience intérieure.* Paris: Gallimard, 1954.

Baudrillard, Jean. *L'autre par lui-même.* Paris: Éditions Galilée, 1987.

———. *Pour une critique de l'économie politique du signe.* Paris: Gallimard, 1972.

———. *La société de consommation: ses mythes, ses structures.* Paris: Editions Denoël, 1970. Translated as *The Consumer Society: Myths and Structures.* London: Sage, 1998.

Beckett, Samuel. *Watt.* London: Picador, 1988.

Bernstein, Charles. "The Academy in Peril: William Carlos Williams Meets the MLA." In *Content's Dream: Essays 1975–1984.* Los Angeles: Sun and Moon, 1986.

————. *A Poetics*. Cambridge: Harvard University Press, 1992.

————. *Content's Dream: Essays 1975–1984*. Los Angeles: Sun and Moon, 1986.

————. "Pound and the Poetry of Today." *Yale Review* [new series] 75 (summer 1986): 635–40.

————. *Veil*. Madison: Xexoxial Editions, 1987.

Bischoff, Bernhard. *Latin Paleography: Antiquity and the Middle Ages*. Translated by Dáibhí Ó Cróinín and David Ganz. Cambridge: Cambridge University Press, 1990.

Blake, William. *Complete Writings*. Edited by Geoffrey Keynes. Oxford: Oxford University Press, 1966.

BLAST. Reprint edition with a foreword by Bradford Morrow. Santa Barbara: Black Sparrow, 1981.

Blyth, Caroline. "Touch Wood: coming to terms with bibliography." *Word & Image* 9, no. 1 (1993).

Bourget, Paul. *Essais de psychologie contemporaine*. 2 vols. Paris: Plon, 1924.

Bowlt, John E. "Kazimir Malevich and the Energy of Language." In *Kazimir Malevich: 1875–1935*, edited by Jeanne D'Andrea. Los Angeles, 1990.

Boym, Svetlana. *Common Places: Everyday Life in Russia*. Cambridge: Harvard University Press, 1994.

Bracken, Len. *Guy Debord: Revolutionary*. Venice, Calif.: Feral House, 1997.

Brakhage, Stan. *Brakhage Scrapbook: Collected Writings 1964–1980*. Edited by Robert A. Haller. New York: Documentext, 1982.

————. *Metaphors on Vision*. Edited by P. Adams Sitney. 2nd ed. New York(?): Film Culture, 1976.

Bristol, Evelyn. *A History of Russian Poetry*. New York: Oxford University Press, 1991.

Brito, Manuel. *A Suite of Poetic Voices*. Sta. Brigida: Kadle Books, 1992.

Broodthaers, Marcel. *Un coup de dés jamais n'abolira le hasard: image*. Antwerp: Galerie Wide White Space, 1969.

Brown, Bob. *Gems: A Censored Anthology*. Cagnes-sur-Mer, Fr.: Roving Eye, 1931.

————. *Readies for Bob Brown's Machine*. Cagnes-sur-Mer, Fr.: Roving Eye, 1931.

Bunting, Basil. *Complete Poems*. Edited by Richard Caddel. Oxford: Oxford University Press, 1994.

Cabanne, Pierre. *Dialogues with Marcel Duchamp*. Translated by Ron Padgett. New York: Da Capo, 1979.

Cage, John. "An Autobiographical Statement." *Southwest Review* 76 (winter 1990).

————. *Empty Words: Writings '73–'78*. Middletown, Conn.: Wesleyan University Press, 1979.

————. *John Cage: Writer: Previously Uncollected Pieces*. Edited by Richard Kostelanetz. New York: Limelight, 1993.

———. *M: Writings '62–'72.* Middletown, Conn.: Wesleyan University Press, 1973.

———. *Silence.* Middletown, Conn.: Wesleyan University Press, 1961.

———. *Writing Through Finnegans Wake.* Simultaneous publication as a special issue of the *James Joyce Quarterly* (vol. 15) and University of Tulsa Monograph Series no. 16, 1989.

———. *X: Writings '79–'82.* Middletown, Conn.: Wesleyan University Press, 1983.

Camille, Michael. "Obscenity under Erasure: Censorship in Medieval Illuminated Manuscripts." In *Obscenity: Social Control and Artistic Creation in the European Middle Ages,* edited by Jan M. Ziolkowski, 139–54. Leiden: Brill, 1998.

Campbell, Ken. *Father's Garden.* Self-produced artists' book, 1989.

Cavendish, Anthony. *Inside Intelligence.* London: Collins, 1990.

Clark, David L. "Monstrosity, Illegibility, Denegation: De Man, Nichol, and the Resistance to Postmodernism." In *Negation, Critical Theory, and Postmodern Textuality,* edited by Daniel Fischlin. Dordrecht: Kluwer Academic Publishers, 1994.

Clark, Thomas, and Colin Stern. *The Geological Evolution of North America: A Regional Approach to Historical Geology.* New York: Ronald, 1960. 2nd rev. ed. (nonuniform subtitle), 1968. 3rd rev. ed., coauthored with Robert Carroll, NewYork: Wiley, 1979.

Cocteau, Jean. "Le secret professionel." In *Le rappel à l'ordre,* vol. 7 of *Oeuvres complètes.* Geneva: Éditions Marguerat, 1946.

Compton, Susan B. *The World Backwards: Russian Futurist Books 1912–16.* London: British Library, 1978.

Crary, Jonathan. "Eclipse of the Spectacle." In *Art after Modernism: Rethinking Representation,* edited by Brian Wallis, 283–94. New York: New Museum of Contemporary Art, 1984.

———. "Modernizing Vision." In *Vision and Visuality,* edited by Hal Foster. DIA Art Foundation Discussions in Contemporary Culture 2. Seattle: Bay, 1988.

———. *Techniques of the Observer: On Vision and Modernity in the Nineteenth Century.* Cambridge: MIT Press, 1990.

Crevel, René. *Babylon.* Translated and with an afterword by Kay Boyle. Los Angeles: Sun and Moon, 1996.

Crow, Thomas. *The Rise of the Sixties.* New York: Abrams, 1996.

de Bolla, Peter. *The Discourse of the Sublime: Readings in History, Aesthetics, and the Subject.* Oxford: Basil Blackwell, 1989.

Debord, Guy-Ernest. "All the King's Men." In *Situationist International Anthology,* edited and translated by Ken Knabb, 114–17. Berkeley: Bureau of Public Secrets, 1981.

————. *In girum imus nocte et consumimur igni.* Translated by Lucy Forsyth. London: Pelagian, 1991.

————. Introduction to *Documents relatif à la fondation de l'Internationale Situationniste,* edited by Gerard Barreby. Paris: Allia, 1985. Translated by Ken Knabb as "Introduction to a Critique of Urban Geography," in *Situationist International Anthology.* Berkeley: Bureau of Public Secrets, 1981.

————. *Panegyrique: Tome premier.* Paris: Éditions Gérard Lebovici, 1989. Translated by James Brook as *Panegyric.* New York: Verso, 1991.

————. "Report on the Construction of Situations and the International Situationist Tendency's Conditions of Organization and Action." In *Situationist International Anthology,* edited and translated by Ken Knabb, 17–25.

————. *La société du spectacle.* Paris: Buchet-Chastel, 1967. Translated by Donald Nicholson-Smith as *The Society of the Spectacle.* New York: Zone Books, 1994.

————. "Théorie de la dérive." *Les lèvres nues* 9 (November 1956). Reproduced in *Documents relatif à la fondation de l'Internationale Situationniste,* edited by Gerard Barreby, 312–16; translated as "Theory of the Dérive" in *Situationist International Anthology,* edited and translated by Ken Knabb, 50–54.

Debord, Guy-Ernest, and Asger Jorn. *Fin de Copenhague.* Copenhagen: Bauhaus Imaginiste, 1957. Facsimile edition by Éditions Allia (Paris), 1986.

————. *Mémoires.* Paris: International Situationniste, 1959. Facsimile edition by Les Belles Lettres (Paris), 1993.

Debord, Guy-Ernest, and Gil J. Wolman. "Mode d'emploi du détournement." *Les lèvres nues* 8 (May 1956). Reproduced in *Documents relatif à la fondation de l'Internationale Situationniste,* edited by Gerard Barreby, 302–9; translated as "Methods of Detournement" in *Situationist International Anthology,* edited and translated by Ken Knabb, 8–14.

de Certeau, Michel. *Arts de faire.* Translated by Steven Rendall as *The Practice of Everyday Life.* Berkeley: University of California Press, 1984.

Deleuze, Gilles. *The Logic of Sense.* Translated by Mark Lester and Charles Stivale, edited by Constantin V. Boundas. New York: Columbia University Press, 1990.

Deleuze, Gilles, and Félix Guattari. *Capitalisme et schizophrenie.* Paris: Éditions de Minuit, 1972/1980. Translated by Brian Massumi as *A Thousand Plateaus.* Minneapolis: University of Minnesota Press, 1987.

De Luca, Vincent A. "A Wall of Words: The Sublime as Text." In *Unnam'd Forms: Blake and Textuality,* edited by Nelson Hilton and Thomas Vogler. Berkeley: University of California Press, 1986.

de Man, Paul. "Phenomenology and Materiality in Kant." In *The Textual Sublime: Deconstruction and Its Differences,* edited by Hugh Silverman and Gary Aylesworth, 86–108. Albany: SUNY Press, 1990.

―――. *The Resistance to Theory.* Minneapolis: University of Minnesota Press, 1986.

Derrida, Jacques. "De l'économie restreinte à l'économie générale: Un Hegelianisme sans réserve." In *L'écriture et la différance.* Paris: Éditions du Seuil, 1967. Translated as "From Restricted to General Economy: A Hegelianism without Reserves." *Semiotext(e)* 2, no. 2 (1976): 25–55.

―――. *Dissemination.* Translated by Barbara Johnson. Chicago: University of Chicago Press, 1981.

―――. "Living On: Border Lines." In *Deconstruction and Criticism,* edited by Harold Bloom, 75–175. New York: Seabury, 1979.

―――. *Of Grammatology.* Translated by Gayatri Spivak. Baltimore: Johns Hopkins University Press, 1974.

De Vinne, T. L. "Masculine Printing." In *United Typothetae of America,* Sixth Annual Convention. 1892.

Dewdney, Christopher. "Fractal Diffusion." In *The L=A=N=G=U=A=G=E Book,* edited by Bruce Andrews and Charles Bernstein. Carbondale: Southern Illinois University Press, 1984.

Drucker, Johanna. *The Century of Artists' Books.* New York: Grannary Books, 1995.

Eliot, T. S. *The Complete Poems and Plays: 1909–1950.* New York: Harcourt Brace Jovanovich, 1971.

Ellmann, Richard. *James Joyce.* New York: Oxford University Press, 1959.

Falon, Janet Ruth. "Speaking with Susan Howe." *The Difficulties* 3, no. 2 (1989).

Ferguson, Frances. *Solitude and the Sublime: Romanticism and the Aesthetics of Individuation.* New York: Routledge, 1992.

Fogg, Peter Walkden. *Elementa Anglicana* (facsimile). Menston: Scolar, 1970.

Foster, Hal, ed. *Vision and Visuality.* DIA Art Foundation Discussions in Contemporary Culture 2. Seattle: Bay, 1988.

Foster, Stephen, ed. *Lettrisme: Into the Present.* Special issue of *Visible Language* (17, no. 3).

Fraenkel, Ernest. *Les dessins trans-conscients de Stéphane Mallarmé: À propos de la typographie de "Un coup de dés."* Paris: Nizet, 1960.

Freud, Sigmund. *The Standard Edition of the Complete Psychological Works of Sigmund Freud,* edited by James Strachey. Vol. 23. London: Hogarth, 1959.

Froula, Christine. *To Write Paradise: Style and Error in Pound's "Cantos."* New Haven: Yale University Press, 1984.

Gehr, Ernie. "Interview with Jonas Mekas." *Film Culture* (March 1972): 25–35.

Gelpi, Albert. "The Genealogy of Postmodernism: Contemporary American Poetry." *The Southern Review* (summer 1990): 517–41.

German, Norman. "The Veil of Words in 'The Minister's Black Veil.'" *Studies in Short Fiction* 25, no. 1 (December 1988): 41–47.

Gill, Eric. *An Essay on Typography.* 2nd ed. London: Sheed and Ward, 1936.

Gilman, Claire. "Asger Jorn's Avant-Garde Archives." *October* 79 (winter 1997): 33–48.

Glassgold, Peter. "A Statement from New Directions." In *A Poem Containing History: Textual Studies in "The Cantos,"* edited by Lawrence Rainey, 275. Ann Arbor: University of Michigan Press, 1997.

Gombin, Richard. "French Leftism." *Journal of Contemporary History* 7 (1972): 27–50.

Gregory, R. L. *Eye and Brain: The Psychology of Seeing.* 2nd ed. New York: McGraw-Hill, 1973.

Groupe μ. "Collages." *Revue d'esthétique,* nos. 3–4. Paris: Union Générale d'Éditions, 1978.

Hassan, Ihab. "The Culture of Postmodernism." *Theory, Culture, and Society* 2, no. 3: 119–32.

Hawthorne, Nathaniel. *The Centenary Edition of the Works of Nathaniel Hawthorne.* Vol. 9. Columbus: Ohio State University Press, 1962.

Hobbs, Robert. *Robert Smithson: Sculpture.* Ithaca, N.Y., and London: Cornell University Press, 1981.

Hohnsträter, Dirk. "The Other Side of Memory: Reflections on Censorship." In *The Poetics of Memory,* edited by Thomas Wägenbaur, 299–304. Tübingen: Stauffenberg, 1998.

Home, Stewart. *The Assault on Culture: Utopian Currents from Lettrisme to Class War.* London: Aporia Press and Unpopular Books, 1988.

Howe, Susan. *The Birth-Mark: Unsettling the Wilderness in American Literary History.* Hanover, N.H.: University Press of New England for Wesleyan University Press, 1993.

———. "The Difficulties Interview." *The Difficulties* 3, no. 2: 28–42.

———. *The Europe of Trusts.* Los Angeles: Sun and Moon, 1990.

———. "Melville's Marginalia." In *The Nonconformist's Memorial,* 83–150.

———. *The Nonconformist's Memorial.* New York: New Directions, 1993.

———. *Singularities.* Hanover, N.H.: Wesleyan University Press, 1990.

———. "Statement for the New Poetics Colloquium, Vancouver, 1985." *Jimmy and Lucy's House of 'K'* 5 (1985).

International Business Machines. "IBM Computers Help Men Find Secrets in Stones, History in The Stars—and Answers to Literary Questions" (advertisement). *Art in America* 53, no. 4 (August–September 1965): 3.

Irwin, John T. *American Hieroglyphics: The Symbol of the Egyptian Hieroglyphics in the American Renaissance.* New Haven: Yale University Press, 1980.

I. S. (Les Éditeurs). "Editorial Notes: The Sense of Decay in Art." *October* 79 (winter 1997): 102–8. Unsigned editorial translated by John Shepley from *Internationale Situationniste* 3 (December 1959): 3–8.

James, David E. *Allegories of Cinema: American Film in the Sixties.* Princeton: Princeton University Press, 1989.

Janecek, Gerald. *The Look of Russian Literature: Avant-Garde Visual Experiments, 1900–1930*. Princeton: Princeton University Press, 1984.

———. *Z@um: The Transrational Poetry of Russian Futurism*. Calexi: San Diego State University Press, 1997.

Jay, Martin. *Downcast Eyes: The Denigration of Vision in Twentieth-Century French Thought*. Berkeley: University of California Press, 1993.

———. "Scopic Regimes of Modernity." In *Vision and Visuality*, edited by Hal Foster. DIA Art Foundation Discussions in Contemporary Culture 2. Seattle: Bay, 1988.

Jolas, Eugène. "My Friend James Joyce." In *James Joyce: Two Decades of Criticism*, edited by Seon Givens. New York: Vanguard, 1948.

Joyce, James. *Finnegans Wake*. New York: Penguin, 1976.

———. *Ulysses: The Corrected Text*. Edited by Hans Walter Gabler, Wolfhard Steppe, and Claus Melchior. New York: Random House, 1986.

Junkerman, Charles. "nEw/foRms of living together." In *John Cage: Composed in America*, edited by Marjorie Perloff and Charles Junkerman. Chicago: University of Chicago Press, 1994.

Kaufman, Vincent. "Angels of Purity." Translated by John Goodman. *October* 79 (winter 1997): 49–68.

Kenner, Hugh. "Notes on Amateur Emendations." In *A Poem Containing History: Textual Studies in "The Cantos,"* edited by Lawrence Rainey, 21–32. Ann Arbor: University of Michigan Press, 1997.

———. *The Pound Era*. Berkeley: University of California Press, 1971.

Khayati, Mustapha. "Captive Words: Preface to a Situationist Dictionary." In *Situationist International Anthology*, edited and translated by Ken Knabb, 170–75.

Kinross, Robin. *Modern Typography: An Essay in Critical History*. London: Hyphen, 1992.

Kittler, Friedrich. *Discourse Networks 1800/1900*. Translated by Michael Metteer and Chris Cullens. Stanford: Stanford University Press, 1990.

Knabb, Ken, ed. and trans. *Situationist International Anthology*. Berkeley: Bureau of Public Secrets, 1981.

Kristeva, Julia. *Revolution in Poetic Language*. Translated by Margaret Waller. New York: Columbia University Press, 1984.

Kruchenykh, Aleksei. Взорвалъ [*Vzorval'*]. Moscow, 1914: unpaginated. Facsimile edition in *Livres futuristes russes*, edited by Nina Gurianova. Moscow: Avant-Garde, 1993.

———. "новый путй слова" ["New Ways of the Word"]. In Трое [*The Three*]. Moscow, 1913.

Lageira, Jacinto. "Le poème du langage." In *Poesure et peintre: "D'un art, l'autre,"* edited by Bernard Blistène and Véronique Legrand, 318–33. Avignon: Réunion des Musées Nationaux, Musées de Marseille, 1993.

Lakoff, George, and Mark Johnson. *Metaphors We Live By*. Chicago: University of Chicago Press, 1980.

Lanham, Richard. *The Electronic Word: Democracy, Technology, and the Arts*. Chicago: University of Chicago Press, 1993.

Lautréamont, Comte de (Isidore Ducasse). *Lautréamont's Maldoror*. Translated by Alexis Lykiard. New York: Crowell, 1973.

———. *Poésies*. London: Allison and Busby, 1978.

Lawton, Anna, ed. *Russian Futurism Through Its Manifestoes: 1912–1928*. Ithaca: Cornell University Press, 1988.

Lee, Alwyn. "The Second Chance." Edited by Jesse Birnbaum, researched by Martha McDowell. *Time* (June 2, 1967): 67–74.

Lefebvre, Henri. *Critique de la vie quotidienne*. Rev. ed. Paris: L'Arche, 1958. Paris: Grasset, 1947. Rev. ed. translated by John Moore as vol. 1 of *Critique of Everyday Life*. London: Verso, 1991.

Le Grice, Malcolm. *Abstract Film and Beyond*. London: Studio Vista, 1977.

Lévi-Strauss, Claude. "The Science of the Concrete." In *The Savage Mind*. Chicago: University of Chicago Press, 1966.

Lifton, Robert. *Death in Life: Survivors of Hiroshima*. New York: Random House, 1967.

Lindsay, Jack. *J. M. W. Turner: His Life and Work*. London: Cory, Adams, and Mackay, 1966.

Lipton, Lenny. "A Filmmaker's Column." *Take One* 4, no. 1 (1974).

Lopez, Tony. *False Memory*. Great Barrington: The Figures, 1996.

Lotringer, Sylvère. "The Game of the Name." *Diacritics* 3, no. 2: 2–9.

Lowry, Malcolm. *Under the Volcano*. New York: New American Library, 1971.

Lyotard, Jean-François. *The Inhuman: Reflections on Time*. Translated by Geoffrey Bennington and Rachel Bowlby. Stanford: Stanford University Press, 1991.

Mac Low, Jackson. *Barnesbook: Four Poems Derived from Sentences by Djuna Barnes*. Los Angeles: Sun and Moon, 1996.

———. "Museletter." In *The L=A=N=G=U=A=G=E Book*, edited by Bruce Andrews and Charles Bernstein. Carbondale: Southern Illinois University Press, 1984.

———. "The Poetics of Chance & the Politics of Simultaneous Spontaneity, or the Sacred Heart of Jesus (Revised and Abridged)." In *Talking Poetics from Naropa Institute: Annals of the Jack Kerouac School of Disembodied Poetics*, vol. 1, edited by Anne Waldman and Marilyn Webb, 170–92. Boulder, Colo., and London: Shambhala, 1978.

———. "Seventh Light Poem." In *Representative Works: 1938–1985*, 142. New York: Roof, 1986.

———. *Stanzas for Iris Lezak*. Barton: Something Else, 1971.

———. *Words nd Ends from Ez*. Bolinas: Avenue B, 1989.

Mahaffey, Vicki. "Intentional Error: The Paradox of Editing Joyce's *Ulysses*." In *Representing Modernist Texts: Editing as Interpretation,* edited by Charles Bornstein, 171–91. Ann Arbor: University of Michigan Press, 1991.

Malevich, Kasimir. "From Cubism and Futurism to Suprematism: The New Realism in Painting". In *Essays on Art 1915–1933,* vol. 1, edited by Troels Anderson, translated by Xenia Glowacki-Prus and Arnold McMillin. Copenhagen: Borgen, 1968.

Mallarmé, Stéphane. "The Book: A Spiritual Instrument." In *Selected Poetry and Prose,* edited by Mary Ann Caws. New York: New Directions, 1982.

———. *Le "Livre" de Mallarmé: Premières recherches sur des documents inédits.* Edited by Jacques Scherer. Paris: Gallimard, 1957.

———. *Oeuvres complètes.* Paris: Pléiade, 1945.

Mallock, W. H. *A Human Document: A Novel.* London: Chapman and Hall, 1892.

Marcus, Greil. "Guy Debord's Mémoires: A Situationist Primer." In *on the passage of a few people through a rather brief moment in time: the Situationist International, 1957–1972,* edited by Elizabeth Sussman. Cambridge: MIT Press, 1989.

———. *Lipstick Traces: A Secret History of the Twentieth Century.* Cambridge: Harvard University Press, 1989.

Marin, Louis. *Détruire la peinture.* Paris: Éditions Galilée, 1977.

Markov, Vladimir. *Russian Futurism: A History.* Berkeley: University of California Press, 1968.

Masheck, Joseph. "Alberti's 'Window': Art-Historical Notes on an Antimodernist Misprision." *Art Journal* 50, no. 1 (March 1991): 35–41.

McCaffery, Steve. *North of Intention: Critical Writings 1973–1986.* New York: Roof Books, 1986.

———. *Theory of Sediment.* Vancouver: Talonbooks, 1991.

———. (Untitled Contribution). *Vort: Twenty-First Century Pre-Views* 3, no. 2 (1975).

———. "Zarathrustran 'Pataphysics." *Open Letter: A Canadian Journal of Writing and Theory,* 9th series, no. 7 (winter 1997): 11–22. Special issue on "Millennial 'Pataphysics," edited by Christian Bök and Darren Wershler-Henry.

McDonald, Scott. "Ernie Gehr: Camera Obscura/Lens/Filmstrip." *Film Quarterly* 43, no. 4 (June 1990): 10–16.

McGann, Jerome J. *Black Riders: The Visible Language of Modernism.* Princeton: Princeton University Press, 1993.

———. "Pound's Cantos: A Poem Including Bibliography." In *A Poem Containing History: Textual Studies in "The Cantos,"* edited by Lawrence Rainey, 33–62. Ann Arbor: University of Michigan Press, 1997.

———. *The Textual Condition.* Princeton: Princeton University Press, 1991.

Melnick, David. "A Short Word on My Work." *L=A=N=G=U=A=G=E* 1, no. 1 (February 1978).

Millington, James. *Are We to Read Backwards?* London: Field and Tuer, 1883.

Minear, Richard, ed. *Hiroshima: Three Witnesses.* Princeton: Princeton University Press, 1990.

Monk, Samuel Holt. *The Sublime.* Ann Arbor: University of Michigan Press, 1960.

Morison, Stanley. *First Principles of Typography.* 2nd ed. London: Cambridge University Press, 1976.

Morris, Robert. "The Art of Existence." *Artforum* 9, no. 5 (January 1971): 28–33.

Mosley, James. "The Nymph and the Grot: the revival of the sanserif letter." *Typographica* 12 (1965): 2–19.

Mossin, Andrew. *From Blake's Notebook.* Dyad, 1997.

Nicholls, Peter. *Modernisms: A Literary Guide.* Berkeley: University of California Press, 1995.

Nilsson, Nils. "Krucenych's Poem 'Dyr bul scyl.'" *Scando-Slavica-Tomus* 24: 139–48.

Oppen, George. *Collected Poems.* New York: New Directions, 1975.

Oster, Gerald. "Phosphenes." *Scientific American* 222, no. 2 (February 1980): 82–87.

Ovink, G. W. "150 Years of Book Typography in the Netherlands." In *Book Typography 1815–1965,* edited by Kenneth Day. London: Ernest Benn, 1966.

Panofsky, Erwin. *Renaissance and Renascences in Western Art.* Stockholm: Almqvist and Wiksell, 1960.

Pasler, Jann. "Inventing a Tradition: Cage's 'Composition in Retrospect.'" In *John Cage: Composed in America,* edited by Marjorie Perloff and Charles Junkerman, 123–43. Chicago: University of Chicago Press, 1994.

Paulson, Ronald. "Turner's Graffiti: The Sun and Its Glosses." In *Images of Romanticism: Verbal and Visual Affinities,* edited by Karl Kroeber and William Walling, 167–68. New Haven: Yale University Press, 1978.

Perelman, Bob. *The Trouble with Genius: Reading Pound, Joyce, Stein, and Zukofsky.* Berkeley: University of California Press, 1994.

Perloff, Marjorie. *The Futurist Moment.* Chicago: University of Chicago Press, 1986.

Phillips, Tom. *A Humument: A Treated Victorian Novel.* 1st rev. ed. London: Thames and Hudson, 1987.

———. "Notes on *A Humument.*" In *Tom Phillips: Works and Texts,* 255–60. London: Thames and Hudson, 1992.

Pound, Ezra. *ABC of Reading.* New Haven: Yale University Press, 1934.

———. *The Cantos of Ezra Pound.* New York: New Directions, 1991.

———. *Collected Early Poems.* Edited by Michael John King. New York: New Directions, 1976.

———. *Guide to Kulture.* New York: New Directions, 1970.

———. *Lustra.* New York: Knopf, 1917.

———. *Personae: Collected Shorter Poems.* London: Faber and Faber, 1952.

———. "Retrospect: Interlude." In *Polite Essays.* London: Faber and Faber, 1937.

———. *Selected Poems.* New York: New Directions, 1957.

Proffer, Ellendea, and Carl R. Proffer, eds. *The Ardis Anthology of Russian Futurism.* Ann Arbor: Ardis, 1980.

Quartermain, Peter. *Disjunctive Poetics: From Gertrude Stein and Louis Zukofsky to Susan Howe.* Cambridge: Cambridge University Press, 1992.

Rainey, Lawrence. " 'All I Want You to Do Is to Follow the Orders': History, Faith, and Fascism in the Early Cantos." In *A Poem Containing History: Textual Studies in "The Cantos,"* edited by Lawrence Rainey, 63–116. Ann Arbor: University of Michigan Press, 1997.

Rasula, Jed. "The Politics of, the Politics in." In *Politics and Poetic Value,* edited by Robert von Hallberg, 315–22. Chicago: University of Chicago Press, 1987.

Redman, Tim. *Ezra Pound and Italian Fascism.* Cambridge: Cambridge University Press, 1991.

Richardson, Samuel. *Clarissa, or The History of a Young Lady.* Vol. 5. Oxford, 1930.

Riddel, Joseph N. "From Heidegger to Derrida to Chance: Doubling and (Poetic) Language." *Boundary 2* 4, no. 2 (winter 1976): 571–92. Reprinted in *Early Postmodernism: Foundational Essays,* edited by Paul A. Bové. Durham: Duke University Press, 1995.

Rimbaud, Arthur. *Une saison en enfer/Les illuminations.* London: Oxford University Press, 1973.

Robinson, Kit. "Bob Cobbing's Blade." *Poetics Journal* 1 (January 1982): 75–80.

Rose, Albert. *Vision: Human and Electronic.* New York: Plenum, 1973.

Rothenberg, Jerome, and Pierre Joris. *Poems for the Millennium.* Berkeley: University of California Press, 1995.

Russolo, Luigi. *The Art of Noises.* Translated by Barclay Brown. New York, 1986.

Sabatini, Arthur J. "Silent Performances: On Reading John Cage." In *John Cage at Seventy-Five,* edited by Richard Fleming and William Duckworth. Special issue of the *Bucknell Review* 32, no. 2 (1989).

Schwerner, Armand. *The Tablets I–XV.* New York: Grossman, 1971.

Selinger, Eric. " 'I composed the holes': Reading Ronald Johnson's *Radi Os.*" *Contemporary Literature* 33, no. 1 (spring 1992): 46–74.

Senn, Fritz. "Joyce's Misconducting Universe." In *International Perspectives on James Joyce,* edited by Gottlieb Gaiser, 161–70. Troy: Whitson, 1986.

Serres, Michel. *Le parasite.* Paris: B. Grasset, 1980. Translated by Lawrence R. Schehr as *The Parasite.* Baltimore: Johns Hopkins University Press, 1982.

Shapiro, Gary. *Earthwards: Robert Smithson and Art after Babel.* Berkeley: University of California Press, 1995.

Shklovskii, Viktor. "Art as Technique." In *Russian Formalist Criticism: Four Essays*, translated by Lee T. Lemon and Marion J. Reis. Lincoln: University of Nebraska Press, 1965: 3–24.

Sieburth, Richard. "In Pound We Trust: The Economy of Poetry/The Poetry of Economics." *Critical Inquiry* 14 (autumn 1987): 142–72.

Silliman, Ron. *The New Sentence*. New York: Roof, 1989.

Smithson, Robert. *Robert Smithson: The Collected Writings*. Edited by Jack Flam. Berkeley: University of California Press, 1996.

Snyder, Joel. "Picturing Vision." *Critical Inquiry* 60, no. 3 (March 1990): 499–526.

Sola, Agnès. *Le futurisme russe*. Paris: Presses Universitaires de France, 1989.

Starobinski, Jean. *Les mots sous les mots: Les anagrammes de Ferdinand de Saussure*. Paris: Éditions Gallimard, 1971.

Stein, Gertrude. *The Geographical History of America, or The Relation of Human Nature to the Human Mind*. New York: Random House, 1936.

———. *Paris, France*. New York: Liveright, 1996.

———. *Tender Buttons: Objects, Food, Rooms*. Paris: Éditions Claire Marie, 1914.

Tinker, Miles A. *Legibility of Print*. Ames: Iowa State University Press, 1963.

Tschichold, Jan. *The New Typography*. Translated by Rauri McLean. Berkeley: University of California Press, 1995.

Ulmer, Gregory L. "The Object of Post-Criticism." In *The Anti-Aesthetic: Essays on Postmodern Culture*, edited by Hal Foster, 83–110. Seattle: Bay, 1983.

University of California at Berkeley, Graduate Division. "Guidelines for Submitting a Doctoral Dissertation or a Master's Thesis." N.p.: November 1997.

Vallier, Dora. "Intimations of a Linguist: Jakobson as Poet." In *Language, Poetry, and Poetics: The Generation of the 1890s: Jakobson, Trubetzkoy, Majakovskii*, edited by Krystyna Pomorska et al., 291–304. Berlin: Mouton de Grutyer, 1987.

Vroon, Ronald. *Velimir Xlebnikov's Shorter Poems: A Key to the Coinages*. Michigan Slavic Materials no. 22. Ann Arbor: Department of Slavic Languages and Literatures, University of Michigan, 1983.

Waldrop, Rosmarie. *Camp Printing*. Providence(?): Burning Deck, 1970.

Warde, Beatrice. *The Crystal Goblet: Sixteen Essays on Typography*. Edited by Henry Jacob. Cleveland: World Publishing, 1956.

Wees, William C. *Light Moving in Time: Studies in the Visual Aesthetics of Avant-Garde Film*. Berkeley: University of California Press, 1992.

Weiskel, Thomas. *The Romantic Sublime*. Baltimore: Johns Hopkins University Press, 1976.

Weitzer, John S. "The Partial Veto." *Marquette Law Review* 76 (spring 1993): 625–49.

Weststeijn, Willem Gerardus. *Velimir Chlebnikov and the Development of Poetical*

Language in Russian Symbolism and Futurism. Studies in Slavic Literature and Poetics no. 4. Amsterdam: Rodopi, 1983.

White, John. *Literary Futurism: Aspects of the First Avant-Garde.* Oxford: Clarendon, 1990.

Wiggins, R. H. "Effects of Three Typographic Variables on Speed of Reading." *Journal of Typographic Research* 1, no. 1 (1967): 5–18.

Williams, Charles Kenneth. *Flesh and Blood.* New York: Farrar, Straus, and Giroux, 1987.

Williams, Jonathan. *The Loco Logo-Daedalus in Situ: Selected Poems 1968–70.* London: Cape Goliard, 1971.

Wittgenstein, Ludwig. *Philosophical Investigations: The English Text of the Third Edition.* Translated by G. E. M. Anscombe. New York: Macmillan, n.d.

———. *Preliminary Studies for the "Philosophical Investigations," Generally Known as the Blue and Brown Books.* Oxford: Blackwell, 1969.

———. *Remarks on the Foundations of Mathematics.* Edited by G. H. Wright, R. Rhees, and G. E. M. Anscombe, translated by G. E. M. Anscombe. New York: Macmillan, 1956.

———. *Tractatus Logico-Philosophicus.* Translated by C. K. Ogden. London: Routledge, 1990.

Wolman, Gil. "J'écris propre." *Les lèvres nues* 9–10. Reprinted in *Documents relatif à la fondation de l'Internationale Situationniste,* edited by Gerard Barreby, 338 et seq.

Index

Richardson, Samuel, 34–36, 40, 168
Richter, Hans, 175
Riffaterre, Michel, 188
Rimbaud, Arthur, 3, 6, 7, 23, 28, 61, 157, 181, 182
Robert, Jacques, 164
Rot, Dieter, 82, 175
Rothenberg, Jerome, 152–53
Rotman, Brian, 183
Roudiez, Leon, xx, 12, 195
Roussel, Raymond, 157
Rule following, xvi, xxiv, 10, 12, 60, 68, 77, 88–89, 91–92, 93, 94, 96–98, 102, 104, 106, 109–10, 115, 118, 119, 127, 130, 131, 161, 196, 198, 201, 203–4
Runderli, Peter, 188
Russell, Bertrand, 133
Russolo, Luigi, 169
Rzepka, Charles, 194

Sabatini, Arthur, 195
Sacrifice, 25, 49, 80, 81, 132, 166, 191–92, 193, 202. *See also* General economy
Sankichi, Toge, 213
Sappho, 112–13
Saroyan, Aram, 185
Sartre, Jean-Paul, 57
Satan, 9, 80
Scan (ocular), 41, 54, 57, 92, 151, 176–77
Scars, 21, 109, 144, 155
Schefer, Jean-Louis, 185
Scherer, Jacques, 152
Schoenberg, Arnold, 107, 112, 200
Schwerner, Armand, 124 et seq., 133
Schwitters, Kurt, 148–49
Score (musical), 32, 41, 135, 168, 210
Sealts, Merton, 154
Sediment, 69, 123, 124, 125, 126, 132–36, 138, 139, 172, 208, 210

Seduction, 79
Self-promotion, 212
Self-referentiality, 20, 21, 42, 73, 93, 144, 172, 211. *See also* Reflection
Selinger, Eric, 211–12
Senn, Fritz, 116
Serres, Michel, 46–48, 76, 79, 80, 82, 169, 190
Seuss, Dr. (pseudonym), 188
Shakespeare, William, 92
Shapiro, Gary, 131
Sharits, Paul, 176
Shepheard, David, 188
Shift (*sdvig*), 22, 56, 100, 109, 125, 164, 189–90
Shklovskii, Viktor, 14, 54
Sieburth, Richard, 105, 200, 202–3
Signature, xvii, 21–22, 34, 77, 96, 112, 121, 200, 209–10, 212. *See also* Proper names
Silliman, Ron, 54, 58, 72, 178, 183
Situationists, 5–30, 124, 131, 146, 160–62. *See also* Debord, Guy-Ernest
Smithson, Robert, xviii, xix, 104, 124 et seq., 130, 132, 134, 211
Snyder, Joel, 66, 183, 184, 185
Social dialogue, 45, 65, 77, 133, 159
Sound poetry, xxiii–xxiv, 73–74
Spicer, Jack, 209
Stallworthy, John, 168
Starobinski, Jean, 85, 157, 172, 188, 195
Static, 44–45, 46–47, 51, 56, 62, 79, 132. *See also* Noise
Stein, Gertrude, xviii, 28, 54, 60, 90, 95–96, 109, 157, 162, 196, 203, 205, 211
Stern, Colin, 126, 133, 210
Stevens, Wallace, 133, 170
Stevenson, Robert Louis, 27
Stewart, Garrett, 157
Sublime, 82–87, 185, 193–94
Survival Research Labs, 94

Craig Dworkin is an assistant professor of English
at Princeton University.